ISBN 978-0-9915285-4-7
Printed and bound in the USA

Library of Congress Catalog
2014933069

Far Out Press
San Francisco, CA

BEAUTIFUL

A girl's trip through the looking glass

by Marie D'Abreo

The experience of Truth
and Beauty are one and
the same experience.

RUPERT SPIRA

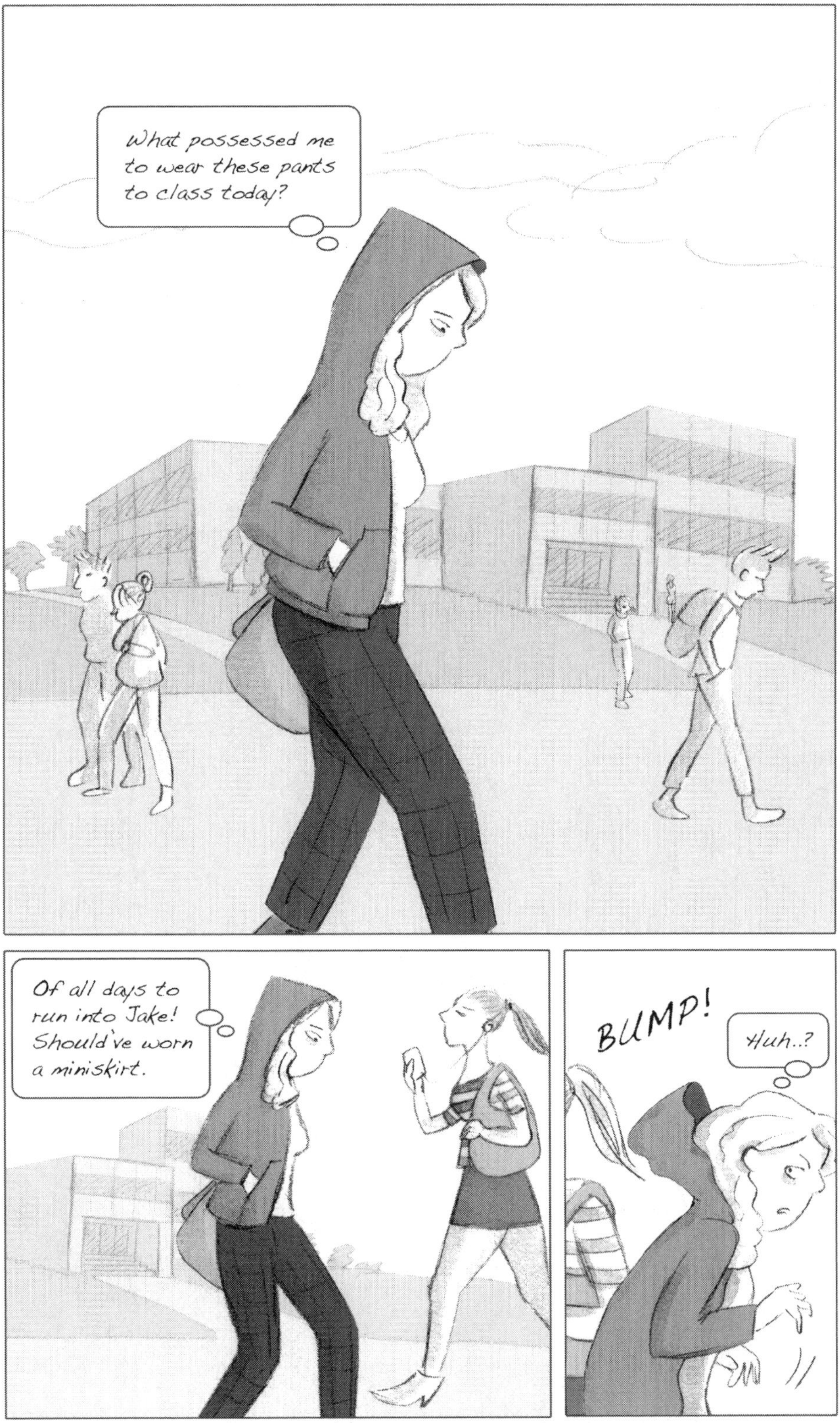
What possessed me to wear these pants to class today?
Of all days to run into Jake! Should've worn a miniskirt.
BUMP!
Huh..?

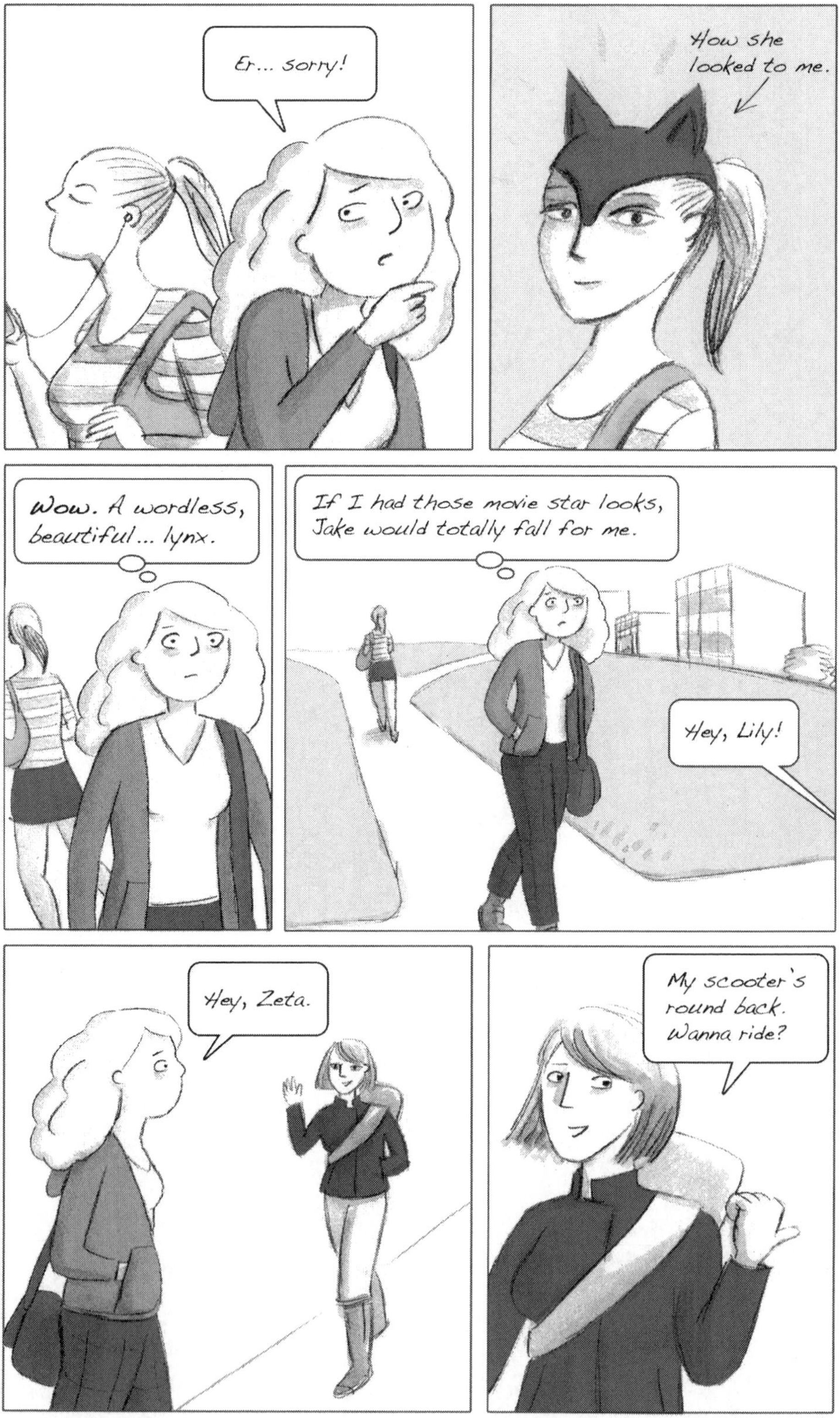
Er... sorry!
How she looked to me.
Wow. A wordless, beautiful... lynx.
If I had those movie star looks, Jake would totally fall for me.
Hey, Lily!
Hey, Zeta.
My scooter's round back. Wanna ride?

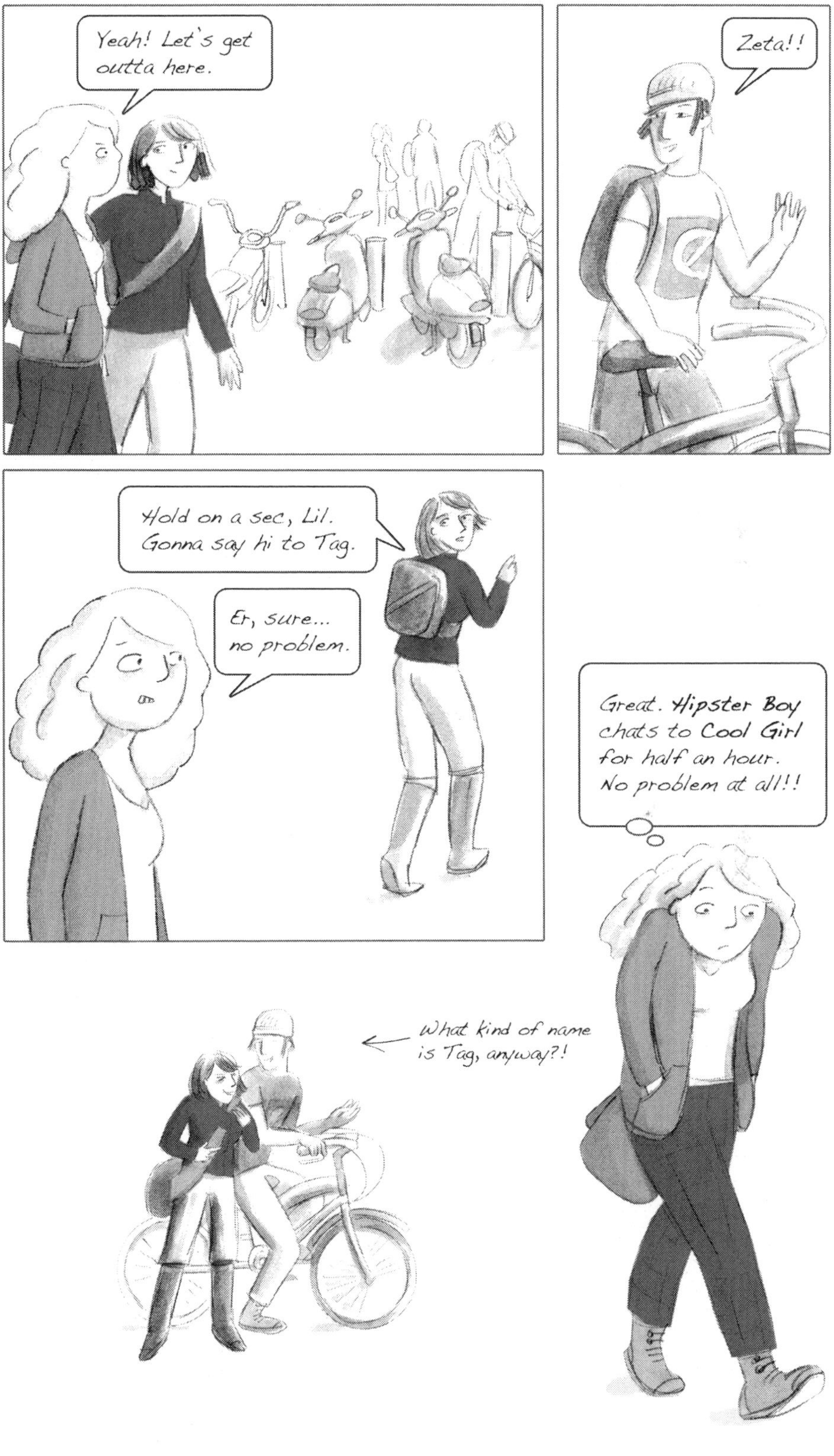
Yeah! Let's get outta here.
Zeta!!
Hold on a sec, Lil. Gonna say hi to Tag.
Er, sure... no problem.
Great. Hipster Boy chats to Cool Girl for half an hour. No problem at all!!
What kind of name is Tag, anyway?!

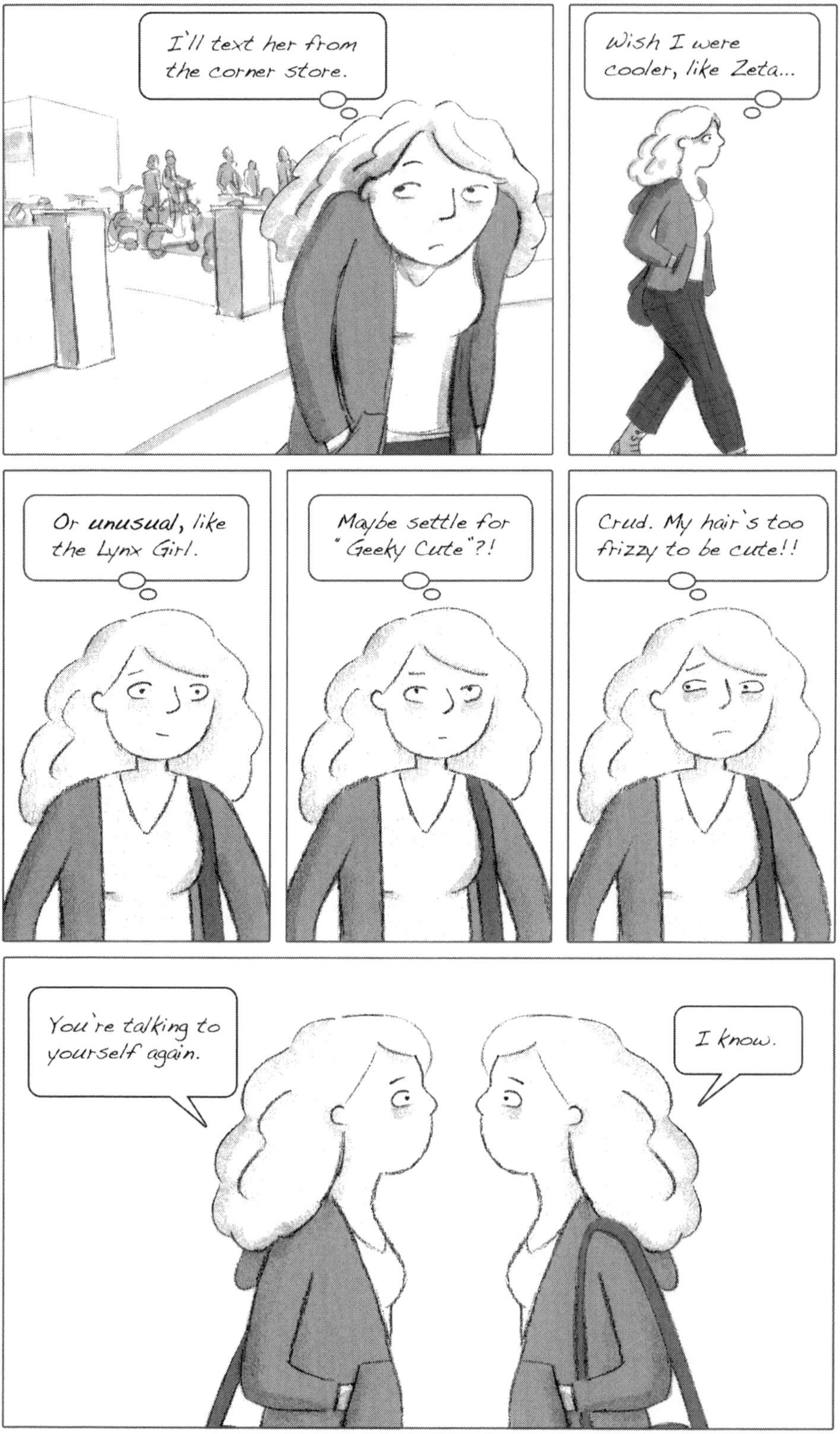
I'll text her from the corner store.
Wish I were cooler, like Zeta...
Or **unusual**, like the Lynx Girl.
Maybe settle for "Geeky Cute"?!
Crud. My hair's too frizzy to be cute!!
You're talking to yourself again.
I know.

SO, IS IT JUST ME? OR IS THERE A VOICE IN EVERYONE'S HEAD?

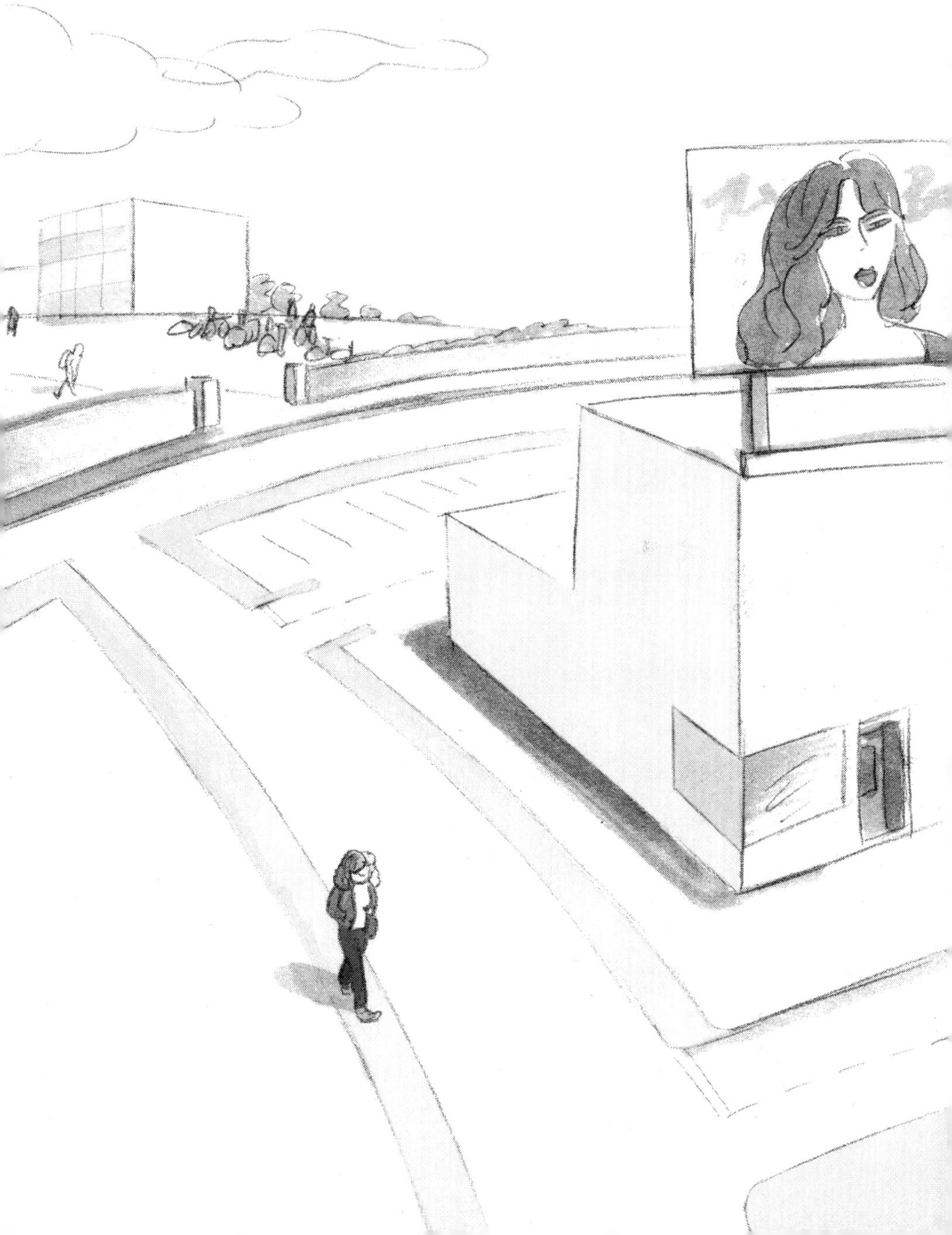

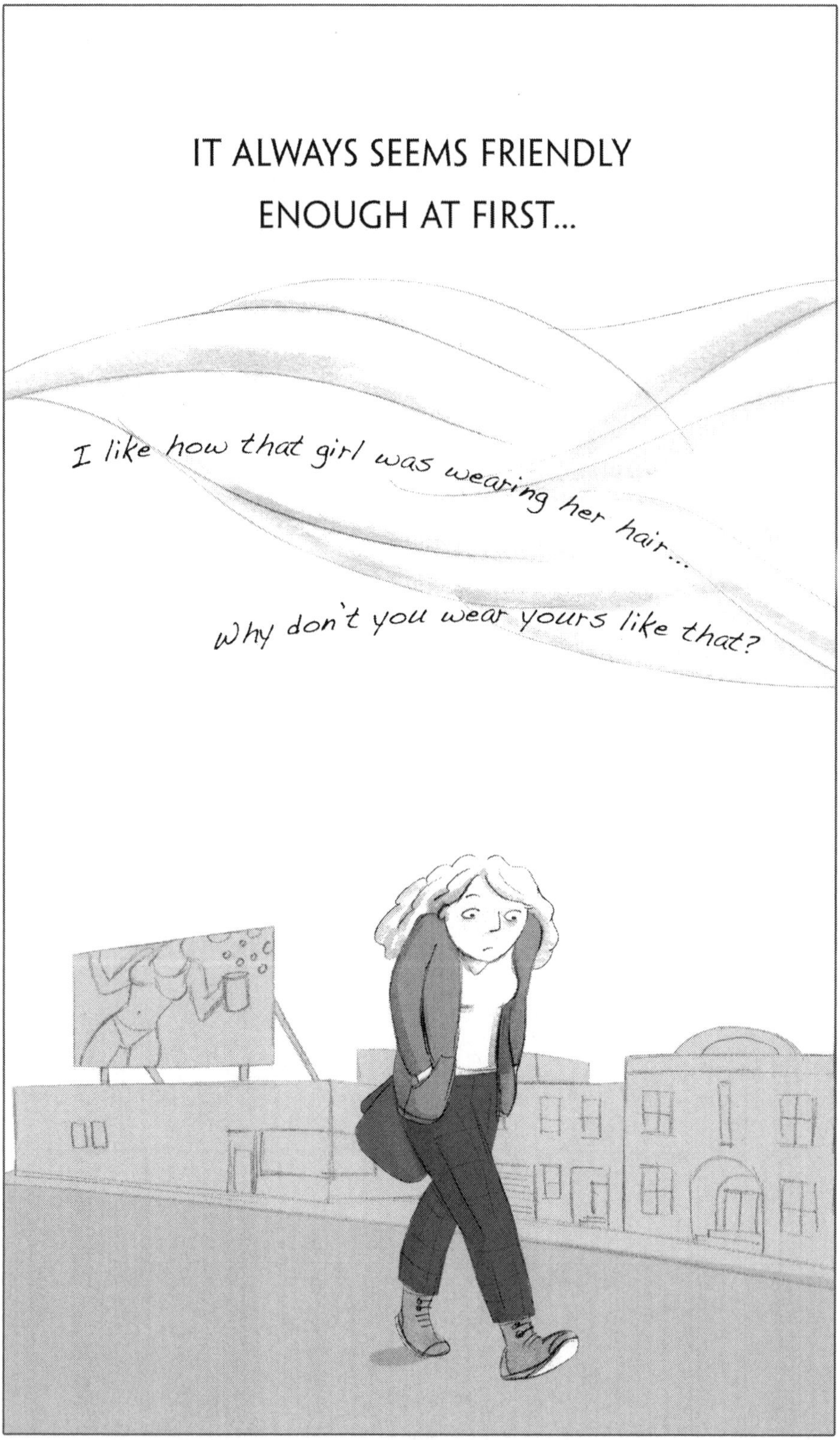
IT ALWAYS SEEMS FRIENDLY ENOUGH AT FIRST...
I like how that girl was wearing her hair...
Why don't you wear yours like that?

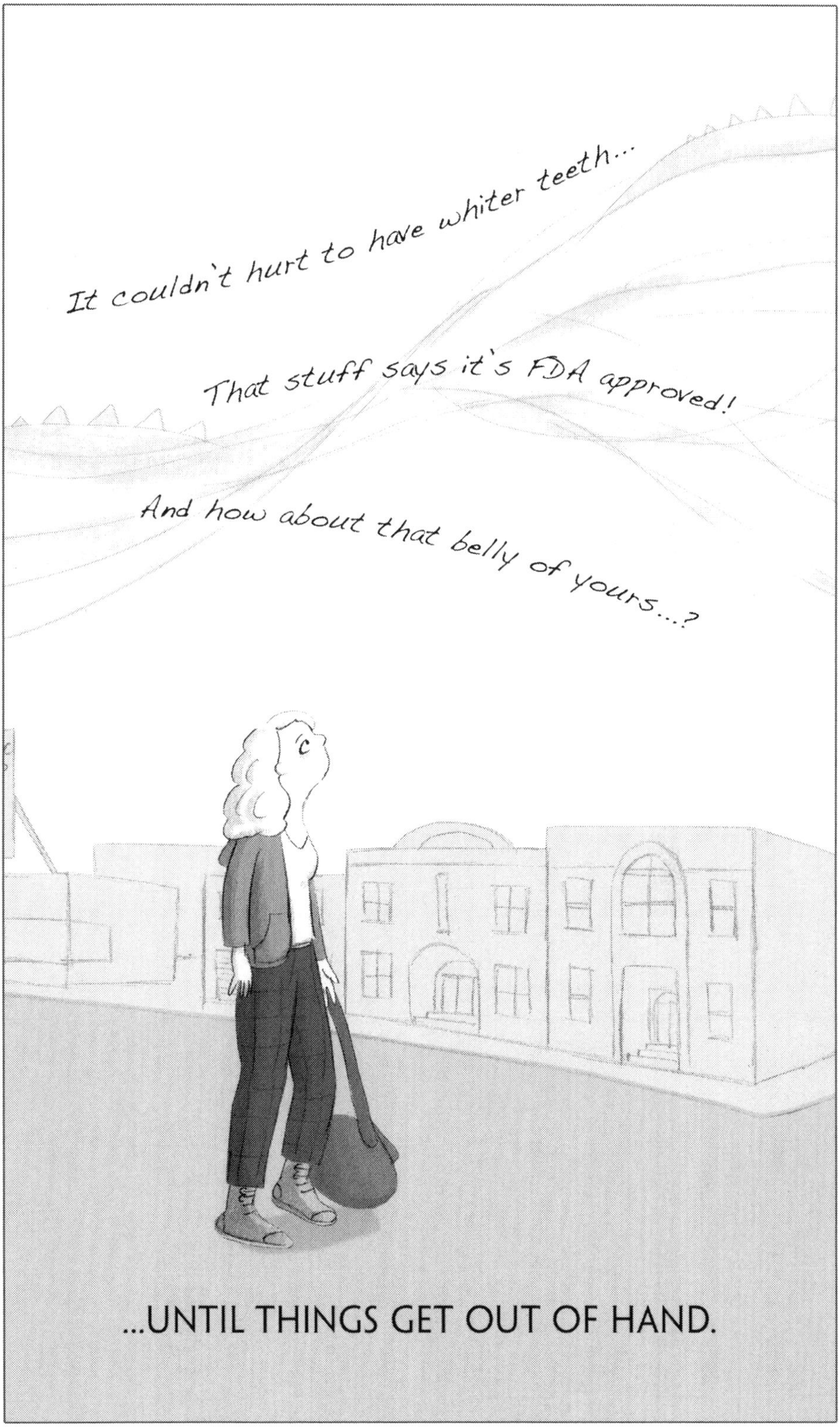
It couldn't hurt to have whiter teeth...
That stuff says it's FDA approved!
And how about that belly of yours...?
...UNTIL THINGS GET OUT OF HAND.

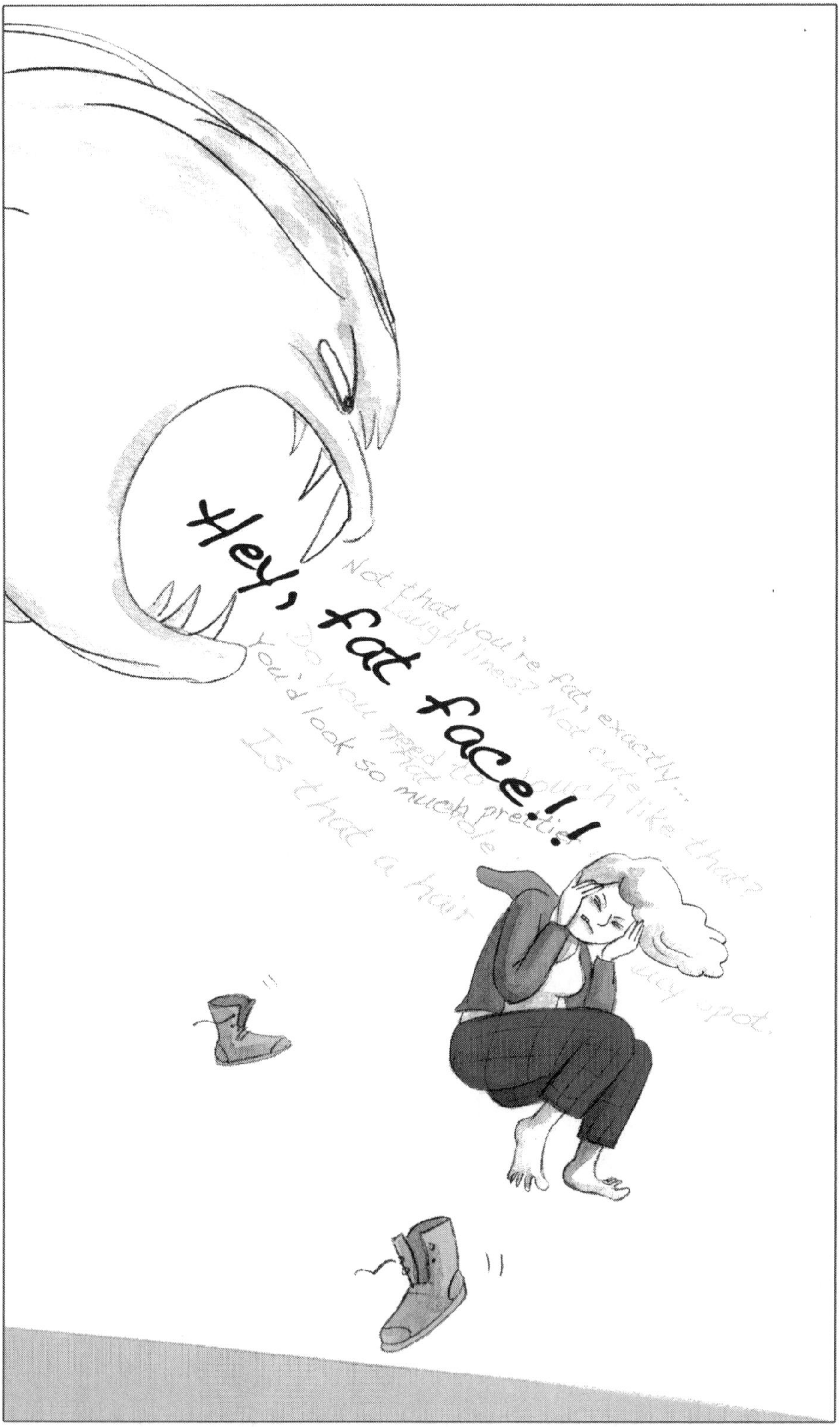
Hey, fat face!!
Not that you're fat, exactly...
Laugh lines? Not cute
like that?
You'd look so much
IS that a hair
spot.

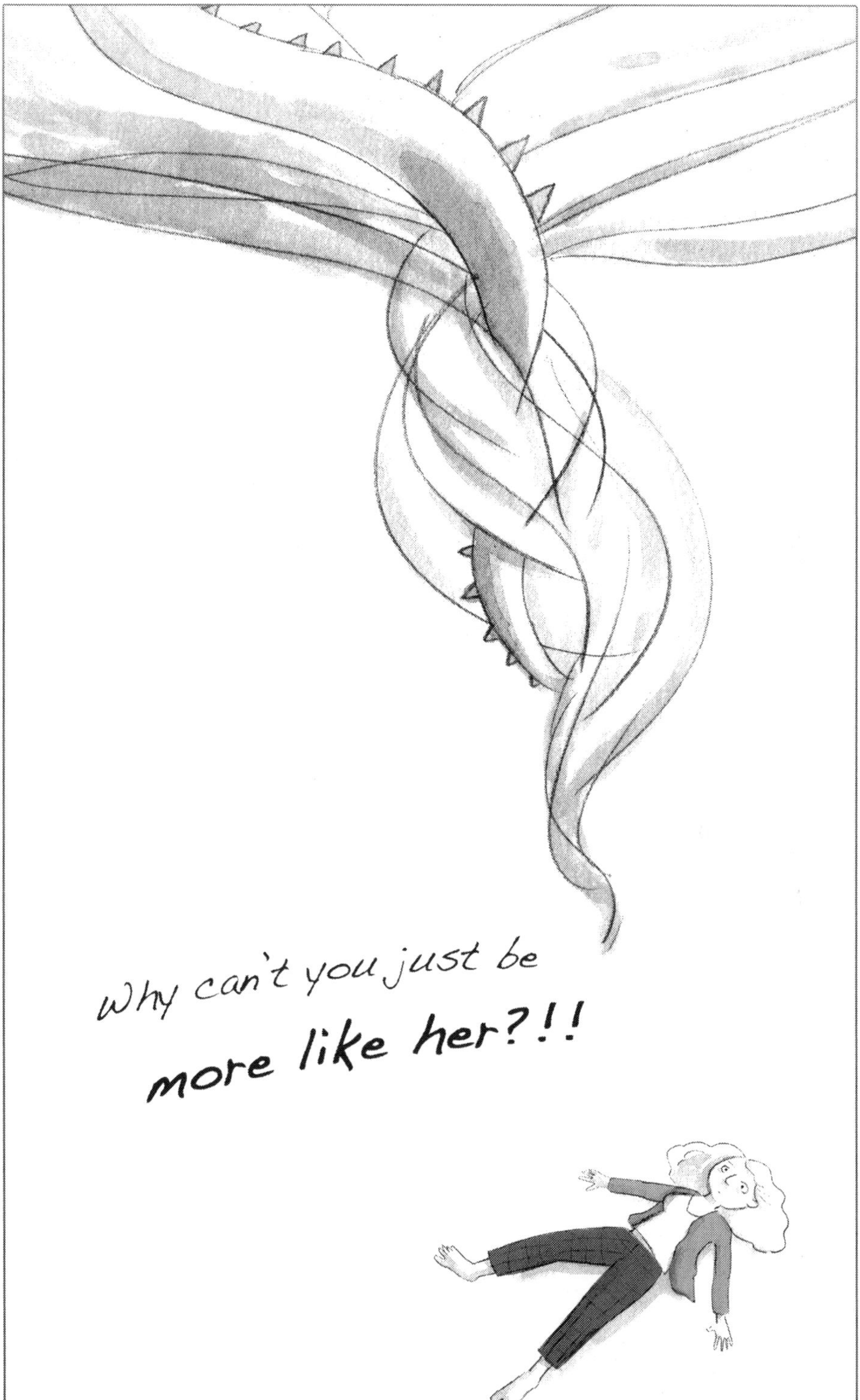
Why can't you just be
more like her?!!

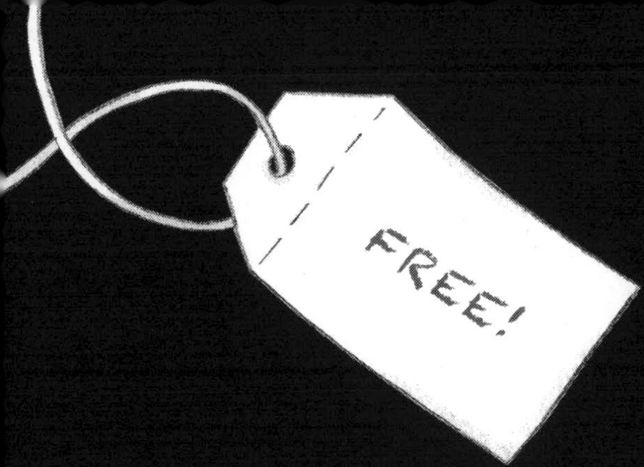
FREE!

Your problem is
you're... too busy
holding onto your
own unworthiness.

RAM DASS

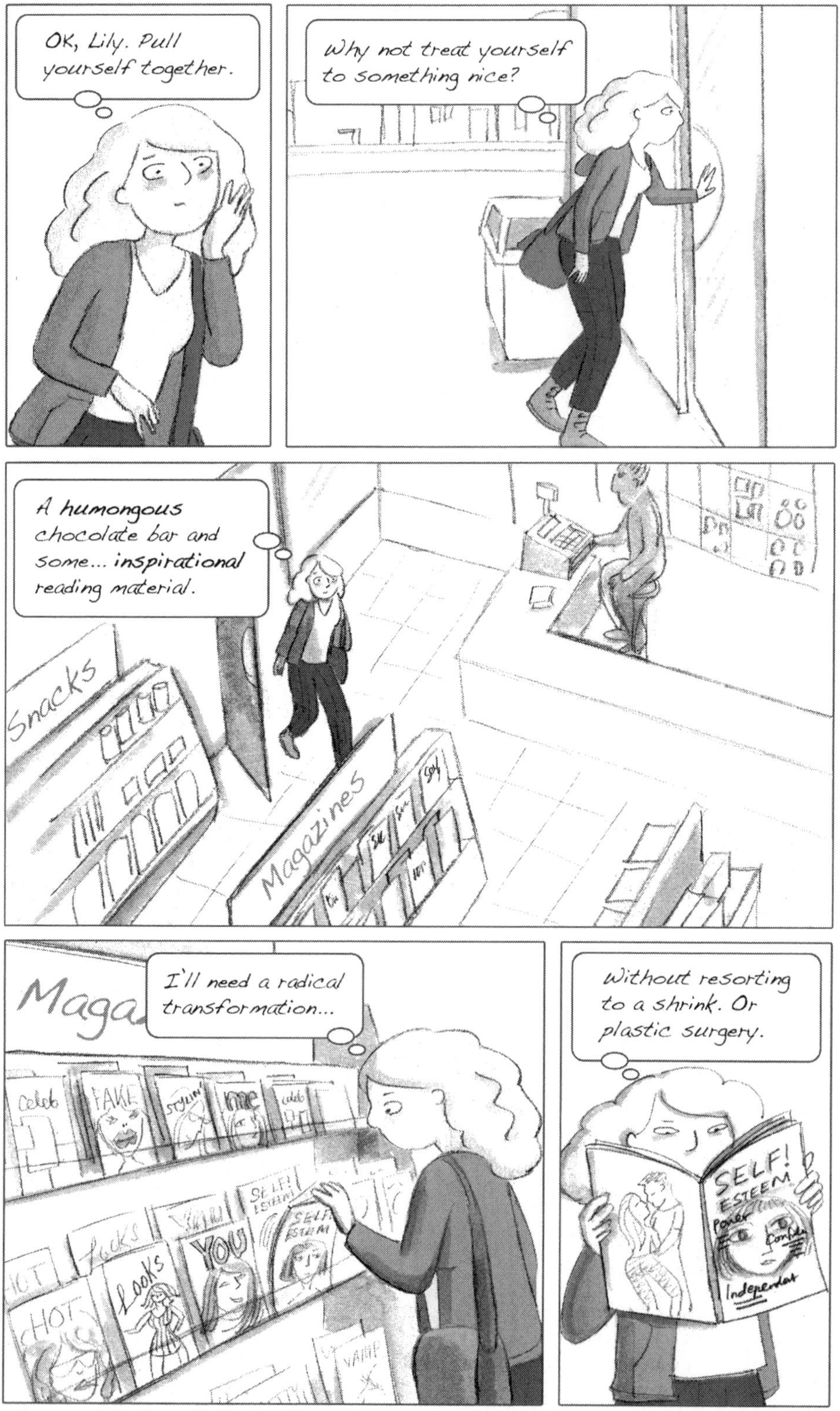
OK, Lily. Pull yourself together.
Why not treat yourself to something nice?
A **humongous** chocolate bar and some... **inspirational** reading material.
Snacks
Magazines
Maga
I'll need a radical transformation...
FAKE
YOU
Looks
HOT
Without resorting to a shrink. Or plastic surgery.
SELF! ESTEEM

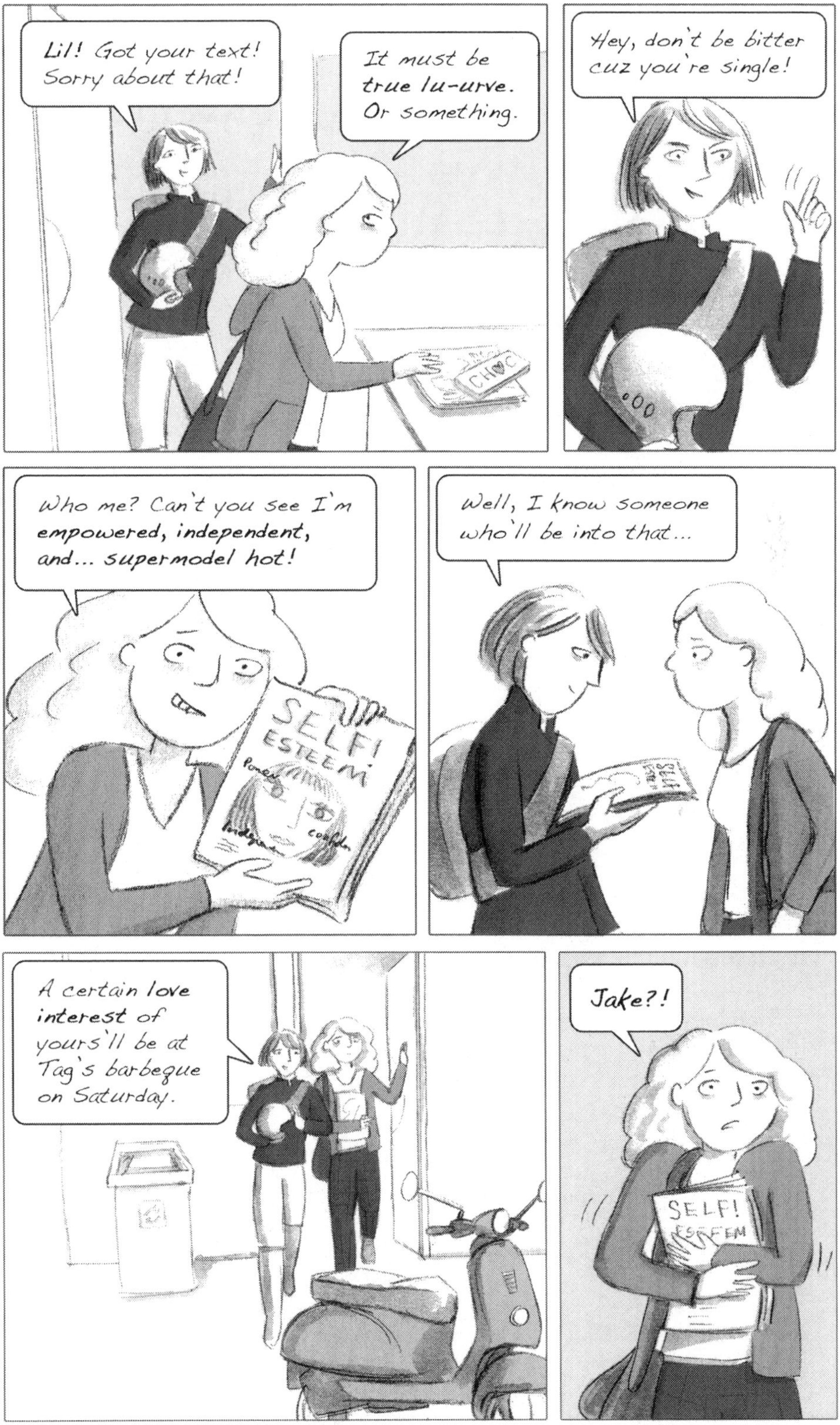
Lil! Got your text! Sorry about that!
It must be **true lu-urve.** Or something.
Hey, don't be bitter cuz you're single!
Who me? Can't you see I'm **empowered, independent,** and... **supermodel hot!**
SELF! ESTEEM
Well, I know someone who'll be into that...
A certain **love interest** of yours'll be at Tag's barbeque on Saturday.
Jake?!
SELF! ESTEEM

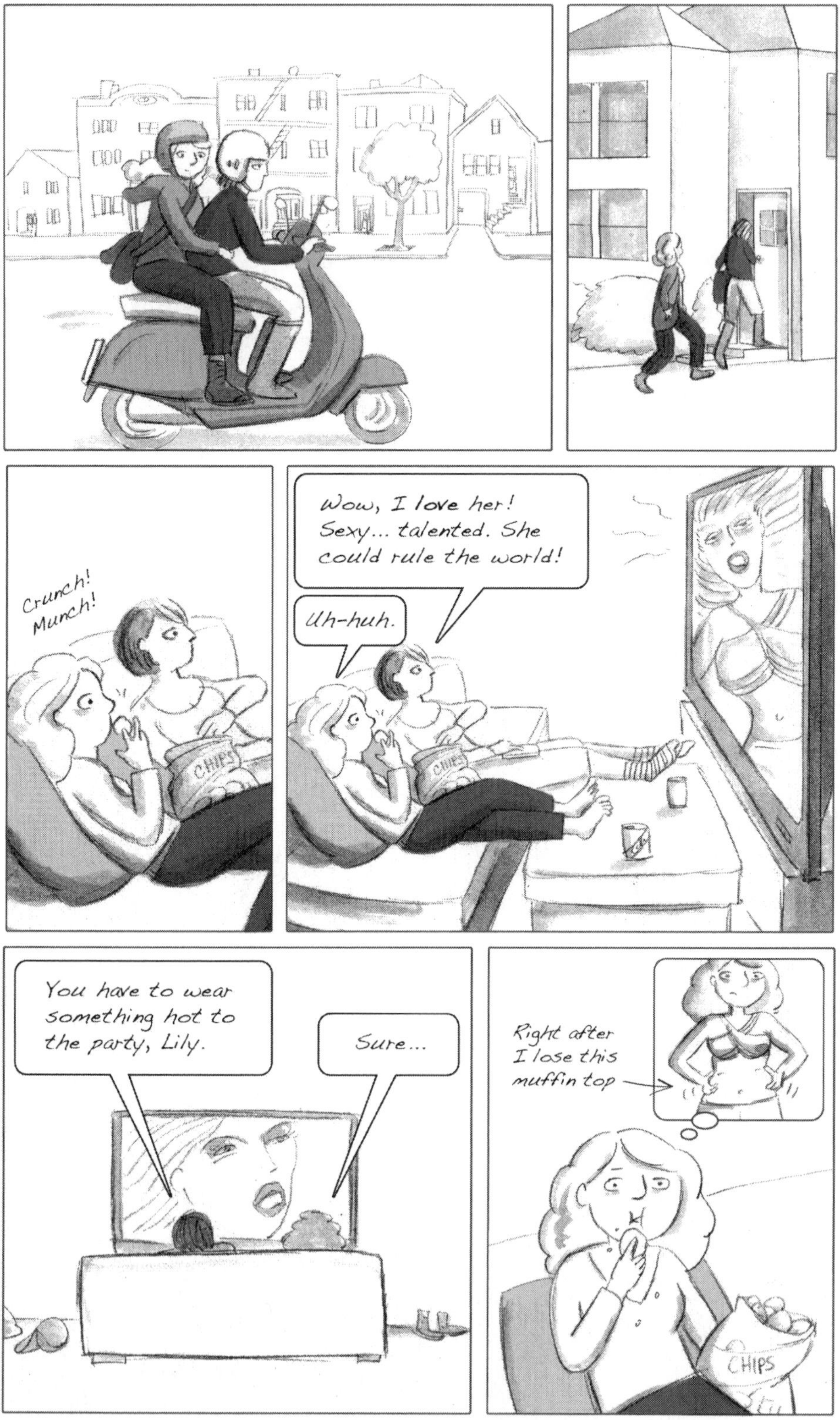
Crunch! Munch!
Wow, I love her! Sexy... talented. She could rule the world!
Uh-huh.
You have to wear something hot to the party, Lily.
Sure...
Right after I lose this muffin top
CHIPS

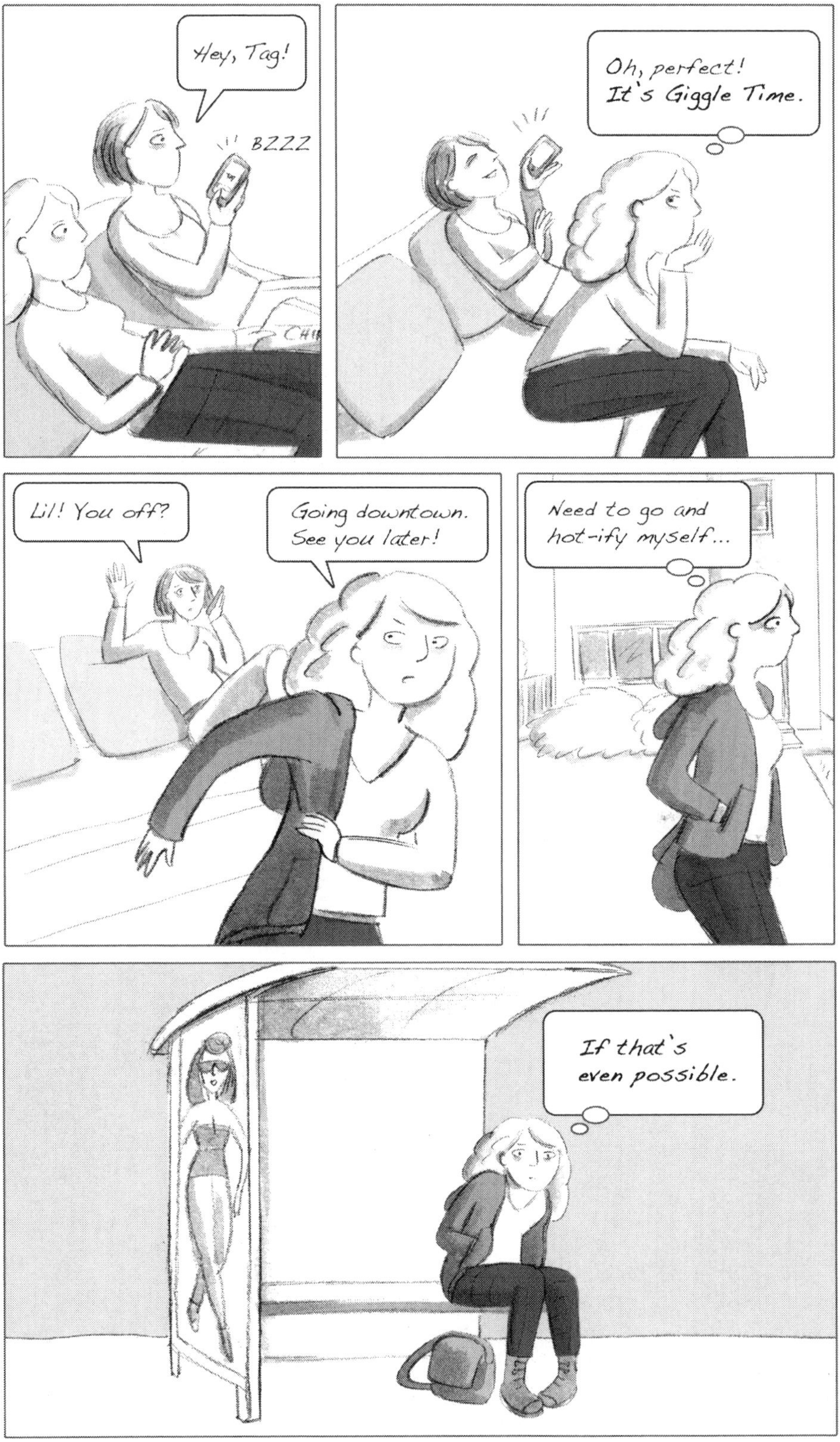
Hey, Tag!
BZZZ
Oh, perfect! It's Giggle Time.
Lil! You off?
Going downtown. See you later!
Need to go and hot-ify myself...
If that's even possible.

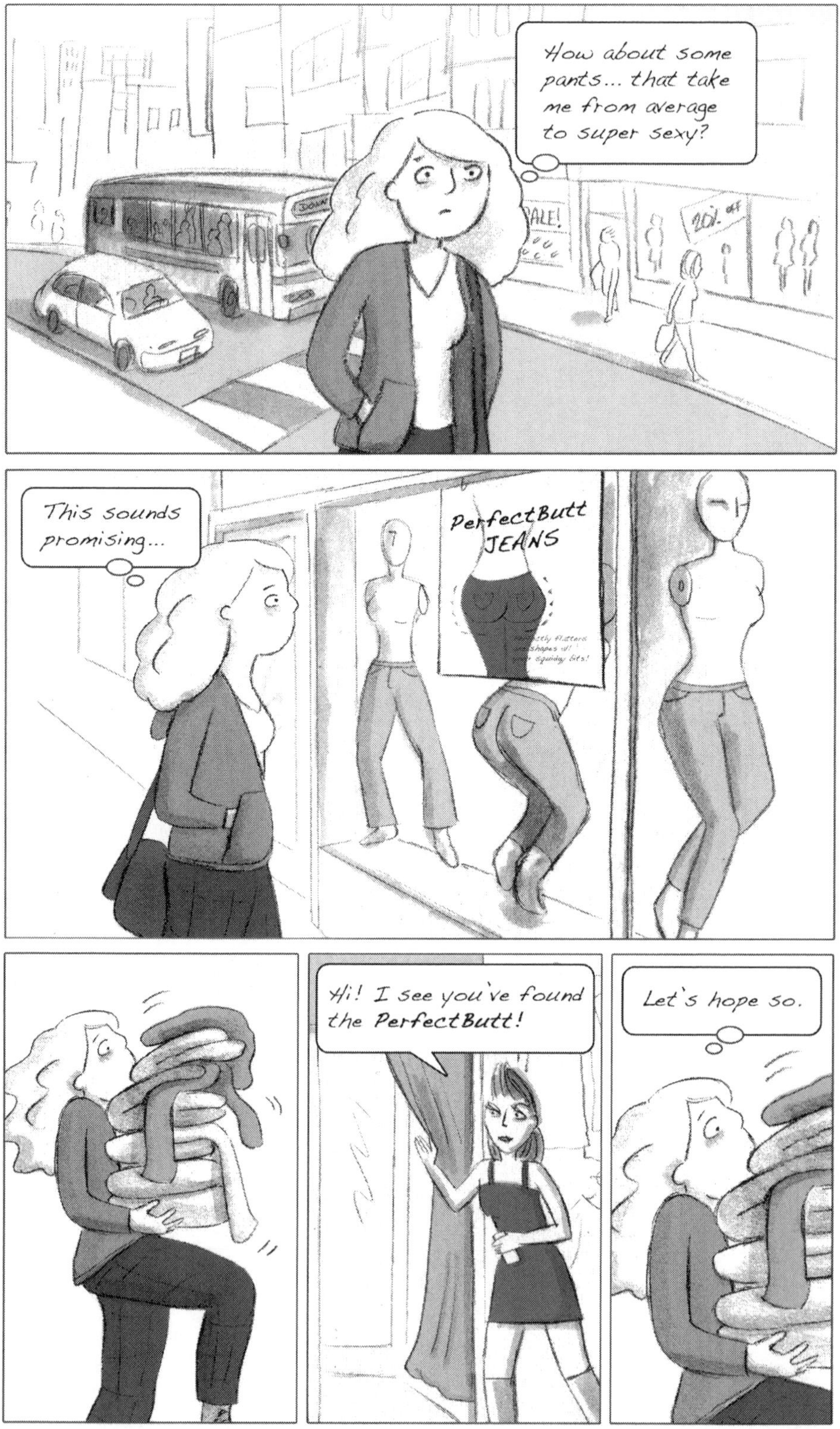
How about some pants... that take me from average to super sexy?
This sounds promising...
PerfectButt JEANS
Hi! I see you've found the PerfectButt!
Let's hope so.

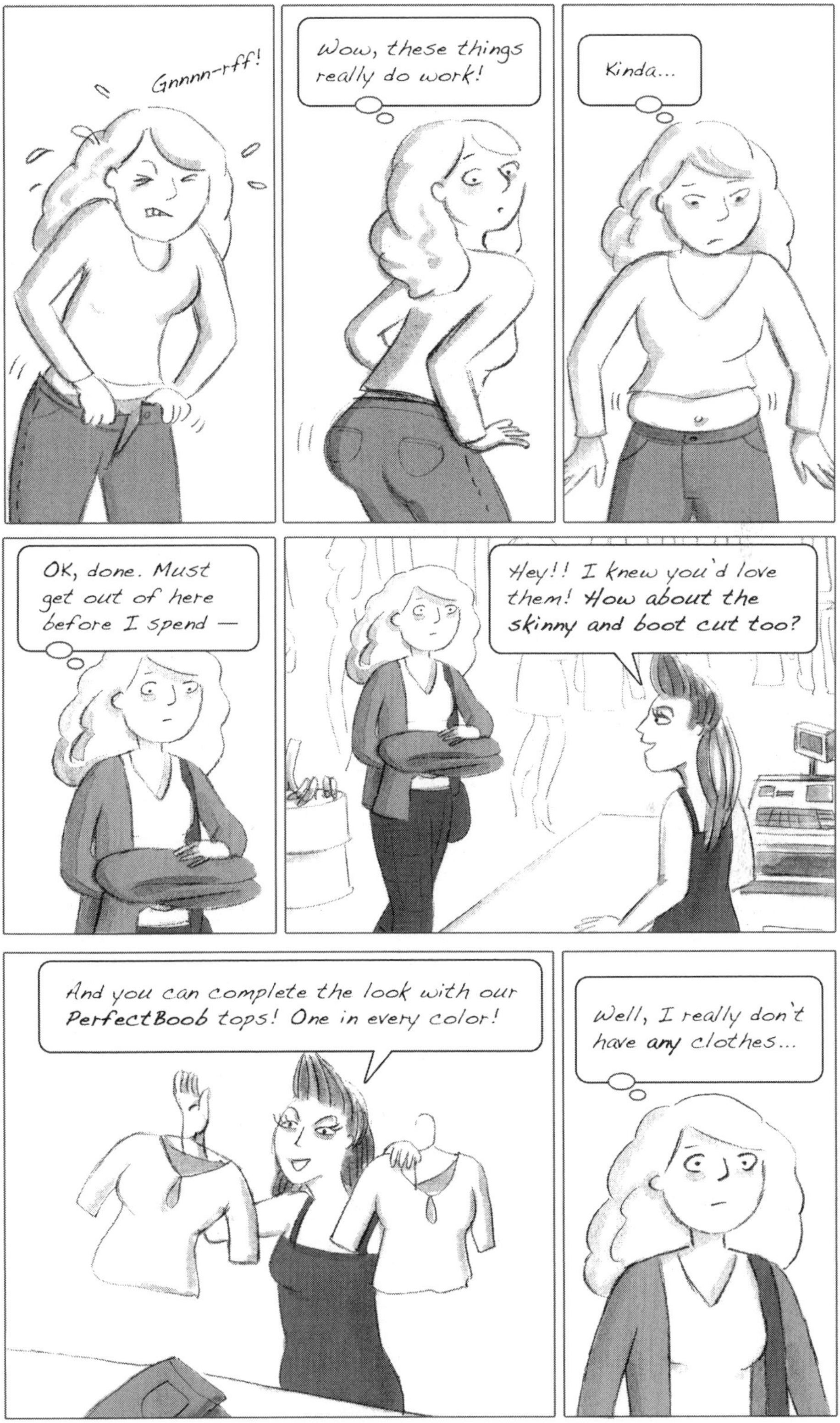
Gnnnn-rff!
Wow, these things really do work!
Kinda...
OK, done. Must get out of here before I spend —
Hey!! I knew you'd love them! How about the skinny and boot cut too?
And you can complete the look with our PerfectBoob tops! One in every color!
Well, I really don't have any clothes...

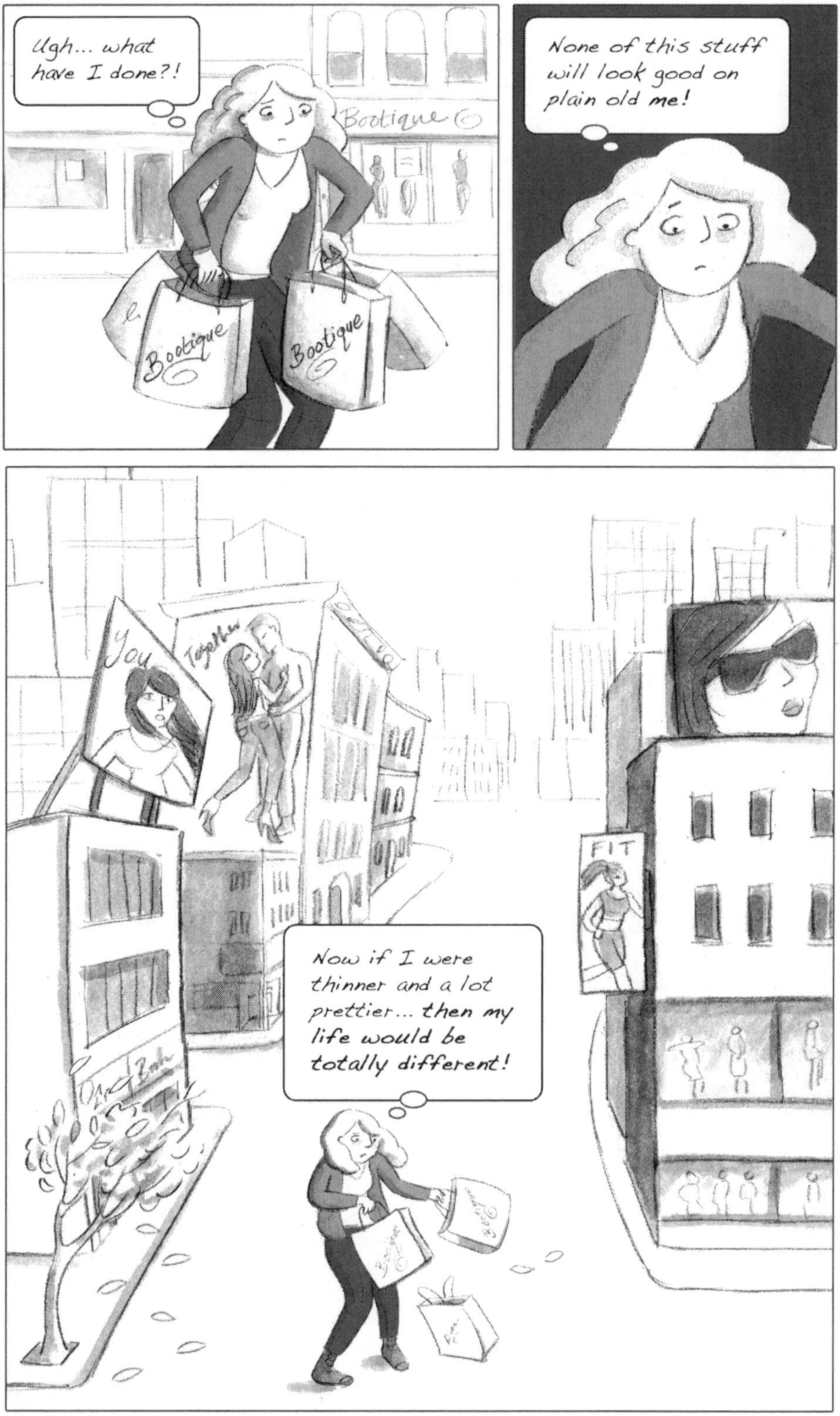
Ugh... what have I done?!
Bootique
Bootique
Bootique
None of this stuff will look good on plain old me!
You
FIT
Now if I were thinner and a lot prettier... then my life would be totally different!

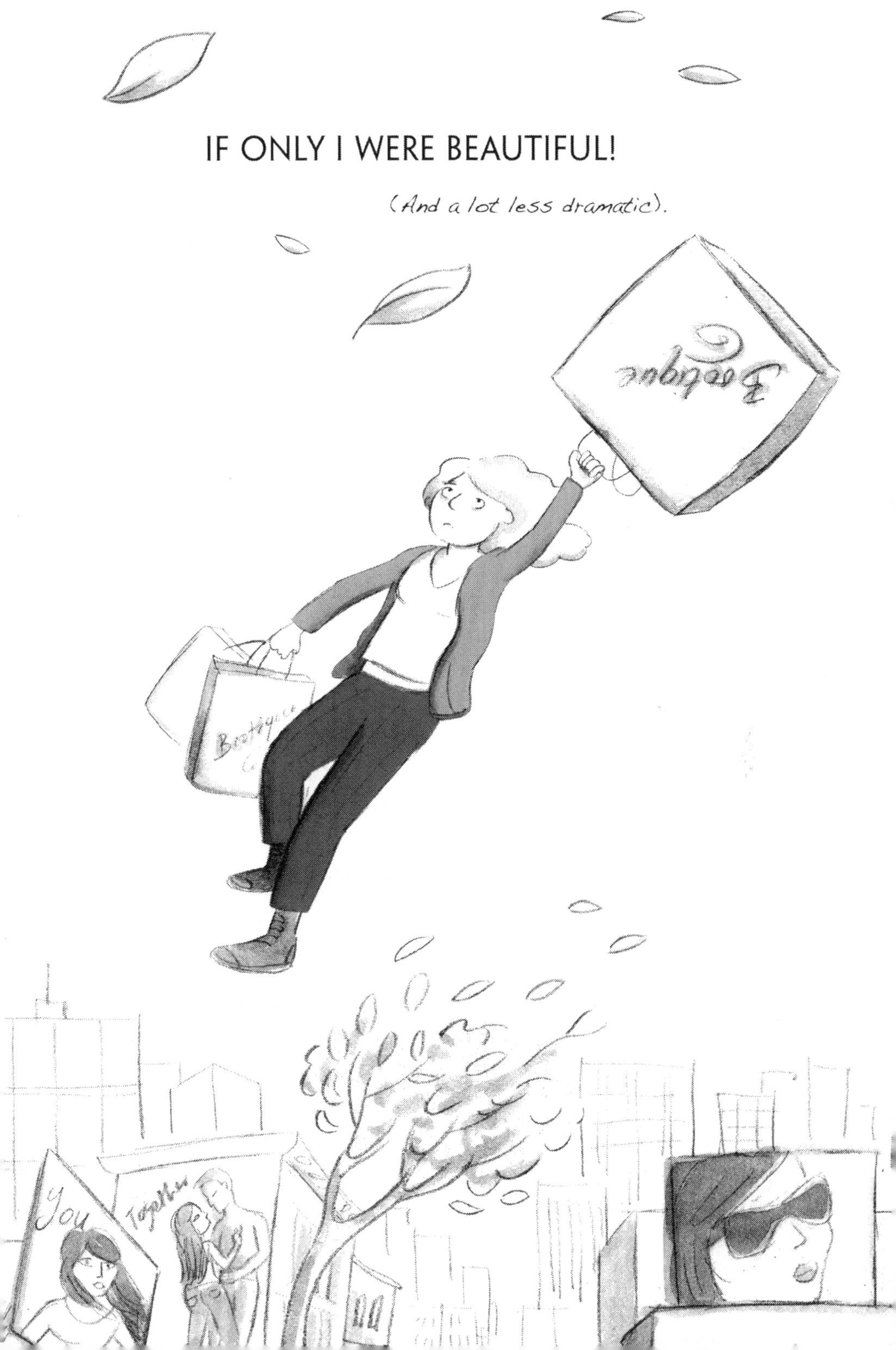
IF ONLY I WERE BEAUTIFUL!
(And a lot less dramatic).
You

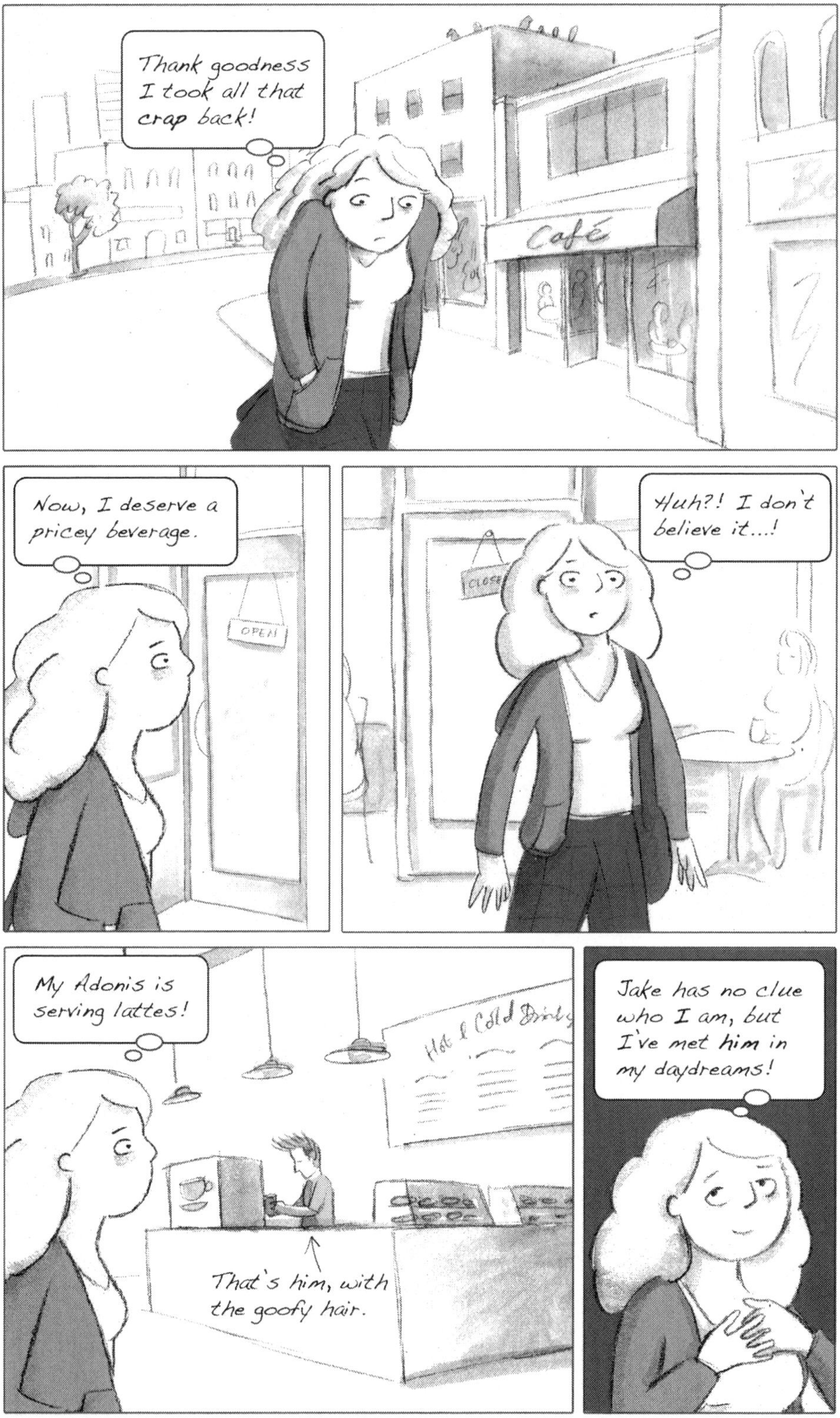
Thank goodness I took all that crap back!
Café
Now, I deserve a pricey beverage.
OPEN
Huh?! I don't believe it...!
My Adonis is serving lattes!
Hot & Cold Drinks
That's him, with the goofy hair.
Jake has no clue who I am, but I've met him in my daydreams!

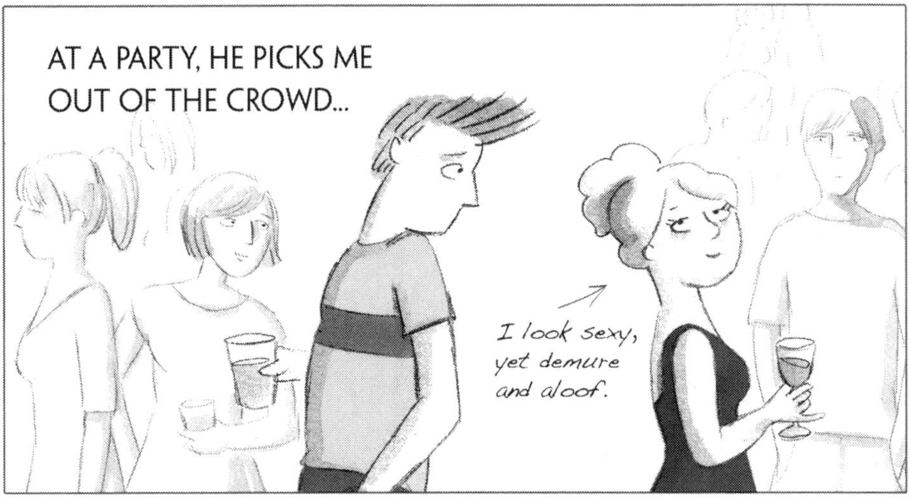
AT A PARTY, HE PICKS ME OUT OF THE CROWD...
I look sexy, yet demure and aloof.

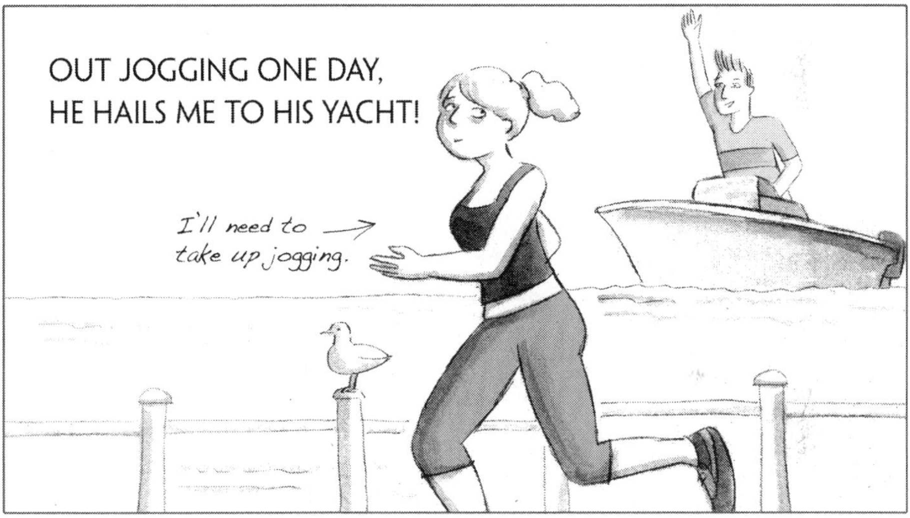
OUT JOGGING ONE DAY, HE HAILS ME TO HIS YACHT!
I'll need to take up jogging.

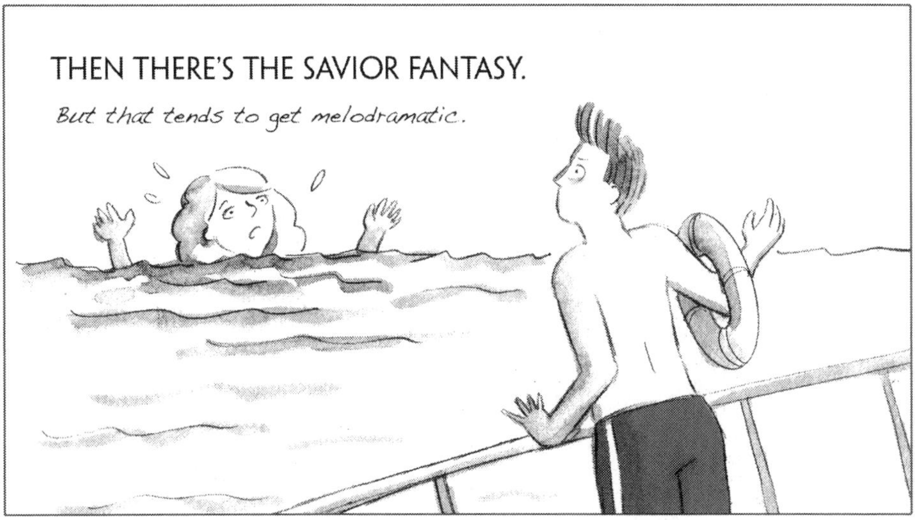
THEN THERE'S THE SAVIOR FANTASY.
But that tends to get melodramatic.

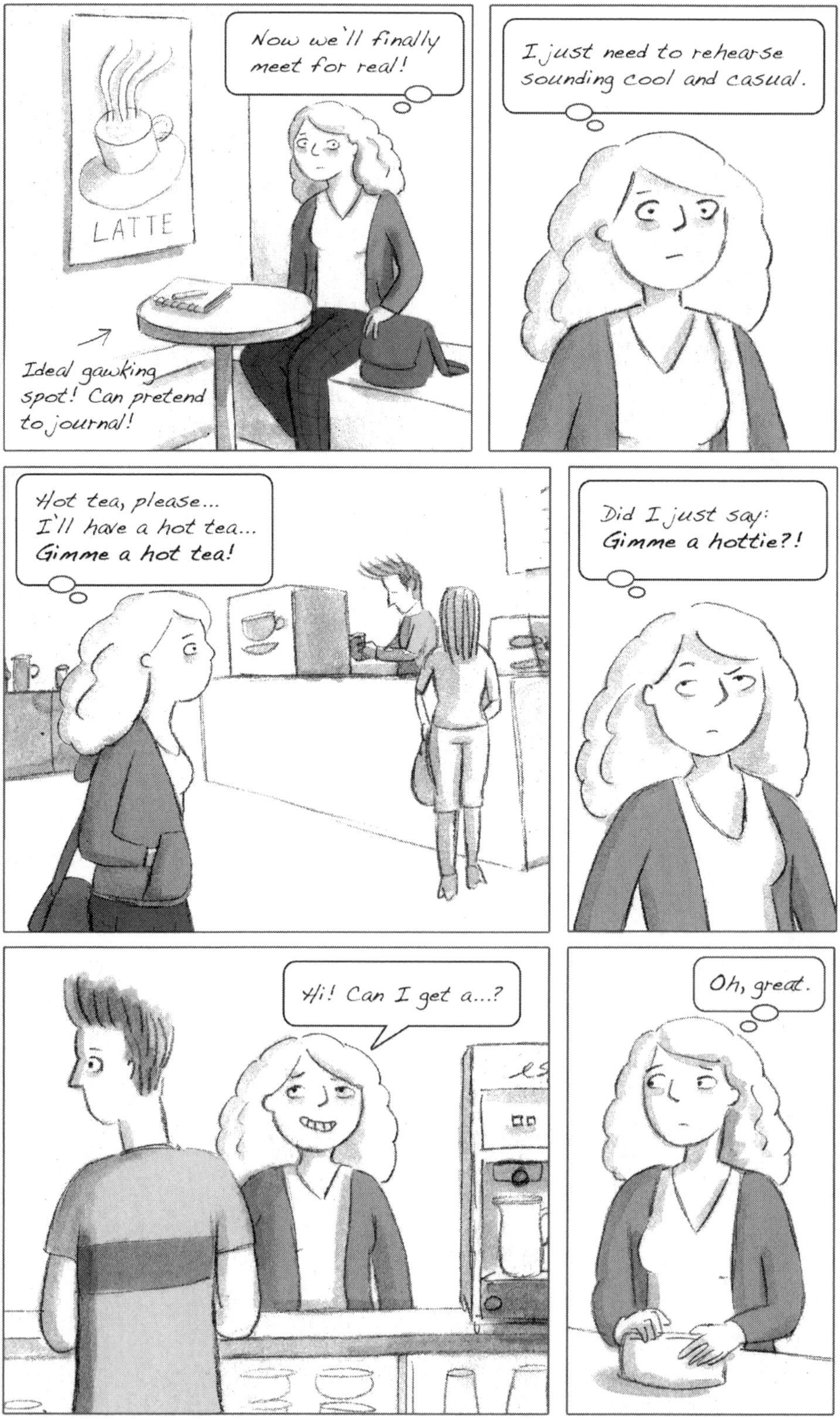
Now we'll finally meet for real!
Ideal gawking spot! Can pretend to journal!
LATTE
I just need to rehearse sounding cool and casual.
Hot tea, please...
I'll have a hot tea...
Gimme a hot tea!
Did I just say:
Gimme a hottie?!
Hi! Can I get a...?
Oh, great.

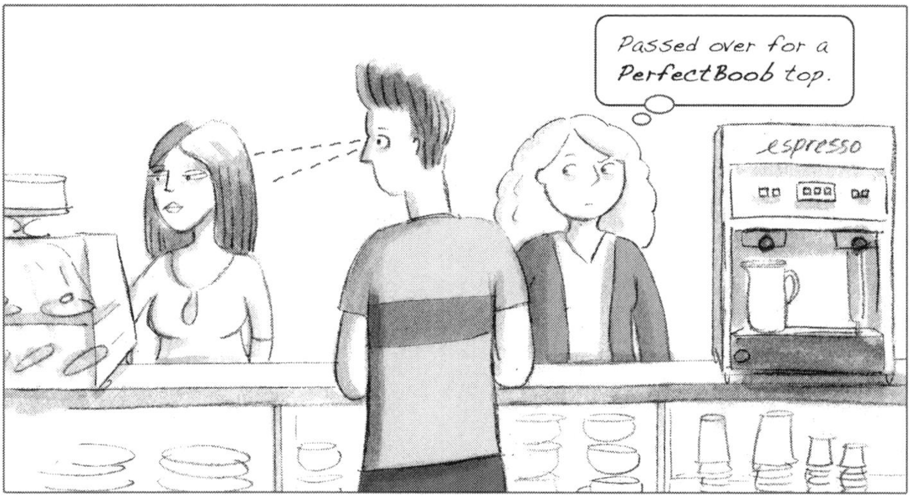
Passed over for a PerfectBoob top.
espresso

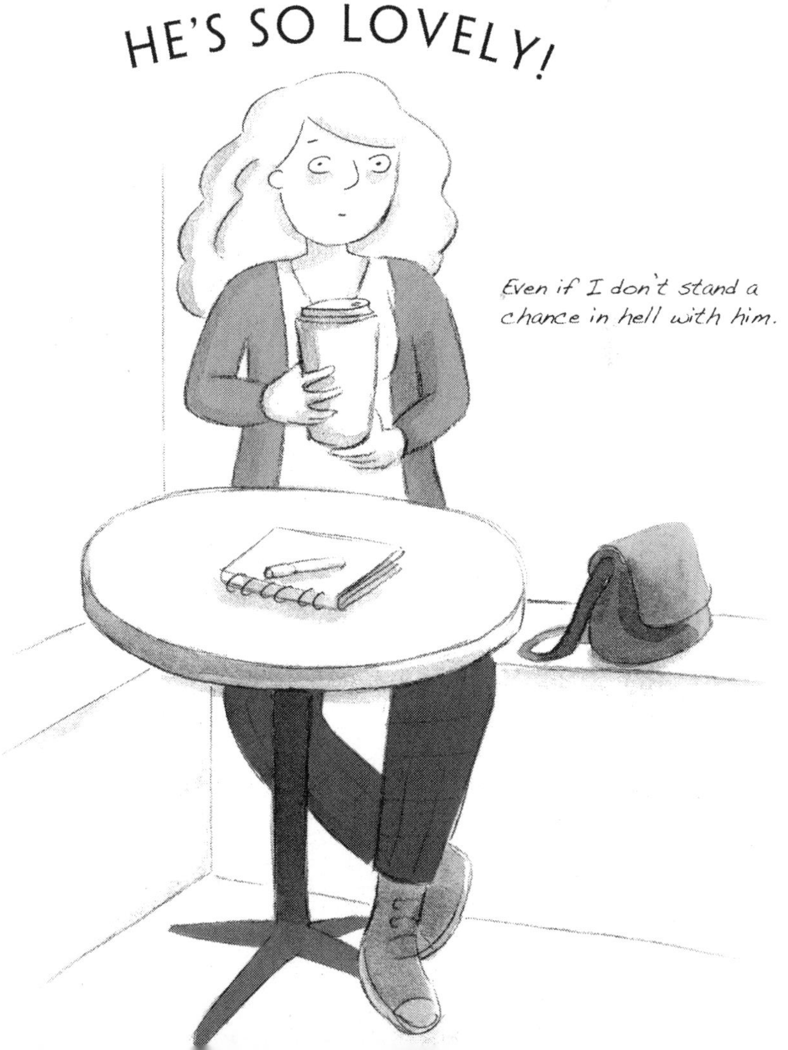
HE'S SO LOVELY!
Even if I don't stand a chance in hell with him.

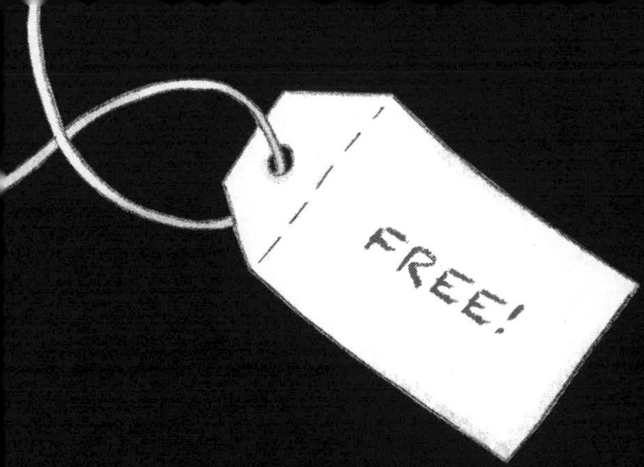
FREE!

There is no secret
that will fix you.
(Remember, there
is nothing wrong
with you.)

CHERI HUBER

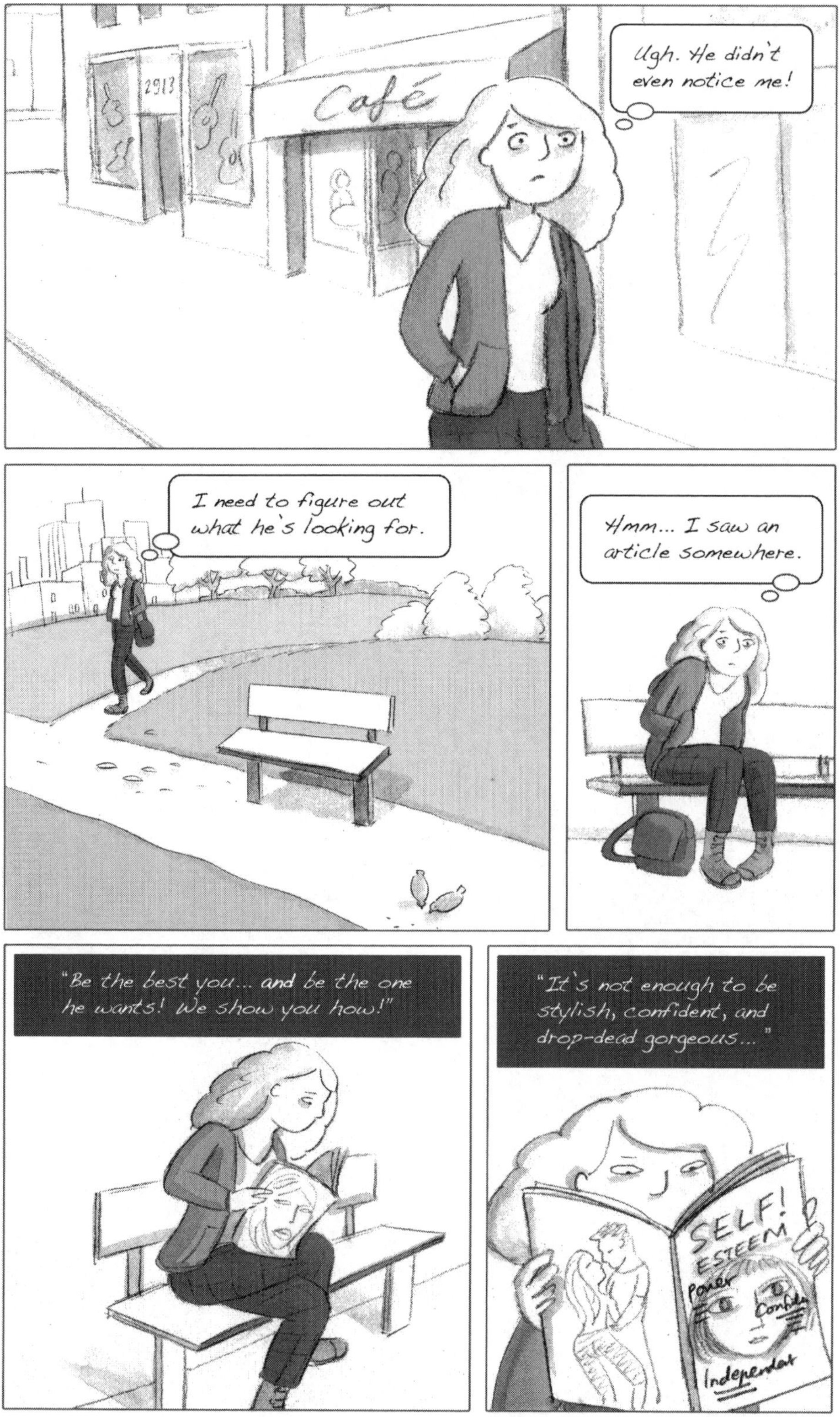
2913
Café
Ugh. He didn't even notice me!
I need to figure out what he's looking for.
Hmm... I saw an article somewhere.
"Be the best you... and be the one he wants! We show you how!"
"It's not enough to be stylish, confident, and drop-dead gorgeous..."
SELF! ESTEEM
Power
Independent

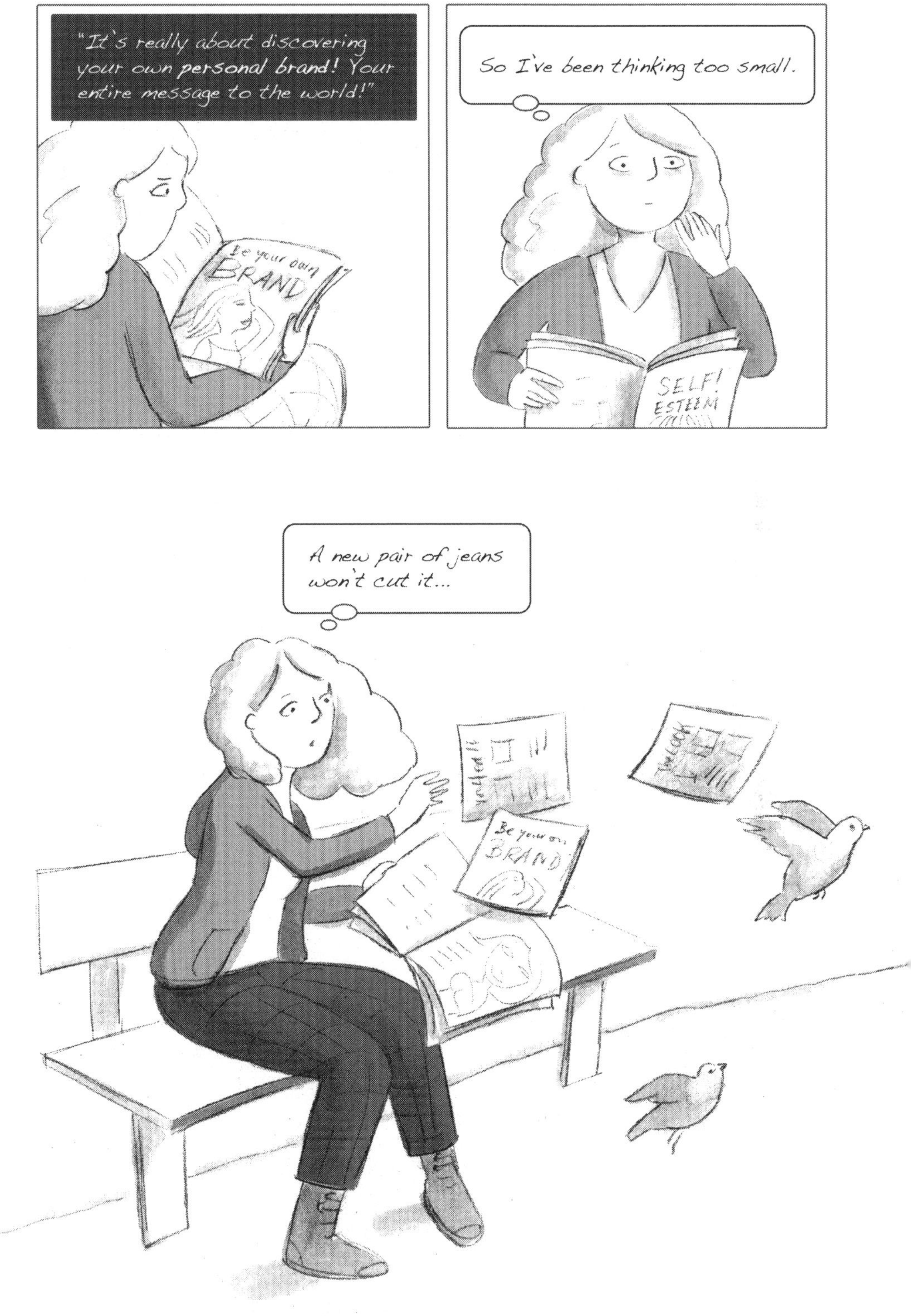
"It's really about discovering your own personal brand! Your entire message to the world!"
Be your own BRAND
So I've been thinking too small.
SELF! ESTEEM
A new pair of jeans won't cut it...
Be your own BRAND

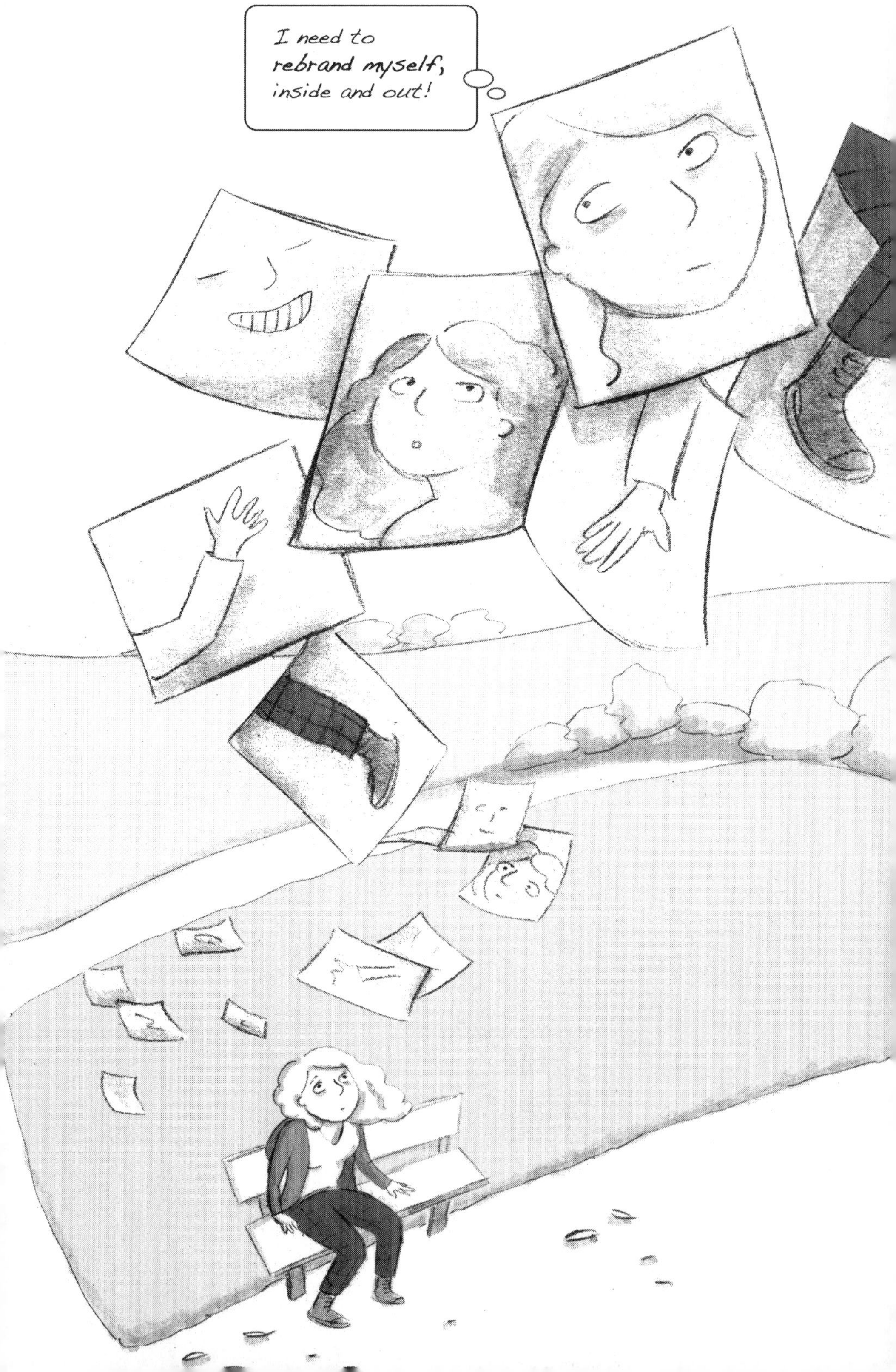
I need to **rebrand myself**, inside and out!

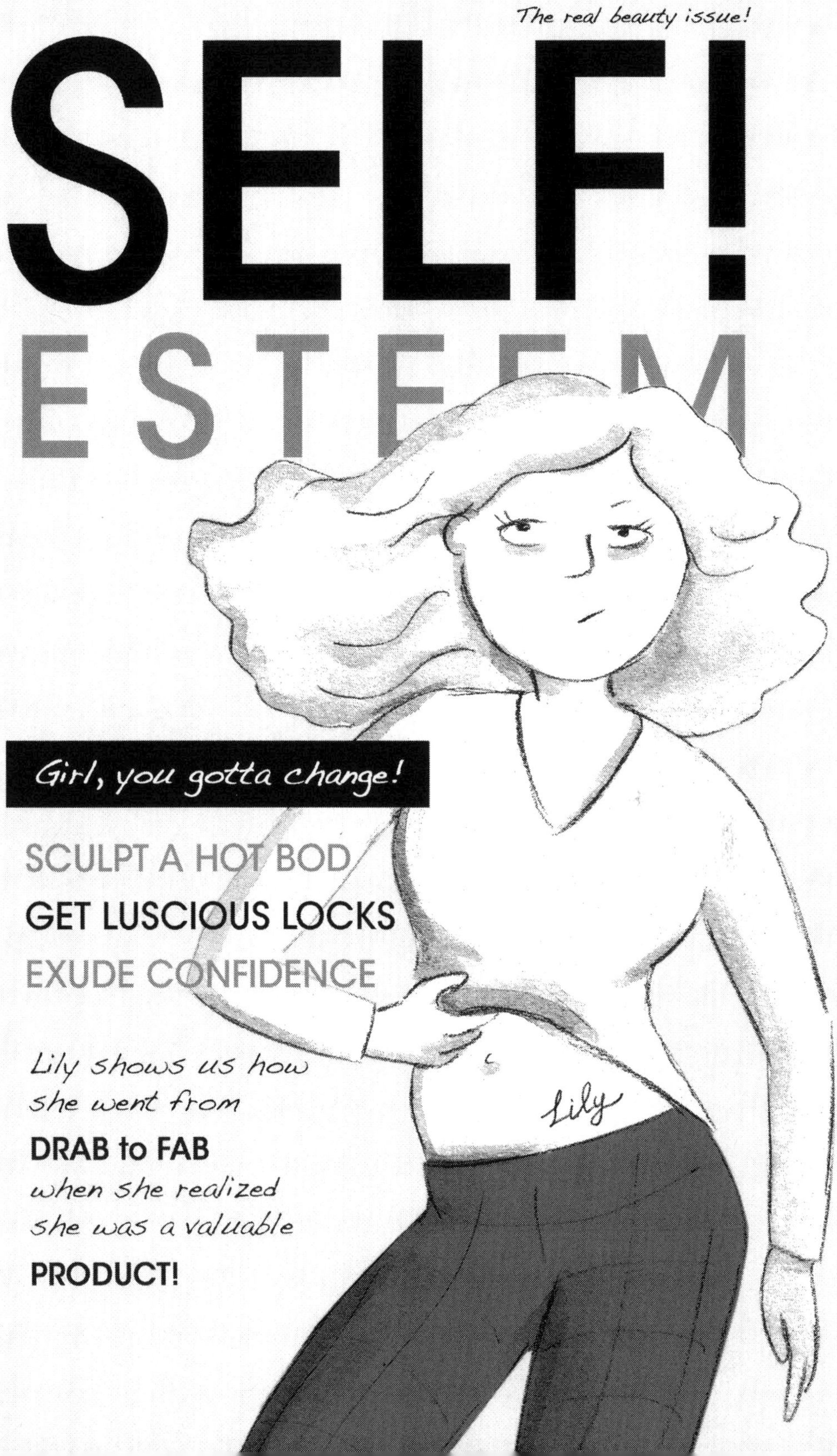

The real beauty issue!
SELF!
ESTEEM
Girl, you gotta change!
SCULPT A HOT BOD
GET LUSCIOUS LOCKS
EXUDE CONFIDENCE
Lily shows us how she went from
DRAB to FAB
when she realized she was a valuable
PRODUCT!
Lily

STEP 1. DESIGN YOUR PACKAGE

FASHION WITH ATTITUDE

It's not just about finding a look that rocks! Inner beauty comes from crafting an identity that'll reach your target market!

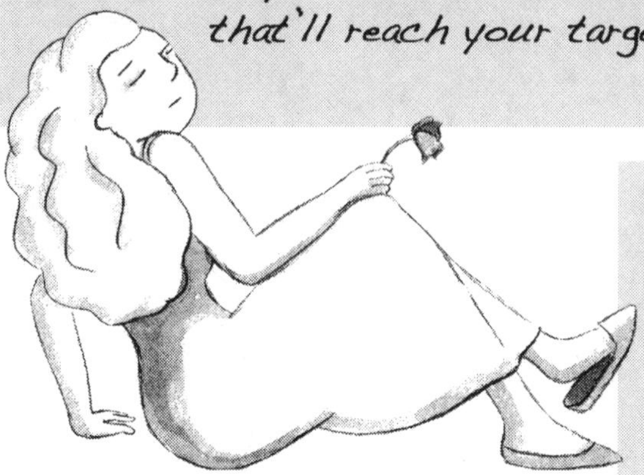

WHIMSICAL GODDESS

She's a romantic dreamer who's just out of reach. Underneath that calm exterior who knows what's bubbling? (Who cares?)

POWER VIXEN

She's like one of the boys. (At least that's what we're meant to think!)

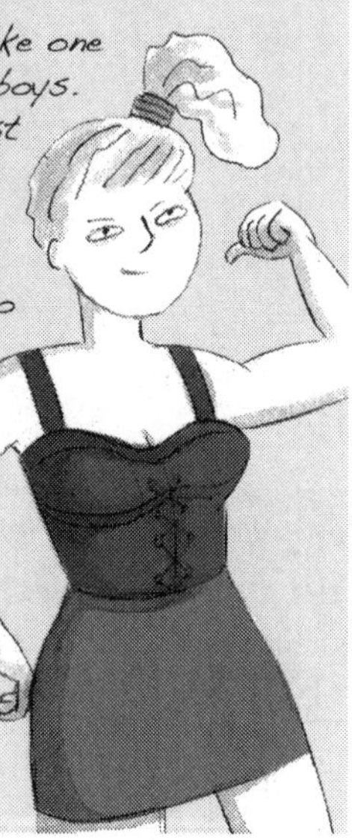

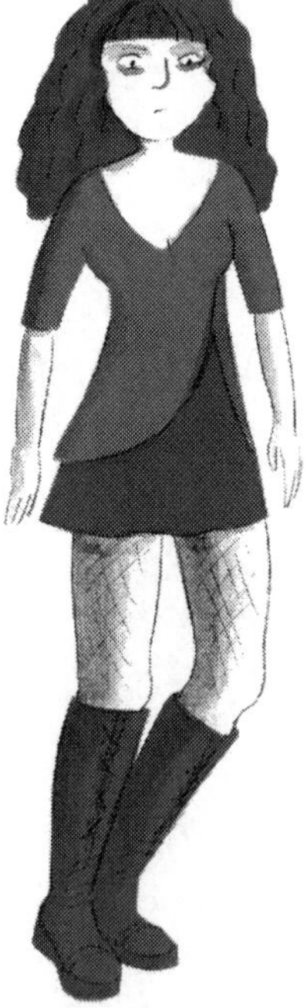

DARK FAIRY

A dose of Gothic cynicism never hurt anyone. (Well, maybe in those boots!)

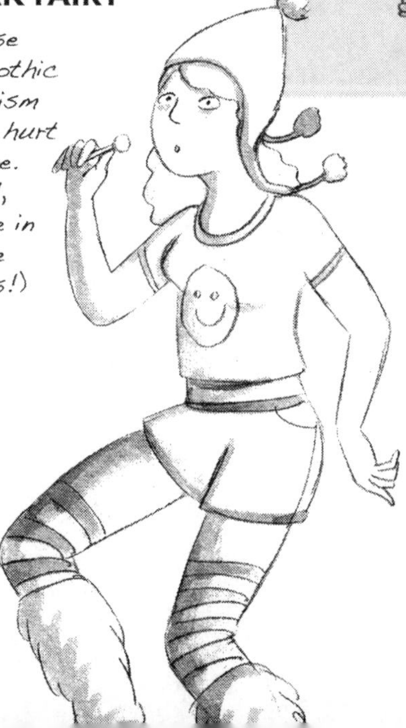

CUTE GIRL-WOMAN

Isn't she so adorable? (Hard to believe, but that lost little girl thing still works!)

DAZZLING TRESSES

Your package will be worthless without gorgeous hair. Perfecting it must be your lifelong quest!

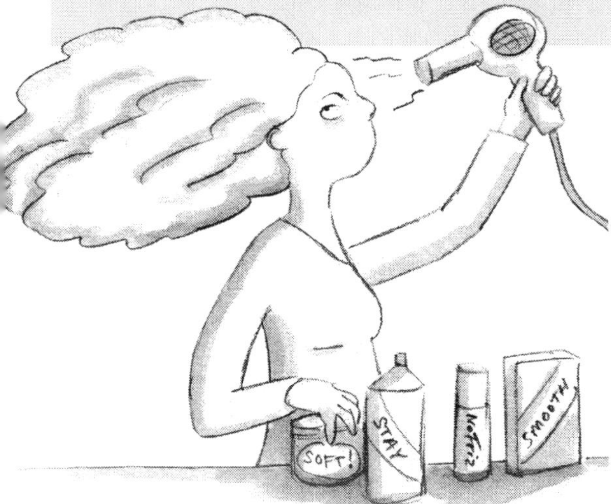
SOFT!
STAY
NoFrizz
SMOOTH

GET VOLUME

Make sure you create fullness, ***not poofiness!***

NO FRIZZ

If you can't get soft, shiny curls, ***steamroll*** *it!*

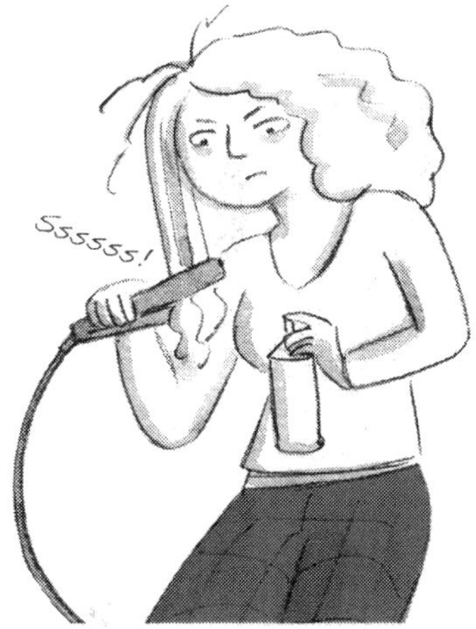
Ssssss!

NO! NEVER! DO NOT!

(Even if you saw how on the internet).

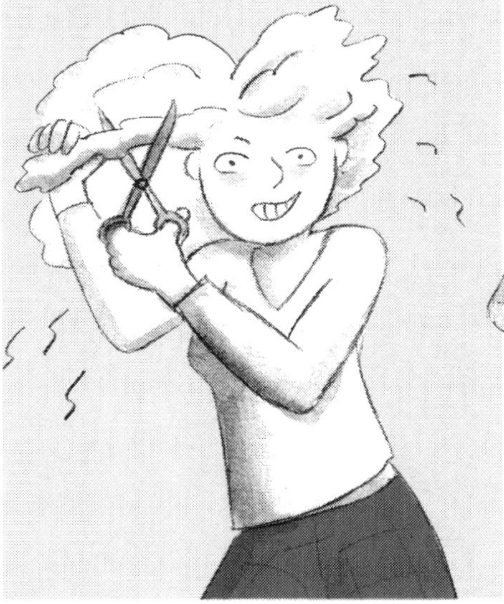

AND NO MATTER WHAT...

Make your alterations look ***natural!***

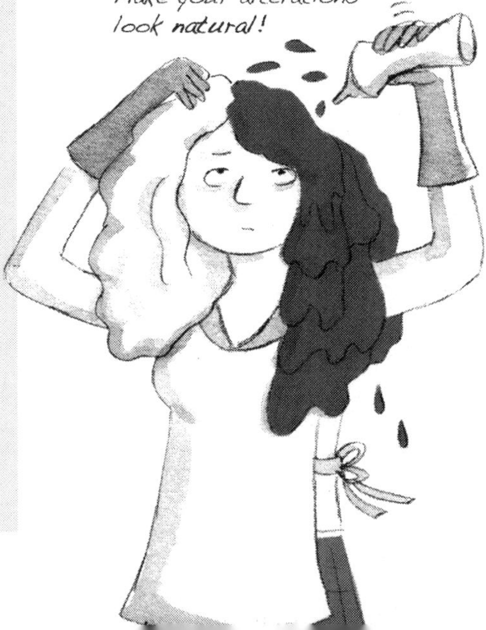

STEP 2. TAKE CONTROL

IT'S A FULL-TIME JOB

Taking care of your physique is your key to success as a woman. Relax for even a minute and it'll all fall apart!

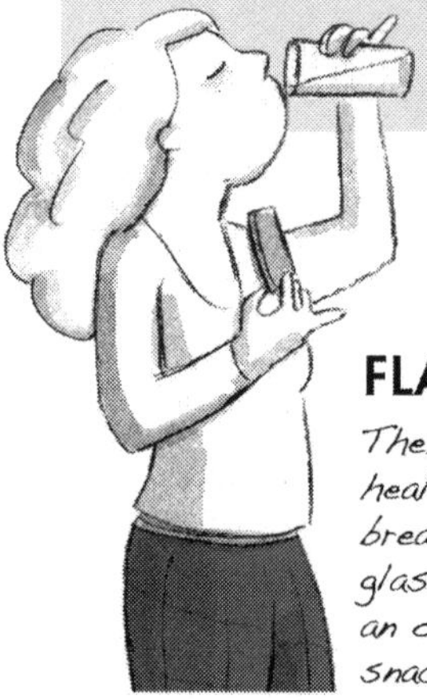

FLAB

There's nothing healthy about breakfast! A full glass of water and an overprocessed snack bar are plenty!

TUCK

Shoot for the ideal belly flatness, shown below.

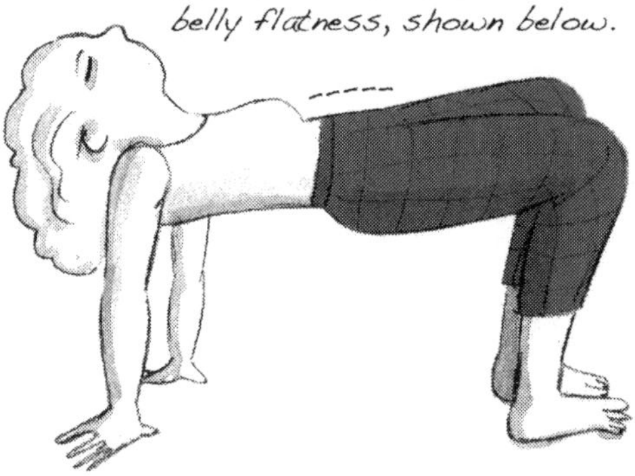

SAG

Lift up those problem wobbly areas (you know what we mean!) with a figure-hugging black dress and the highest heels you can stand in!

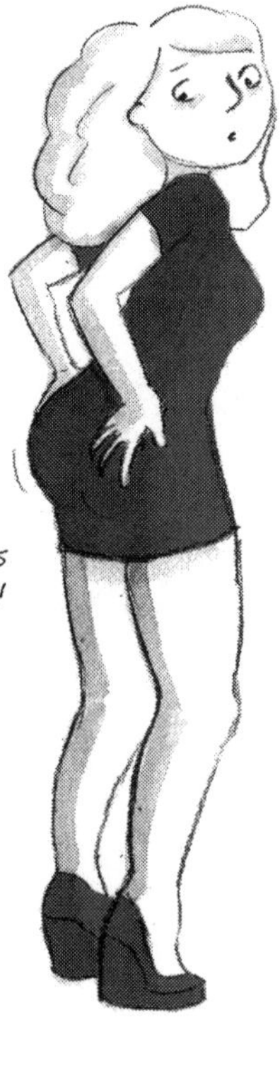

SUCK

Do not let it all hang out!

Practice your skinny!

Whether you're on the beach or alone in your room, remember to ***suck, suck, suck it in!***

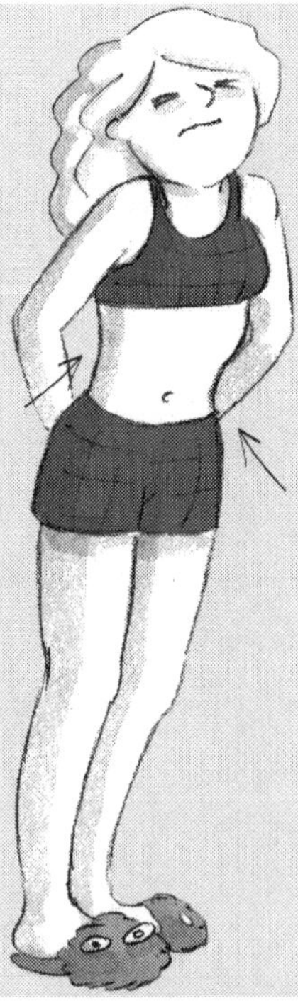

IS YOUR PERSONALITY OVERWEIGHT?

Make sure your mind is as trim as your body! Remove excess baggage.

POSITIVE OUTLOOK

Get control over negative thinking by using yoga or meditation. Be sure to consistently berate yourself when you fail. You're obviously not trying hard enough!

THE PERFECT WOMAN

Find your ideal female role model and constantly try to measure up. It'll help you strive for something better!

We really can't say enough about comparing yourself to others!

Otherwise, who knows what might happen? (You'll become a lazy slob, that's what).

STEP 3. ADVERTISE!

Lily

Sexy

Sassy

Fun

ABOUT ME
I'm really easygoing. No drama here!
(I just repress all my feelings).

WHAT MAKES LILY DIFFERENT?
I have really low expectations.

INTERESTS
Running, hiking, snowboarding, yoga...
Well, on occasion.

CONTACT ME IF
You're reasonably cute.
You like me.

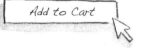

Add to Cart

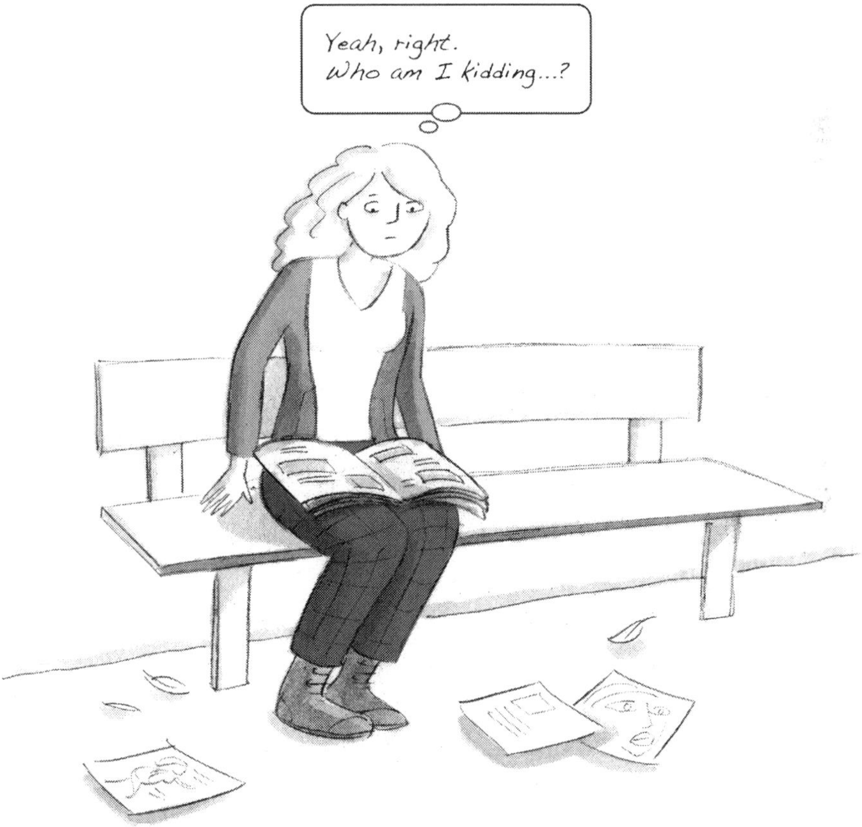
Yeah, right.
Who am I kidding...?

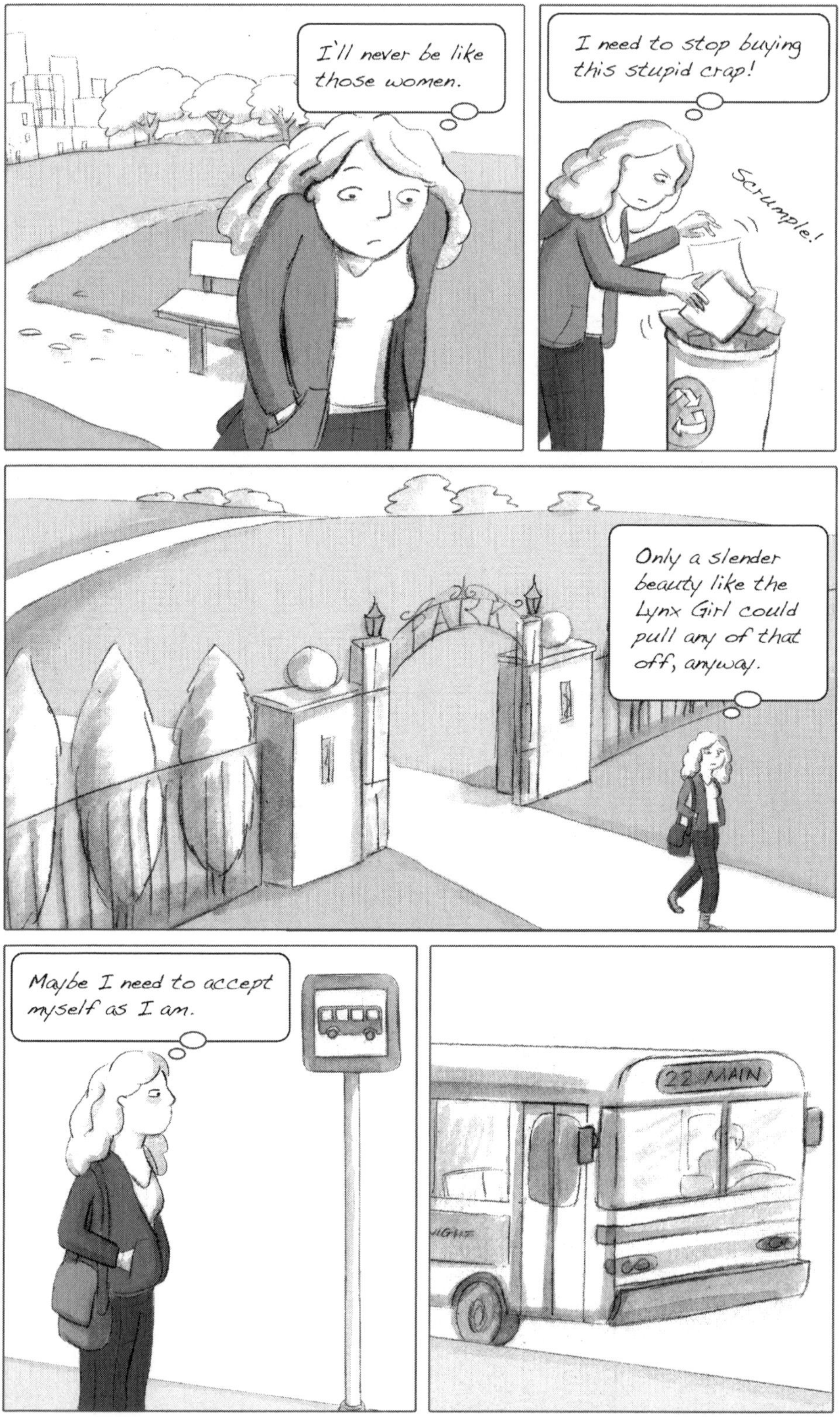
I'll never be like those women.
I need to stop buying this stupid crap!
Scrumple!
Only a slender beauty like the Lynx Girl could pull any of that off, anyway.
PARK
Maybe I need to accept myself as I am.
22 MAIN

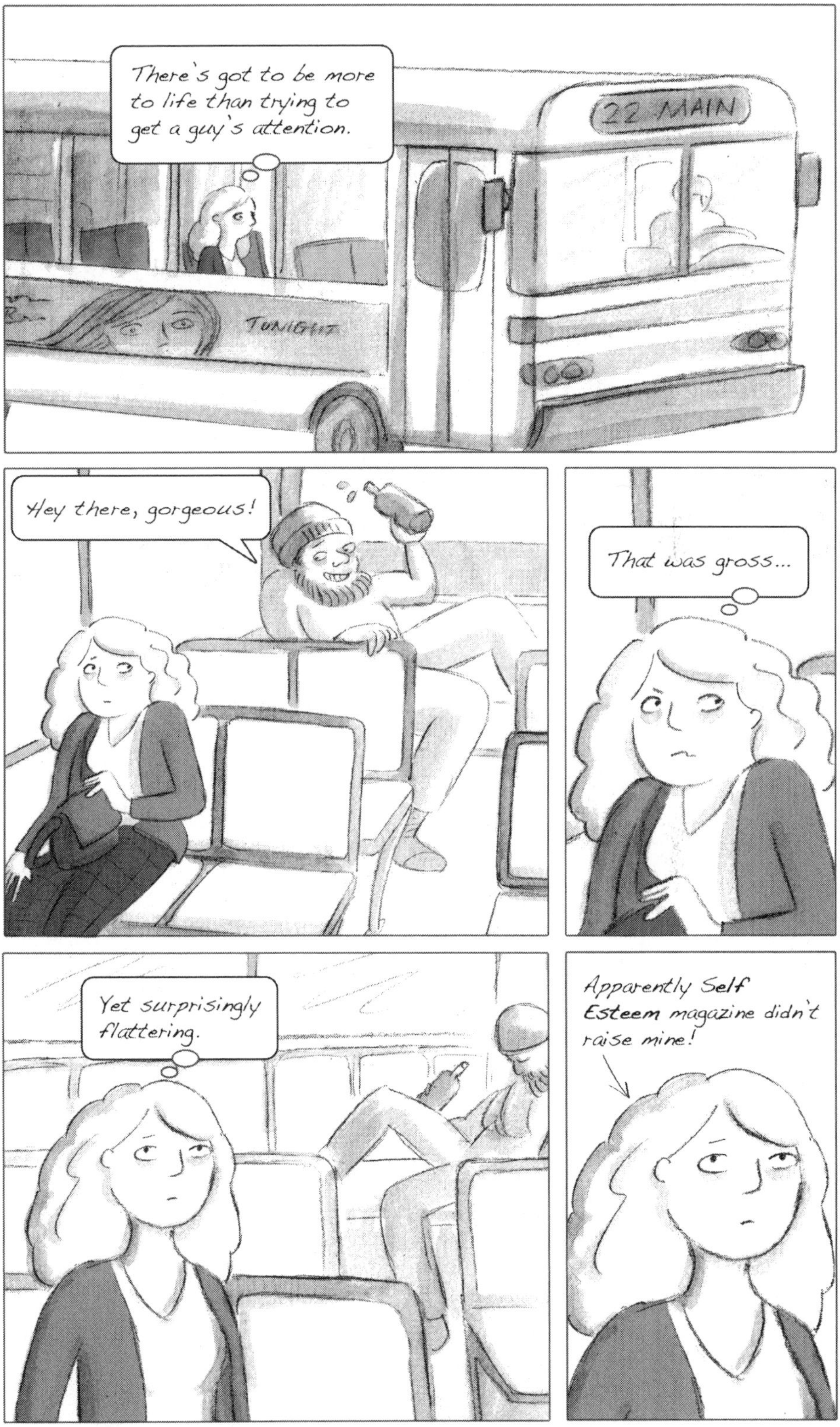
There's got to be more to life than trying to get a guy's attention.
22 MAIN
TONIGHT
Hey there, gorgeous!
That was gross...
Yet surprisingly flattering.
Apparently Self **Esteem** magazine didn't raise mine!

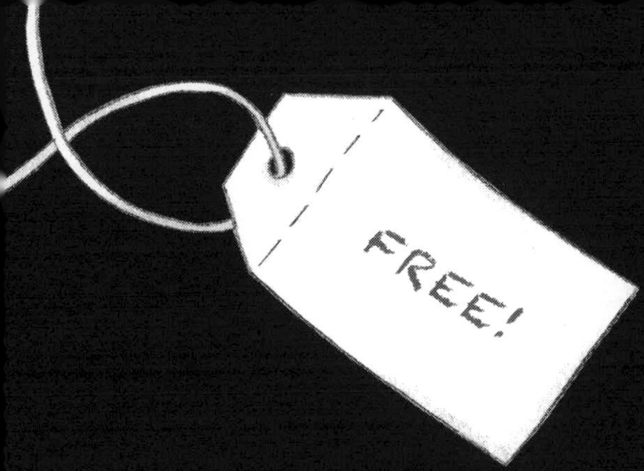
FREE!

Two people have been living inside you all your life. One is the ego...; the other is the hidden spiritual being, whose still voice of wisdom you have only rarely attended to.

SOGYAL RINPOCHE

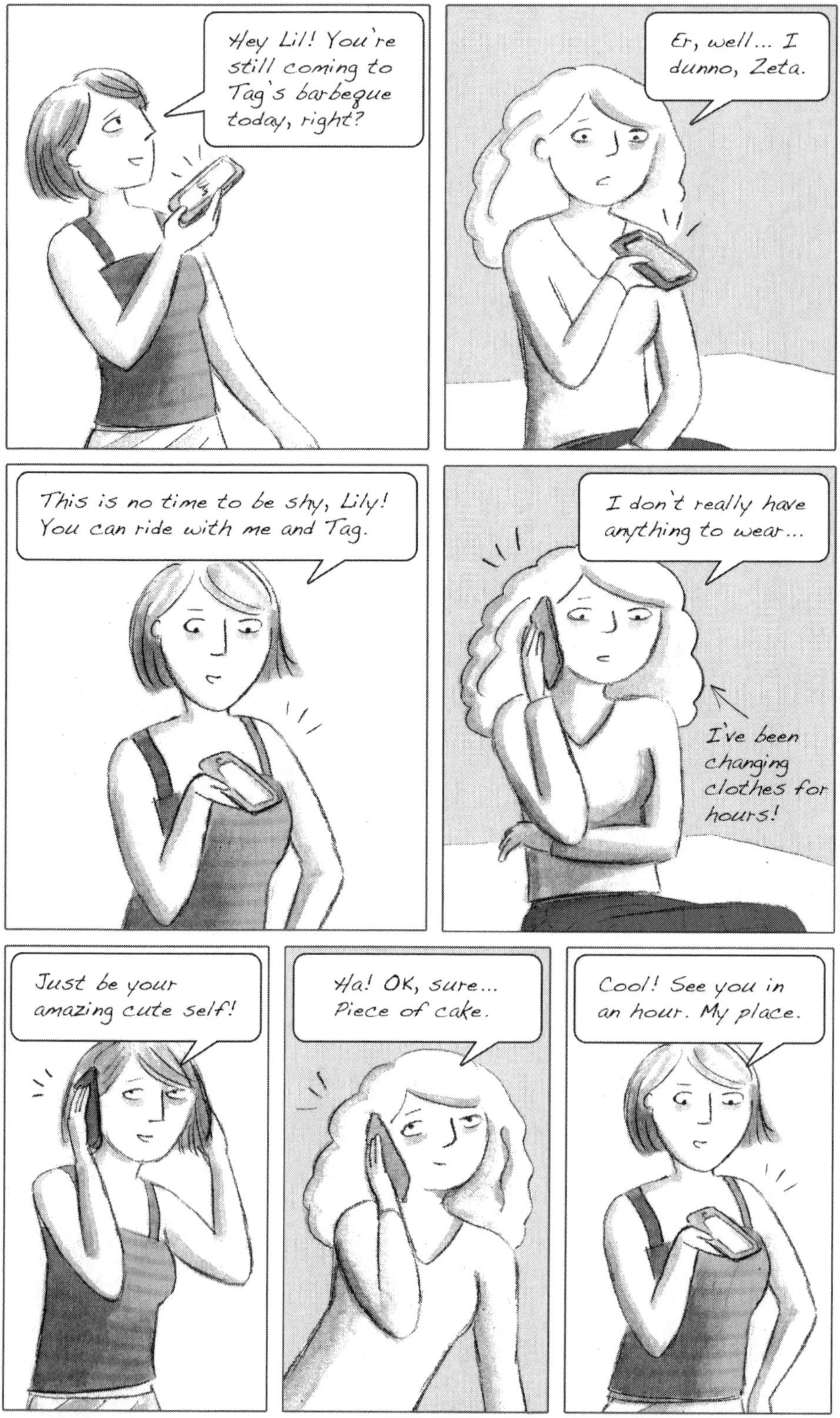
Hey Lil! You're still coming to Tag's barbeque today, right?
Er, well... I dunno, Zeta.
This is no time to be shy, Lily! You can ride with me and Tag.
I don't really have anything to wear...
I've been changing clothes for hours!
Just be your amazing cute self!
Ha! OK, sure... Piece of cake.
Cool! See you in an hour. My place.

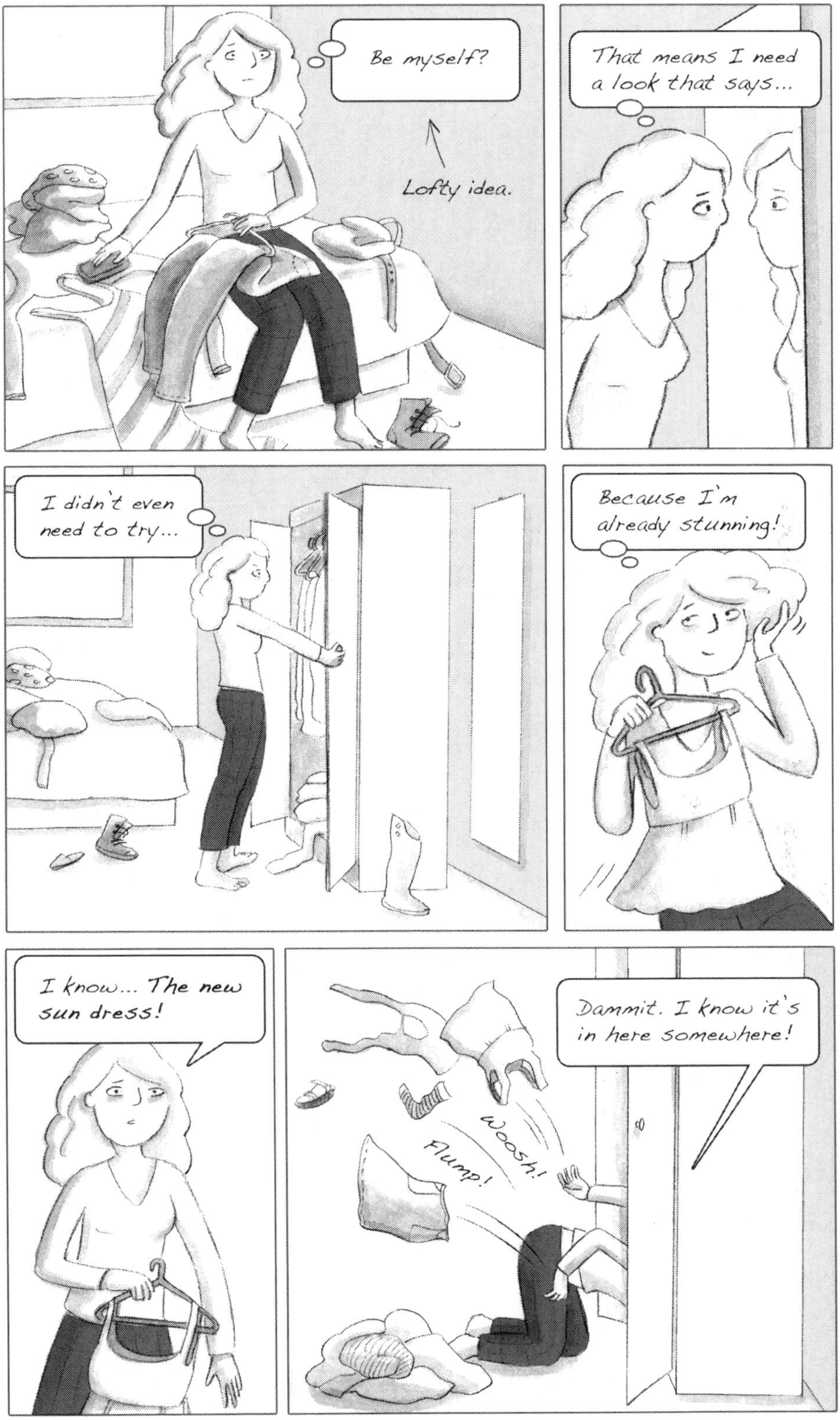
Be myself?
Lofty idea.
That means I need a look that says...
I didn't even need to try...
Because I'm already stunning!
I know... The new sun dress!
Dammit. I know it's in here somewhere!
Wooosh!
Flump!

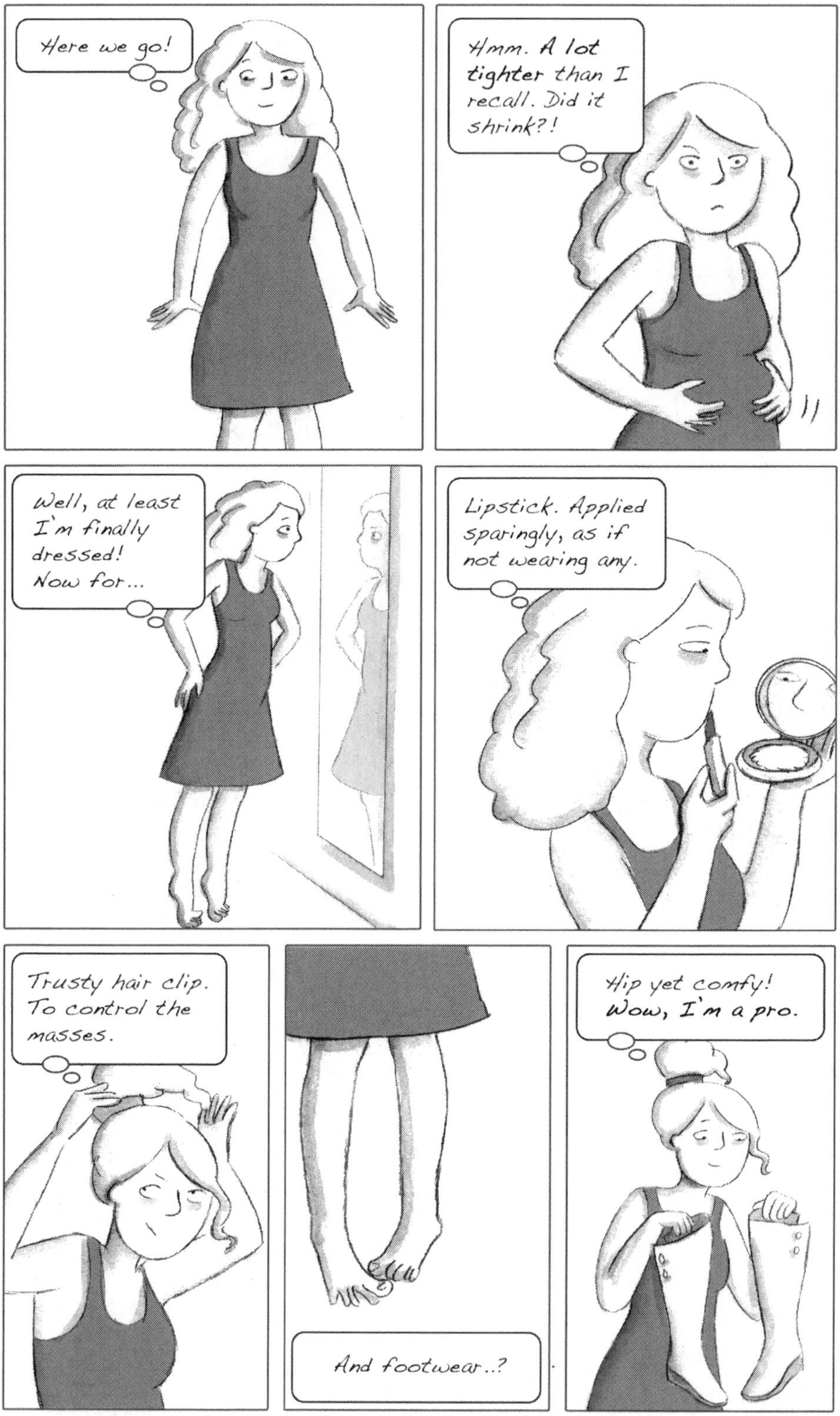
Here we go!
Hmm. A lot tighter than I recall. Did it shrink?!
Well, at least I'm finally dressed! Now for...
Lipstick. Applied sparingly, as if not wearing any.
Trusty hair clip. To control the masses.
And footwear..?
Hip yet comfy! Wow, I'm a pro.

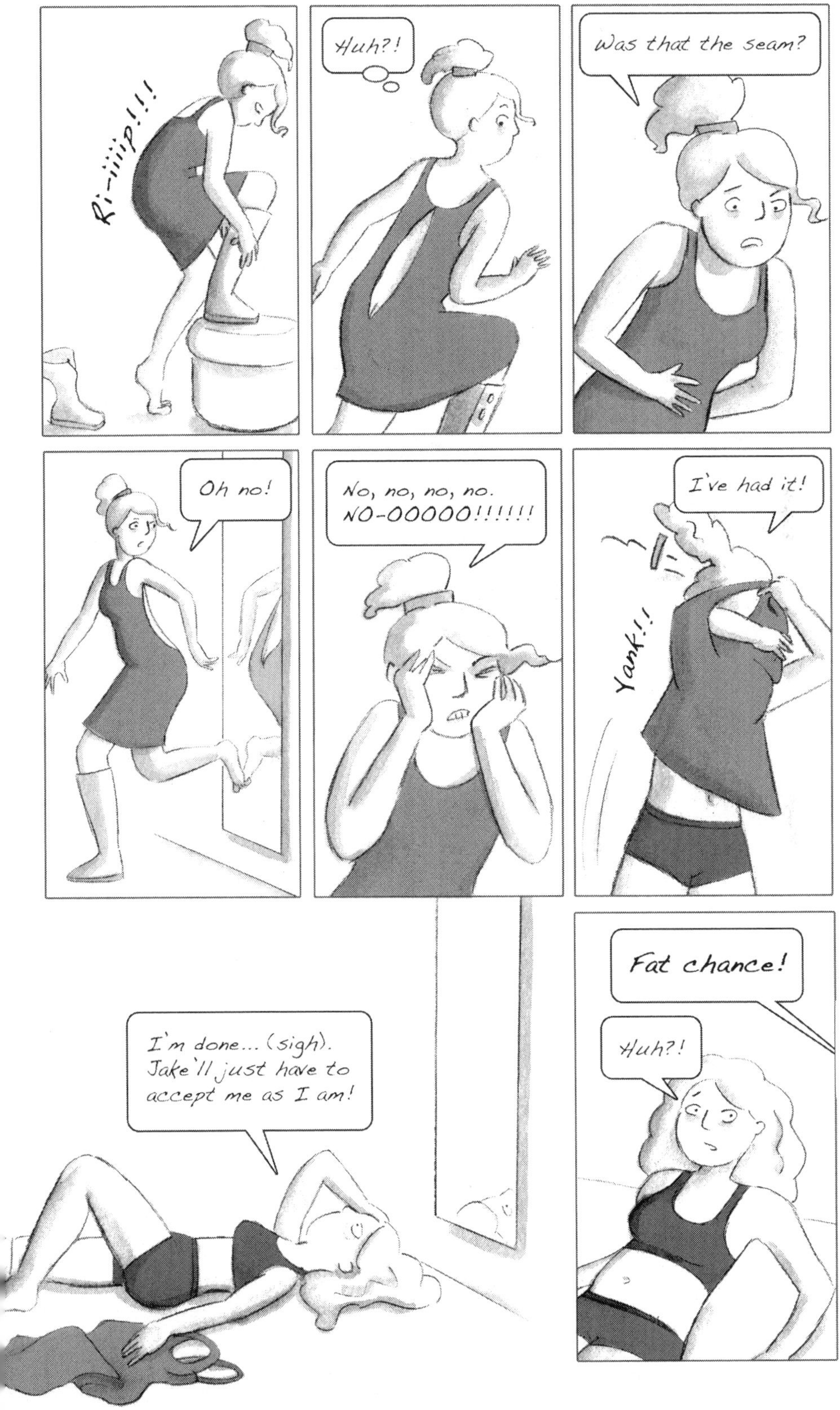
Ri-iiiip!!!
Huh?!
Was that the seam?
Oh no!
No, no, no, no.
NO-OOOOO!!!!!!
I've had it!
Yank!!
I'm done... (sigh).
Jake'll just have to
accept me as I am!
Fat chance!
Huh?!

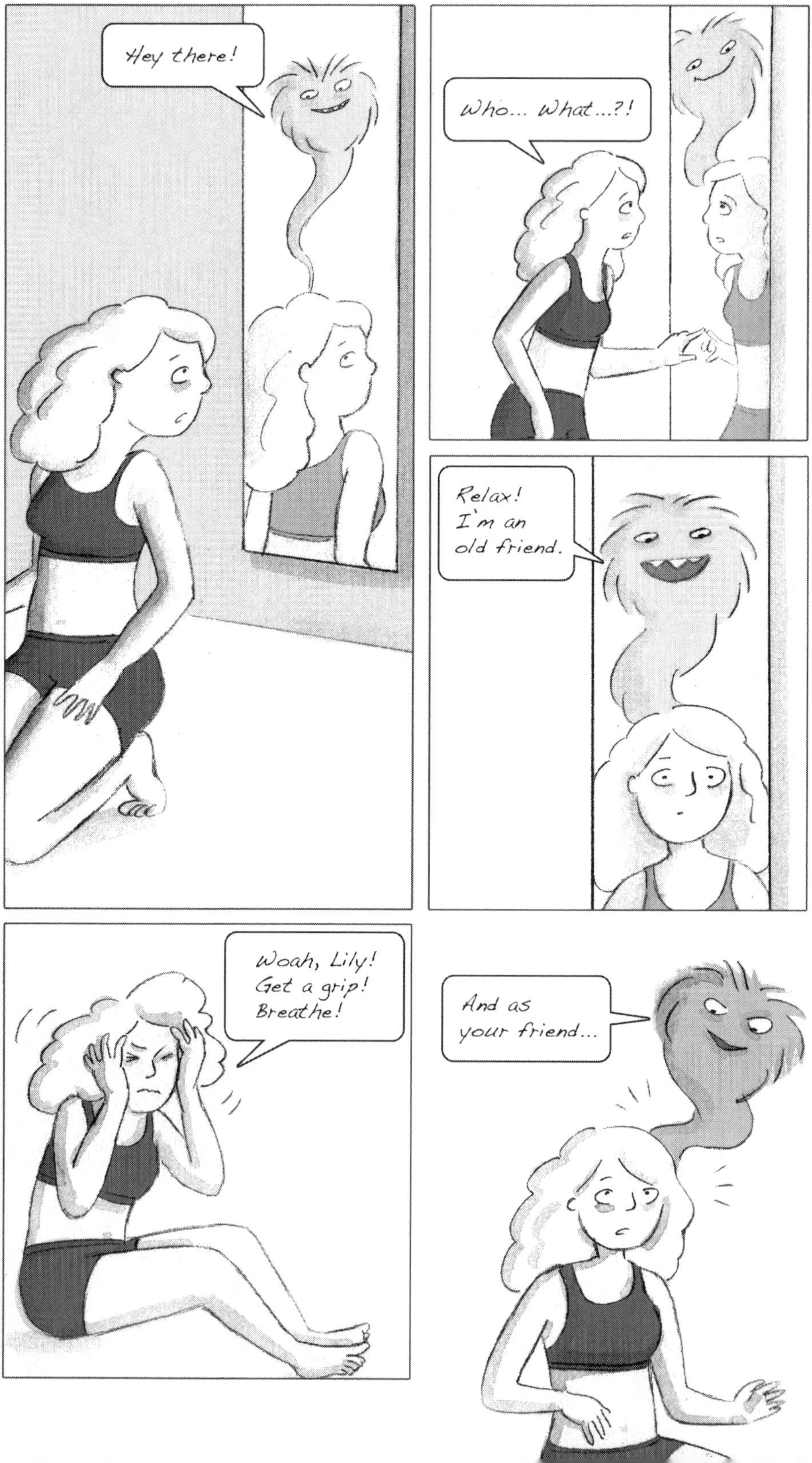
Hey there!
Who... What...?!
Relax! I'm an old friend.
Woah, Lily! Get a grip! Breathe!
And as your friend...

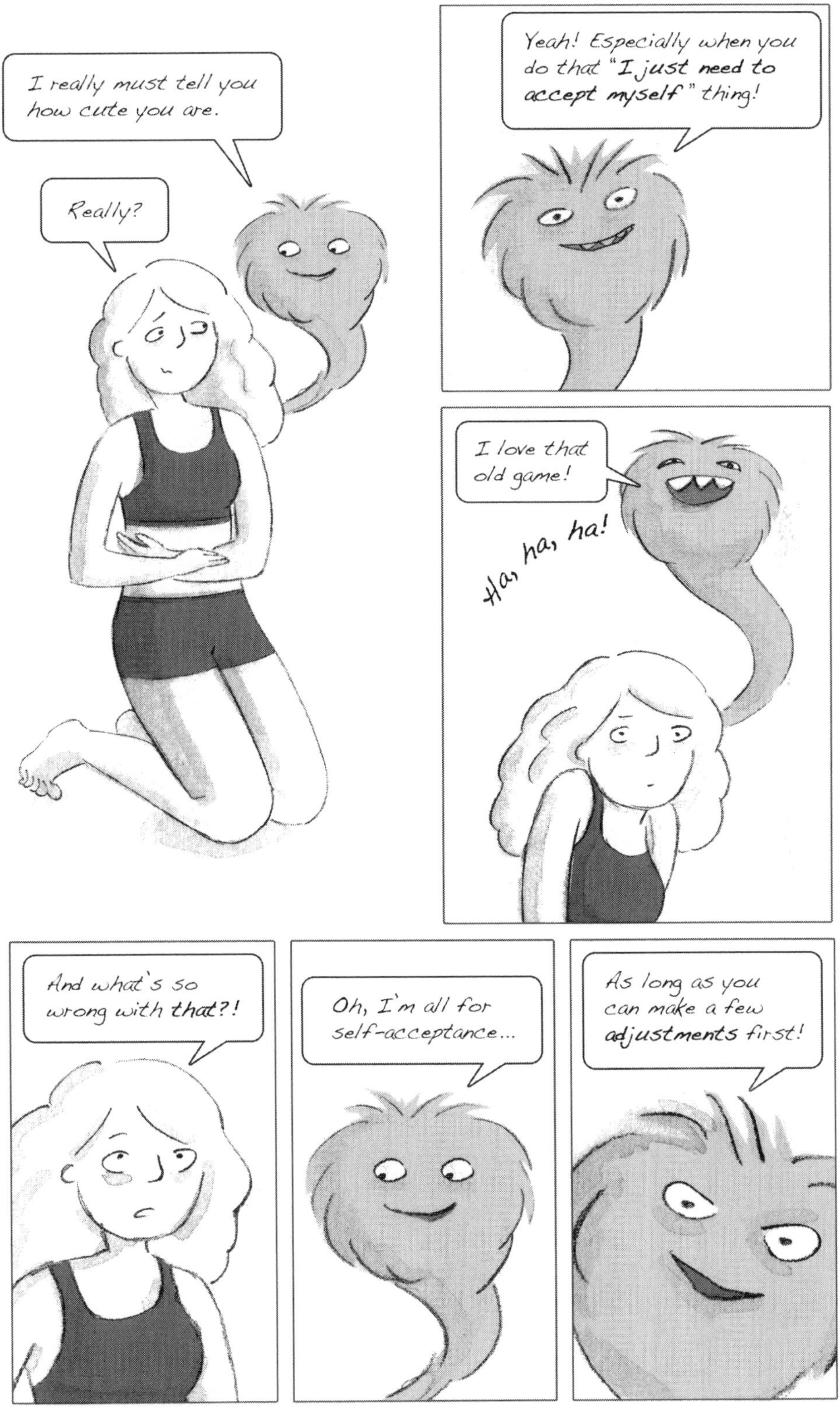
I really must tell you how cute you are.
Really?
Yeah! Especially when you do that "**I just need to accept myself**" thing!
I love that old game!
Ha, ha, ha!
And what's so wrong with **that**?!
Oh, I'm all for self-acceptance...
As long as you can make a few **adjustments** first!

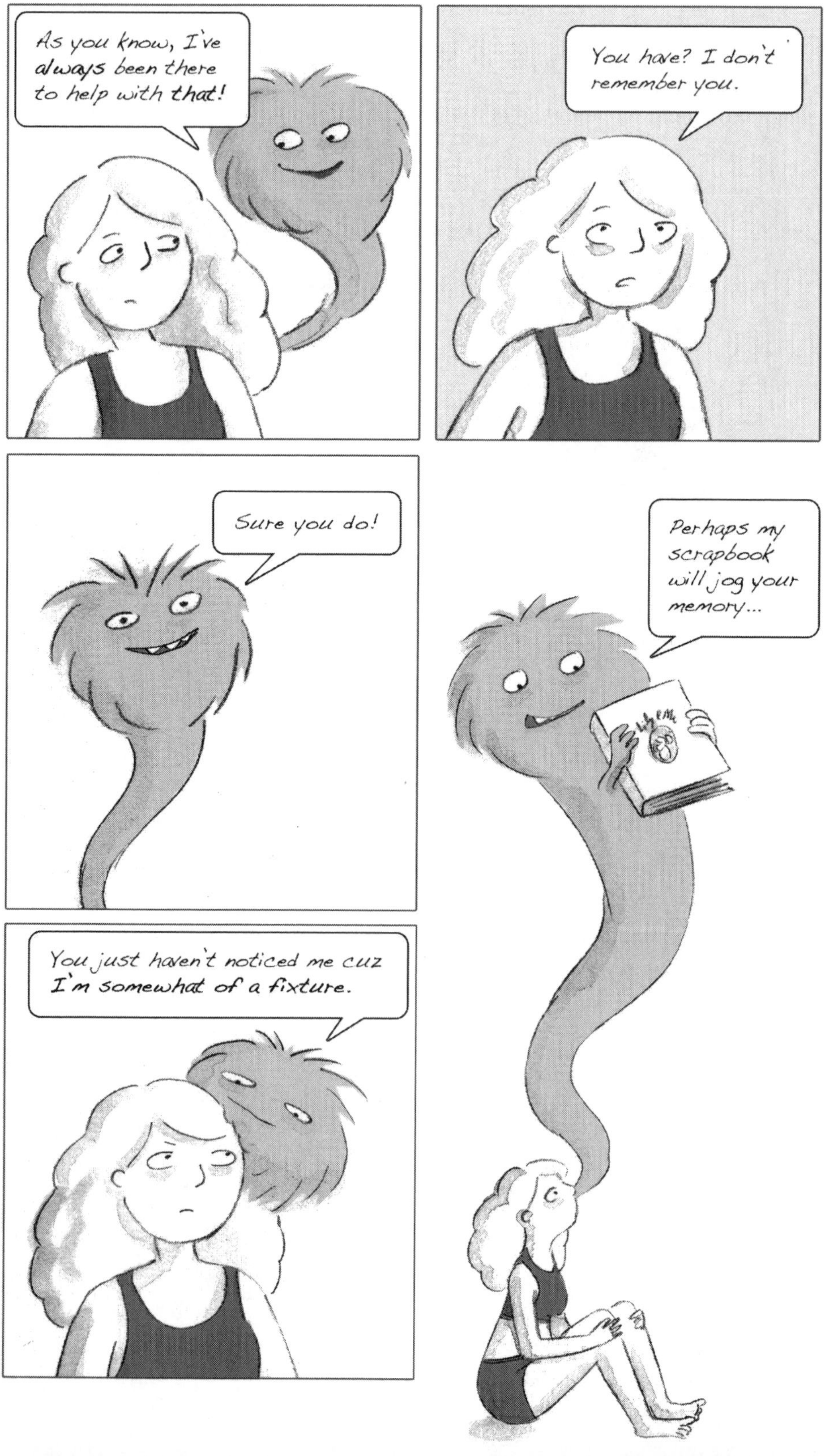
As you know, I've always been there to help with that!
You have? I don't remember you.
Sure you do!
You just haven't noticed me cuz I'm somewhat of a fixture.
Perhaps my scrapbook will jog your memory...

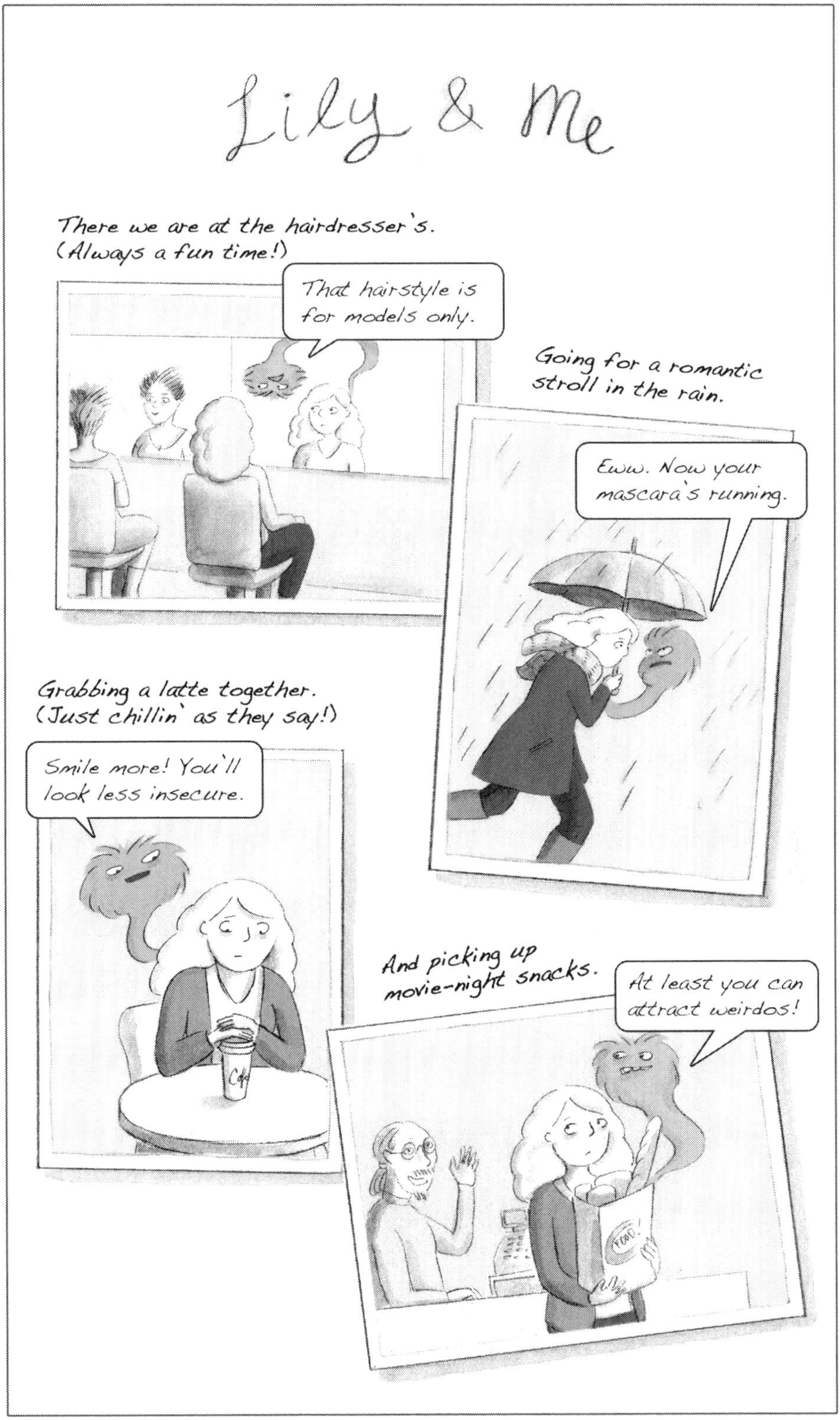
Lily & Me
There we are at the hairdresser's. (Always a fun time!)
That hairstyle is for models only.
Going for a romantic stroll in the rain.
Eww. Now your mascara's running.
Grabbing a latte together. (Just chillin' as they say!)
Smile more! You'll look less insecure.
And picking up movie-night snacks.
At least you can attract weirdos!
FOOD!

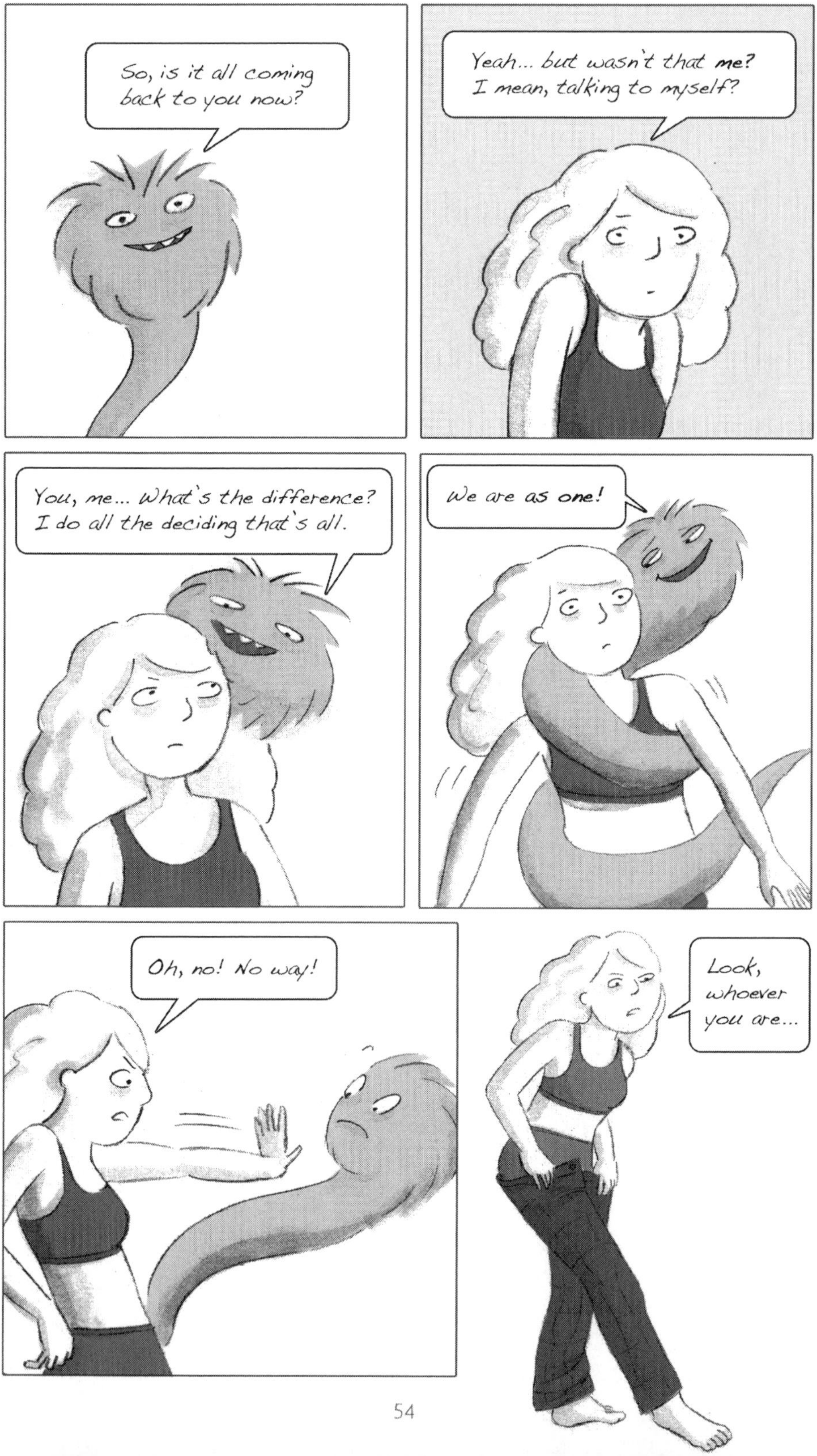
So, is it all coming back to you now?
Yeah... but wasn't that **me**? I mean, talking to myself?
You, me... What's the difference? I do all the deciding that's all.
We are as **one**!
Oh, no! No way!
Look, whoever you are...

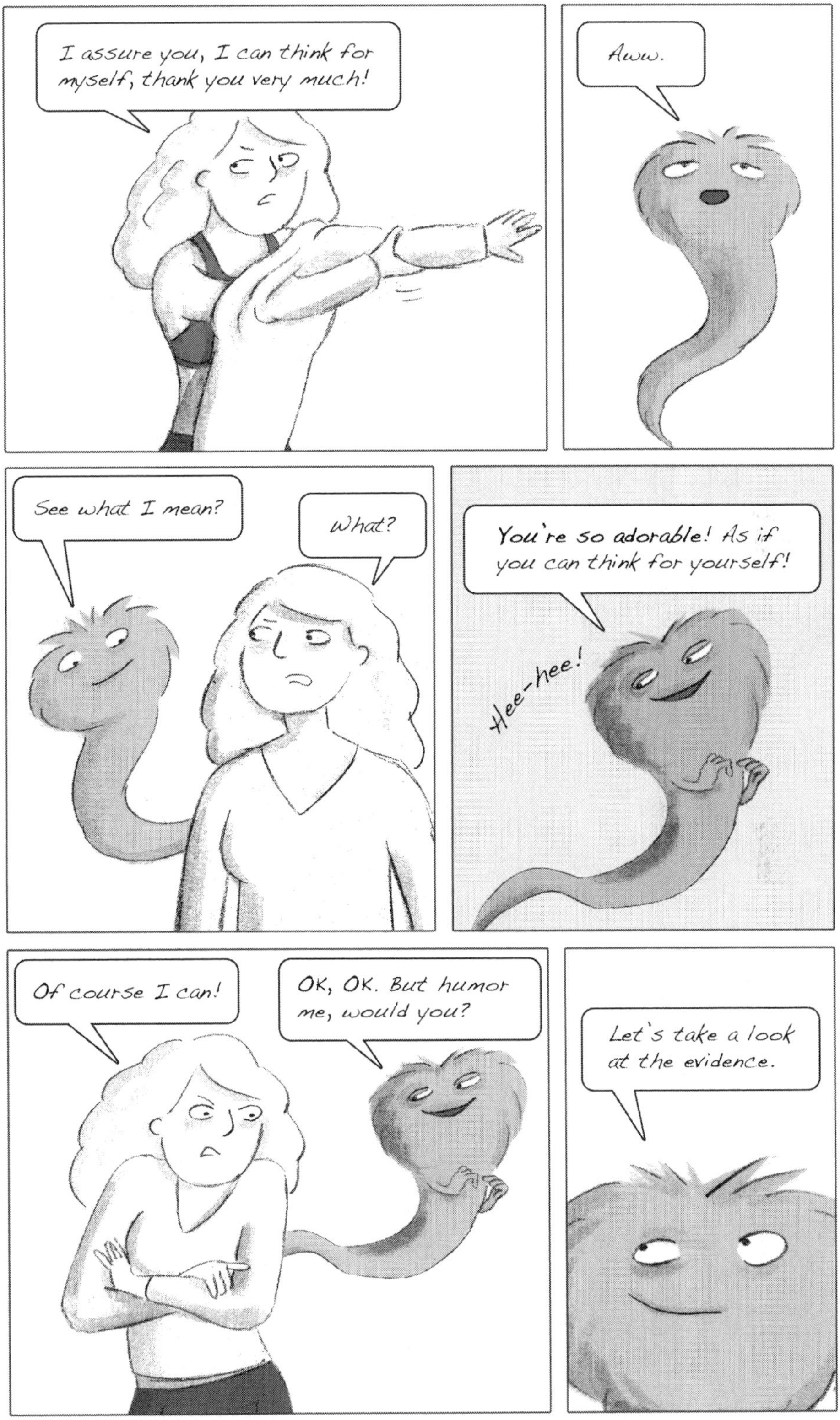
I assure you, I can think for myself, thank you very much!
Aww.
See what I mean?
What?
You're so adorable! As if you can think for yourself!
Hee-hee!
Of course I can!
OK, OK. But humor me, would you?
Let's take a look at the evidence.

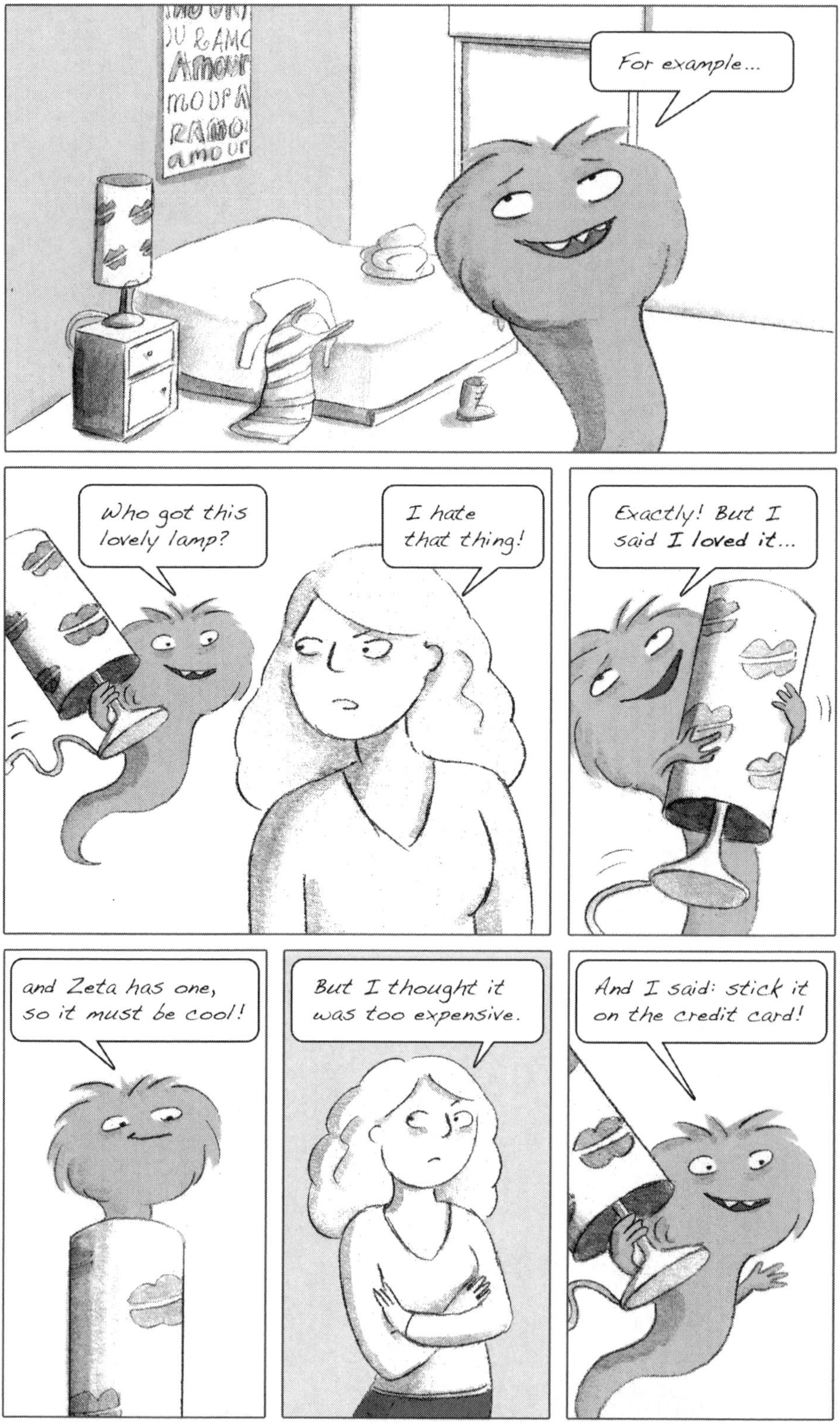
For example...
Who got this lovely lamp?
I hate that thing!
Exactly! But I said **I loved it**...
and Zeta has one, so it must be cool!
But I thought it was too expensive.
And I said: stick it on the credit card!

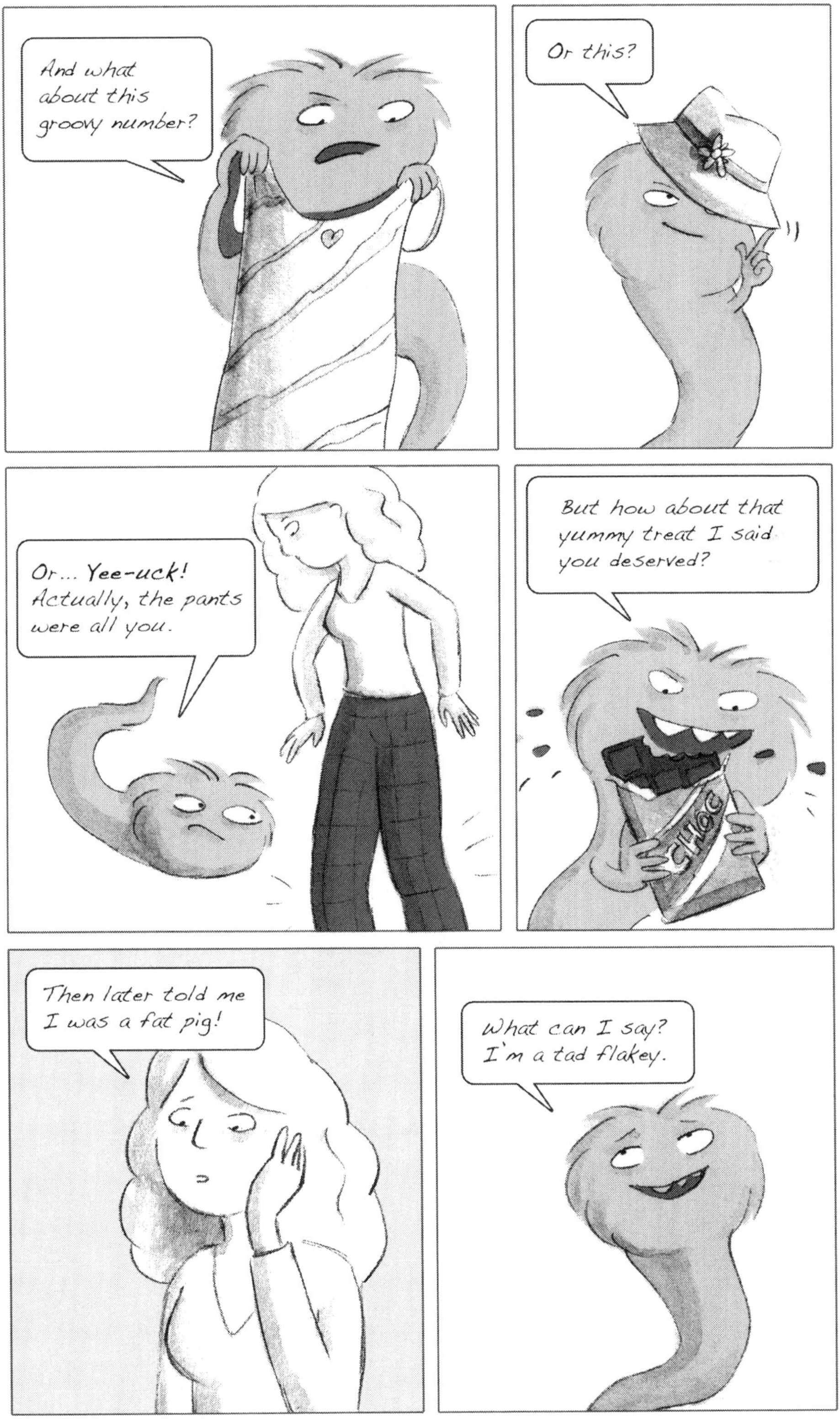
And what about this groovy number?
Or this?
Or... Yee-uck! Actually, the pants were all you.
But how about that yummy treat I said you deserved?
CHOC
Then later told me I was a fat pig!
What can I say? I'm a tad flakey.

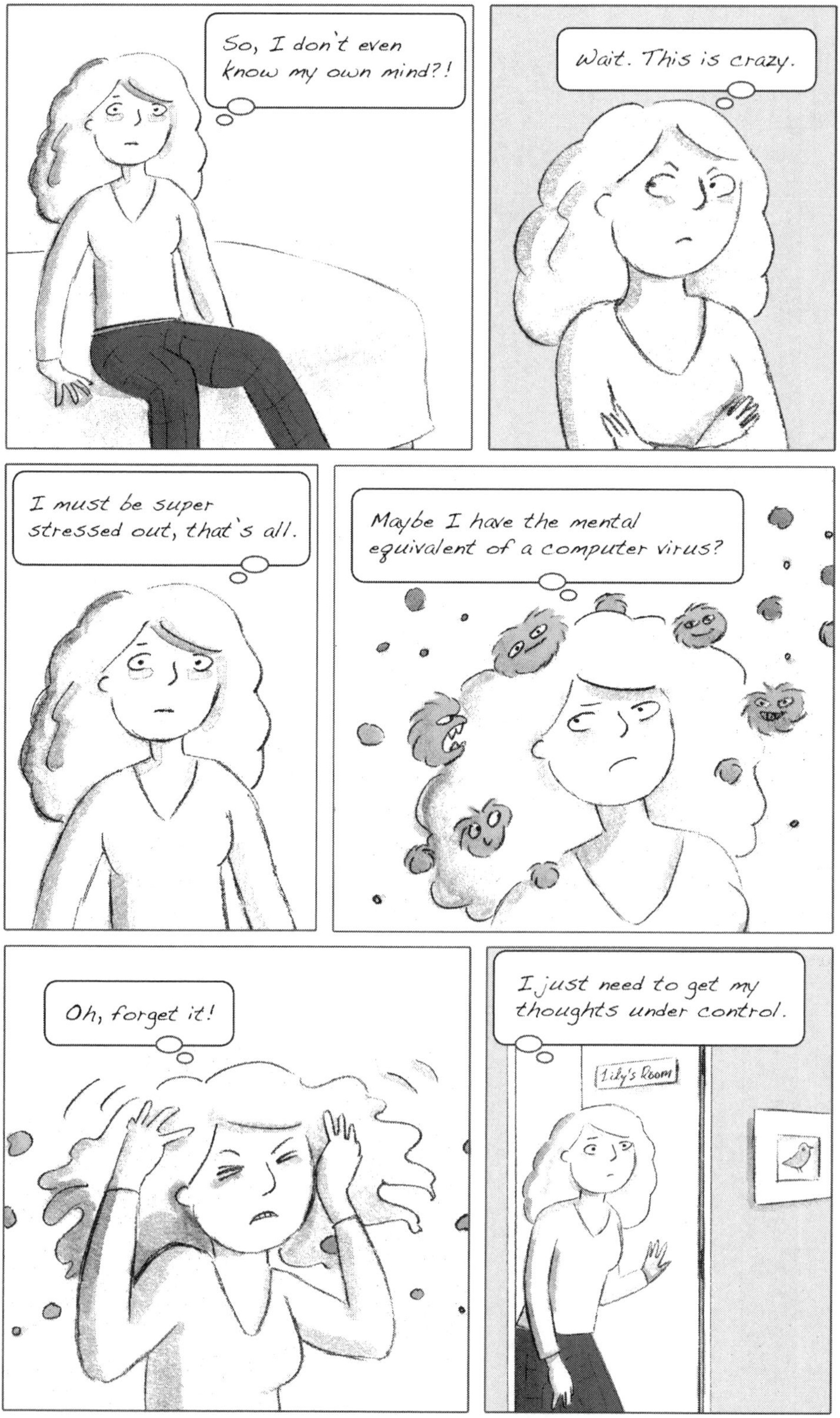
So, I don't even know my own mind?!
Wait. This is crazy.
I must be super stressed out, that's all.
Maybe I have the mental equivalent of a computer virus?
Oh, forget it!
I just need to get my thoughts under control.
Lily's Room

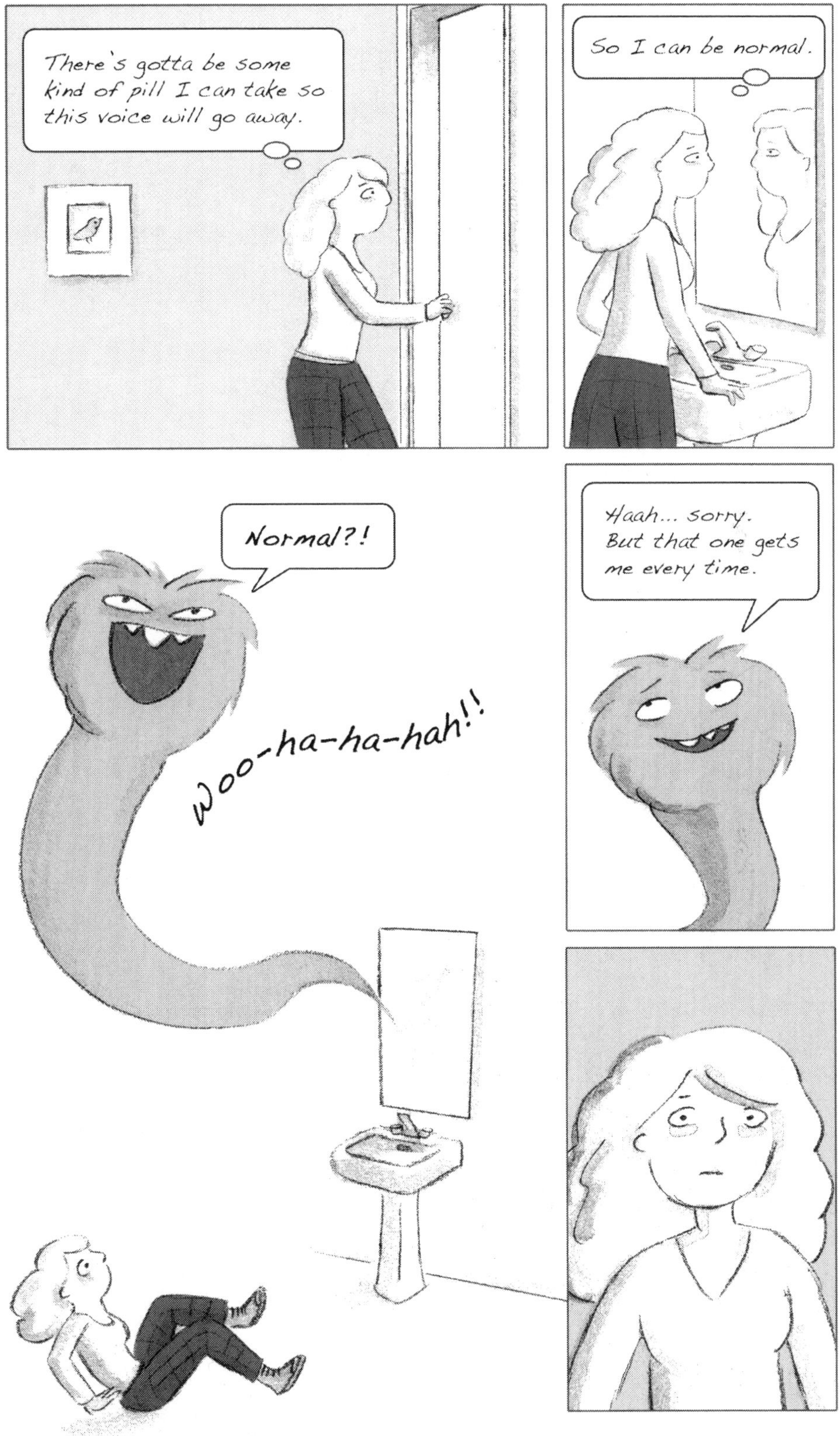
There's gotta be some kind of pill I can take so this voice will go away.
So I can be normal.
Normal?!
Woo-ha-ha-hah!!
Haah... sorry. But that one gets me every time.

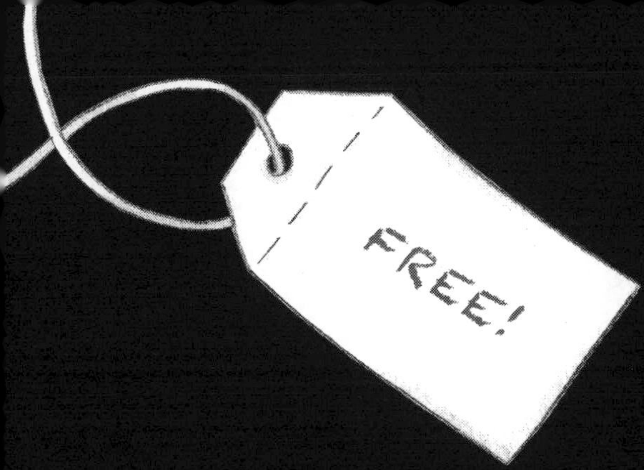
FREE!

One day you finally knew
what you had to do... though
the voices kept shouting.

MARY OLIVER

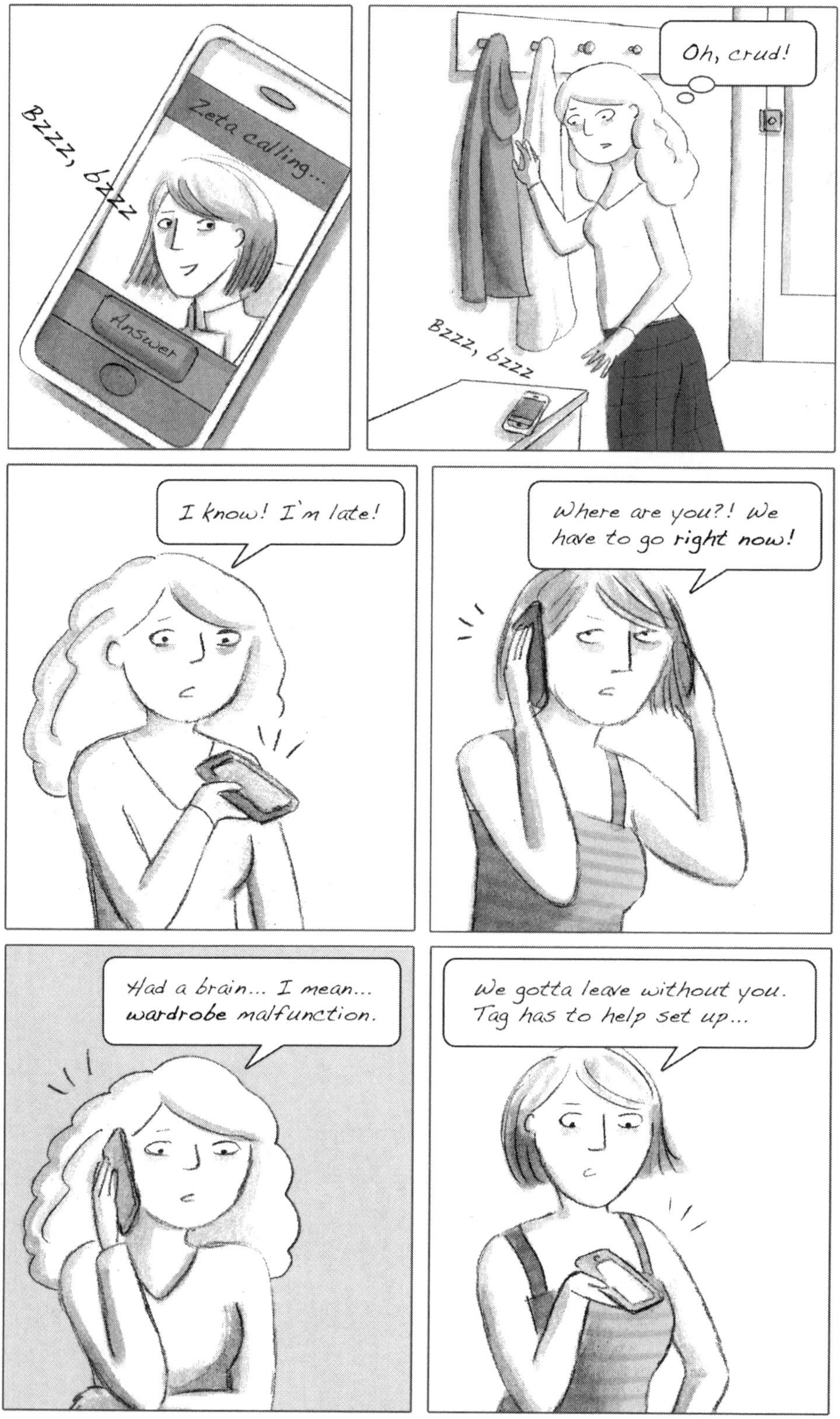
Zeta calling...
Answer
Bzzz, bzzz
Oh, crud!
Bzzz, bzzz
I know! I'm late!
Where are you?! We have to go right now!
Had a brain... I mean... wardrobe malfunction.
We gotta leave without you. Tag has to help set up...

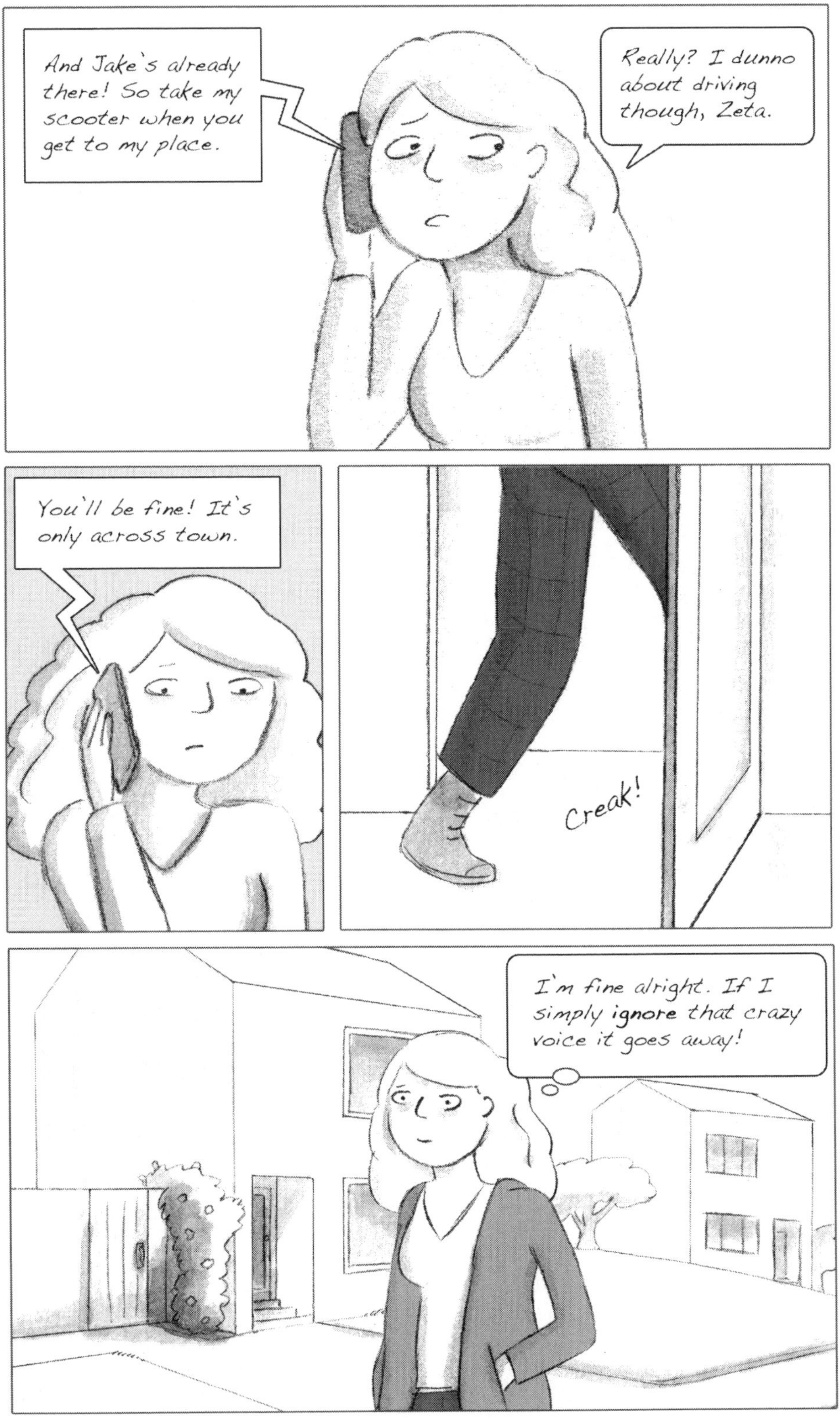
And Jake's already there! So take my scooter when you get to my place.
Really? I dunno about driving though, Zeta.
You'll be fine! It's only across town.
Creak!
I'm fine alright. If I simply **ignore** that crazy voice it goes away!

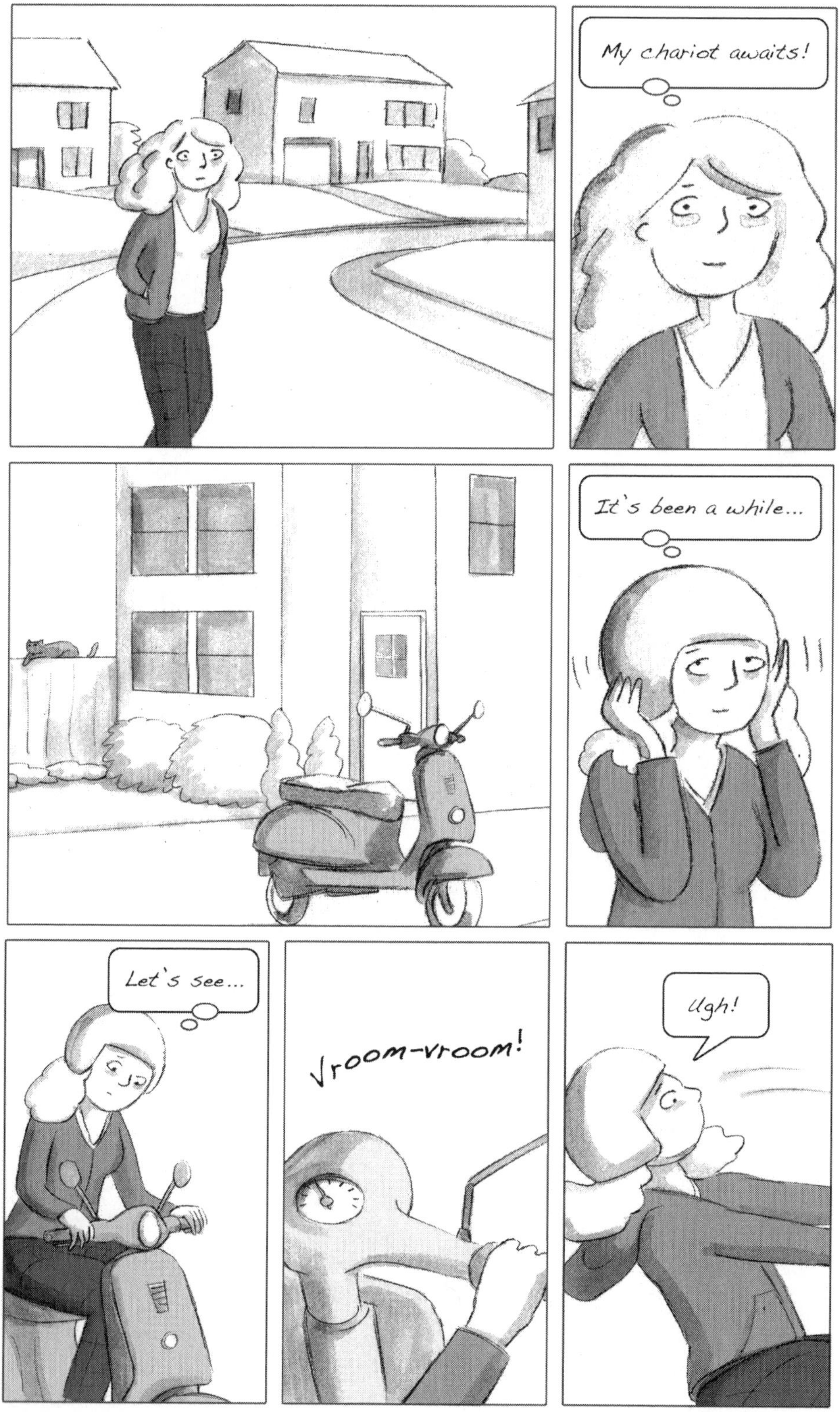
My chariot awaits!
It's been a while...
Let's see...
Vroom-vroom!
Ugh!

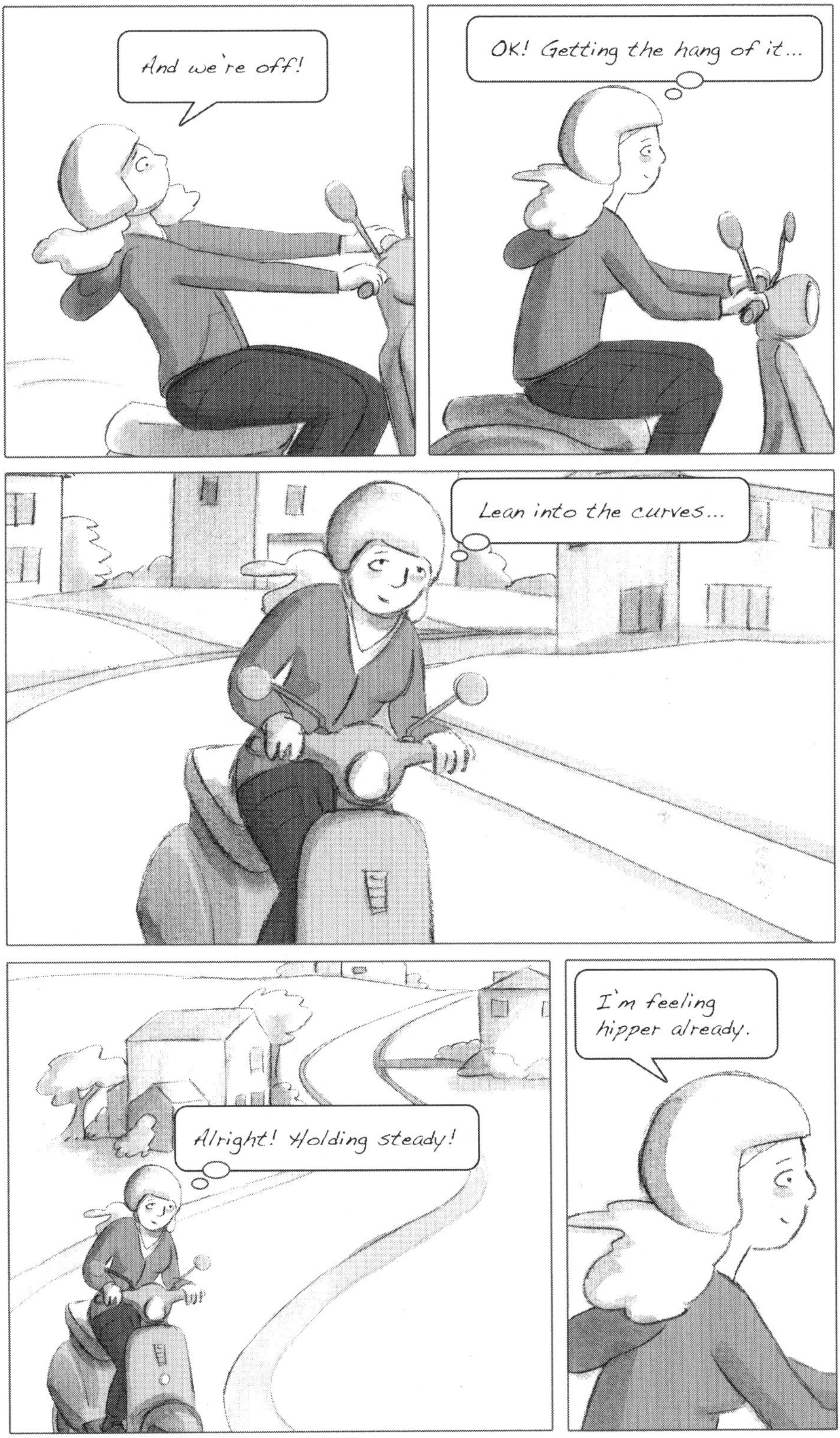
And we're off!
OK! Getting the hang of it...
Lean into the curves...
Alright! Holding steady!
I'm feeling hipper already.

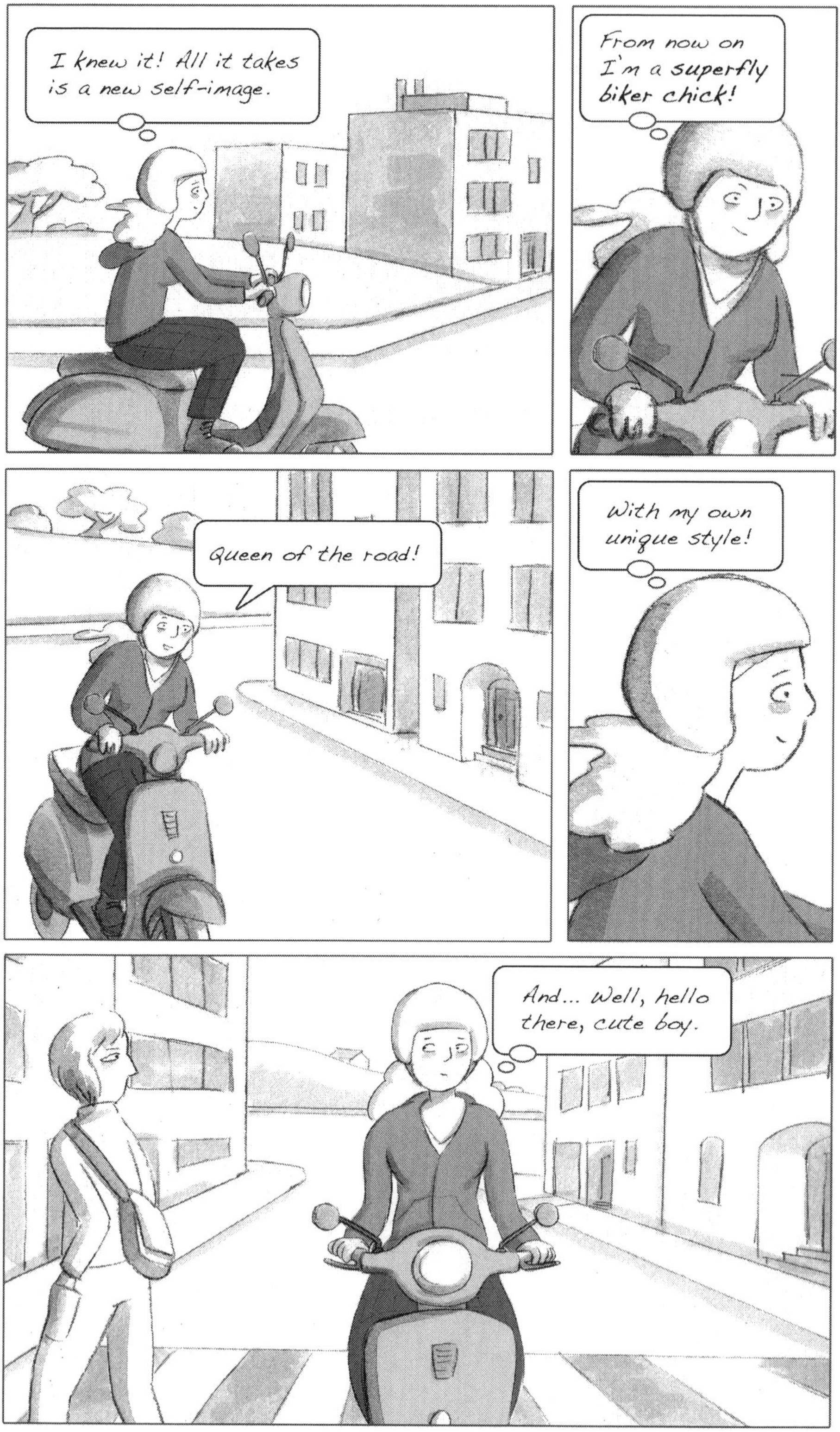
I knew it! All it takes is a new self-image.
From now on I'm a superfly biker chick!
Queen of the road!
With my own unique style!
And... Well, hello there, cute boy.

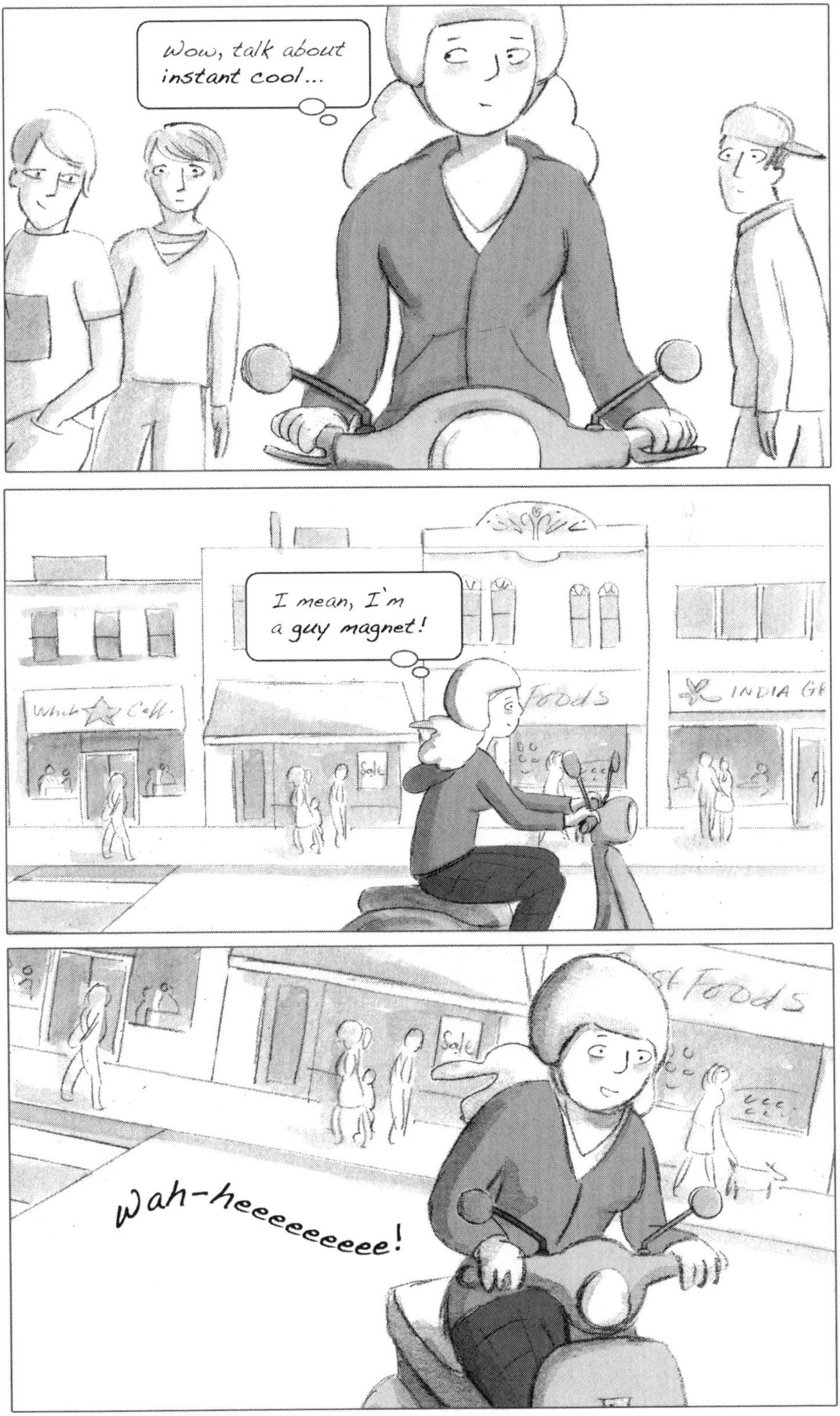
Wow, talk about instant cool...
I mean, I'm a guy magnet!
Foods
INDIA
Sale
Wah-heeeeeeeee!

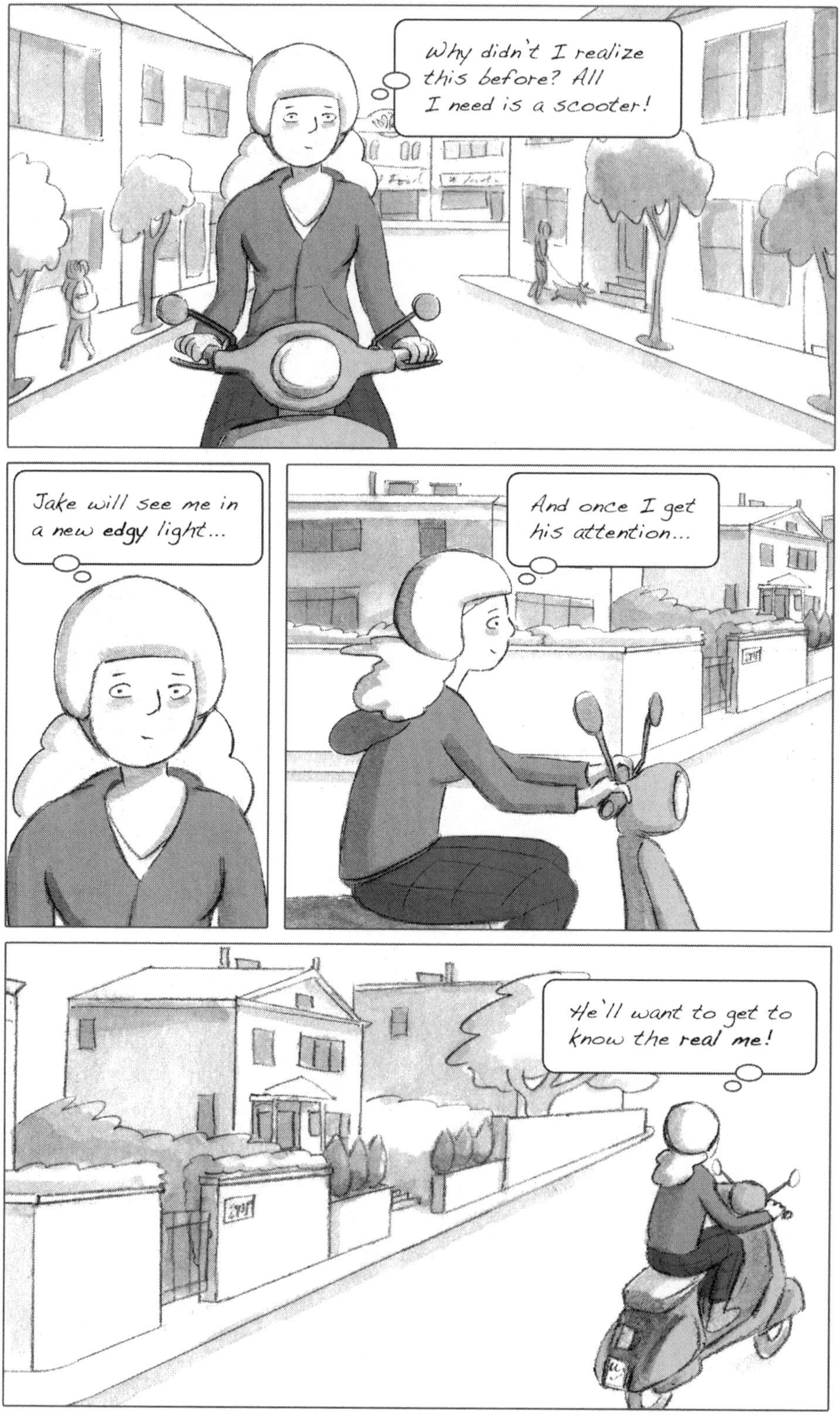
Why didn't I realize this before? All I need is a scooter!
Jake will see me in a new **edgy** light...
And once I get his attention...
He'll want to get to know the **real me**!

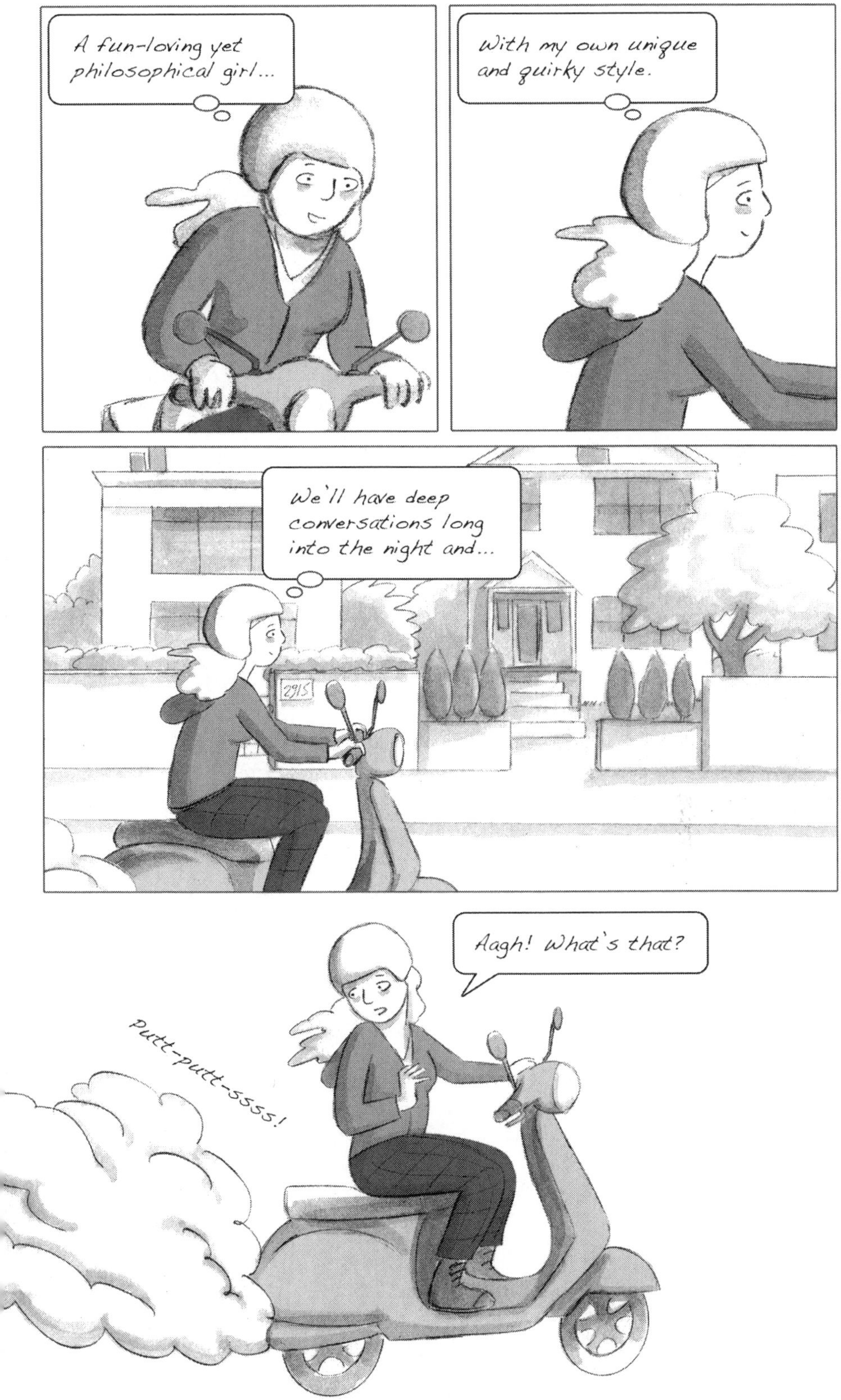
A fun-loving yet philosophical girl...
With my own unique and quirky style.
We'll have deep conversations long into the night and...
2915
Aagh! What's that?
putt-putt-ssss!

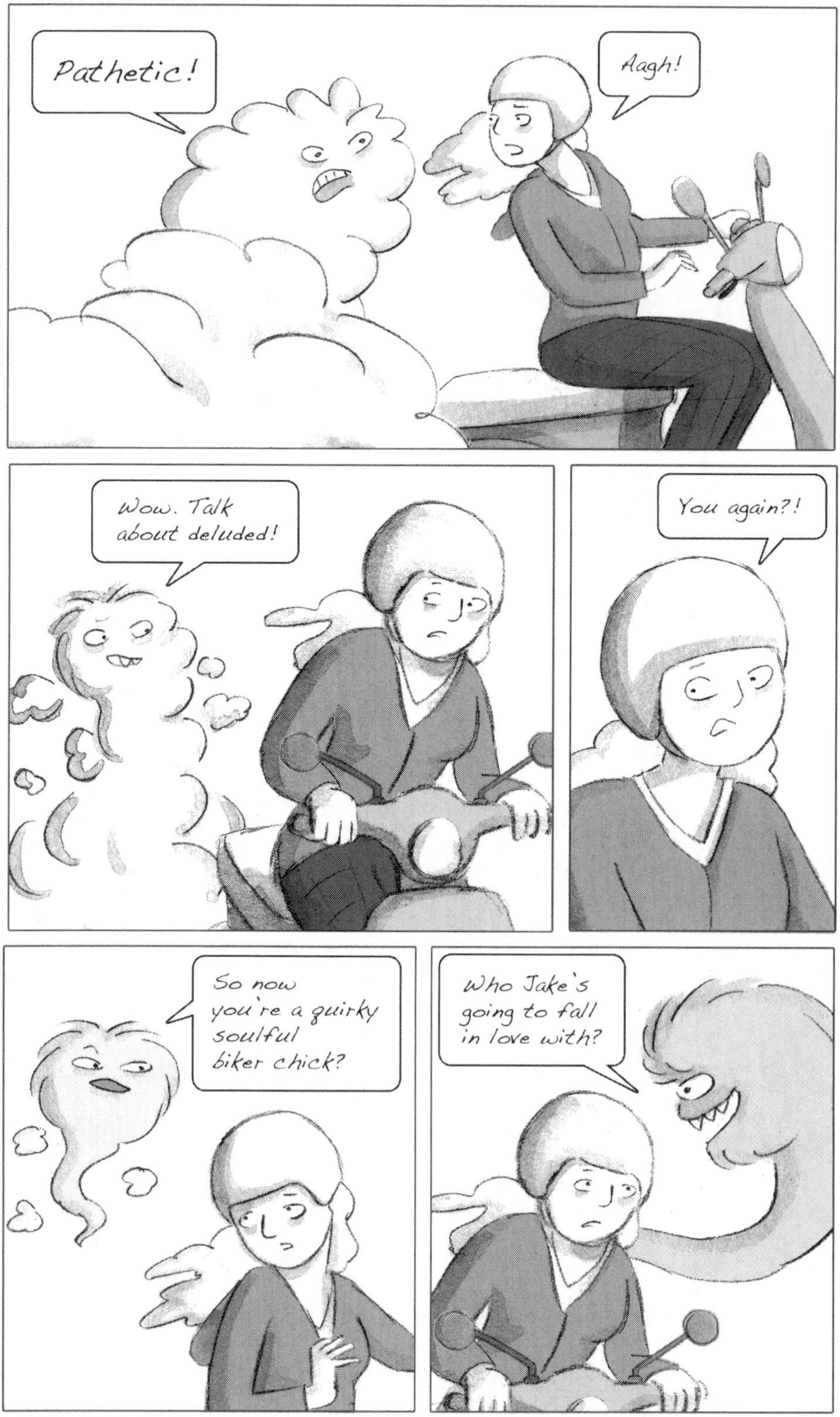
Pathetic!
Aagh!
Wow. Talk about deluded!
You again?!
So now you're a quirky soulful biker chick?
Who Jake's going to fall in love with?

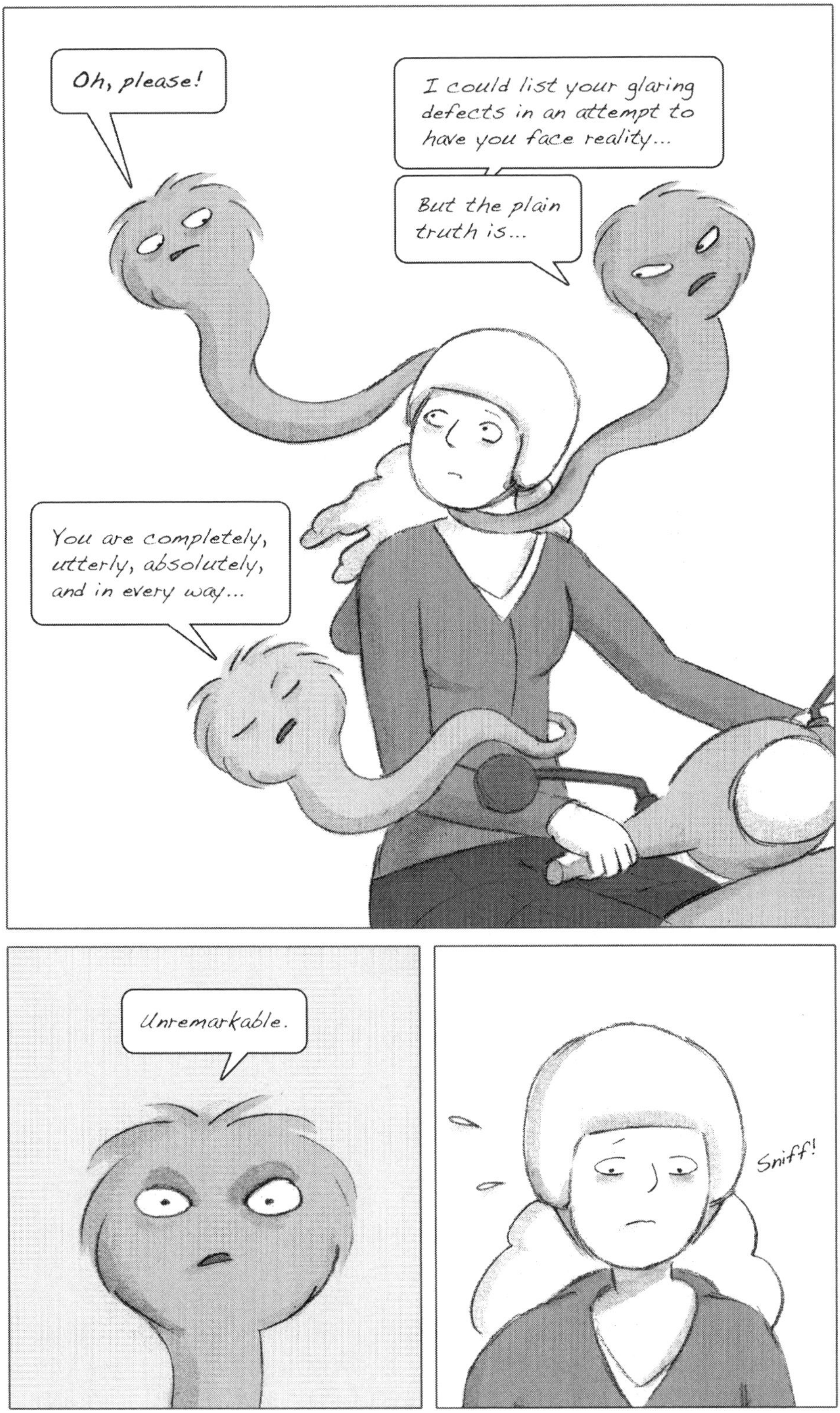
Oh, please!
I could list your glaring defects in an attempt to have you face reality...
But the plain truth is...
You are completely, utterly, absolutely, and in every way...
Unremarkable.
Sniff!

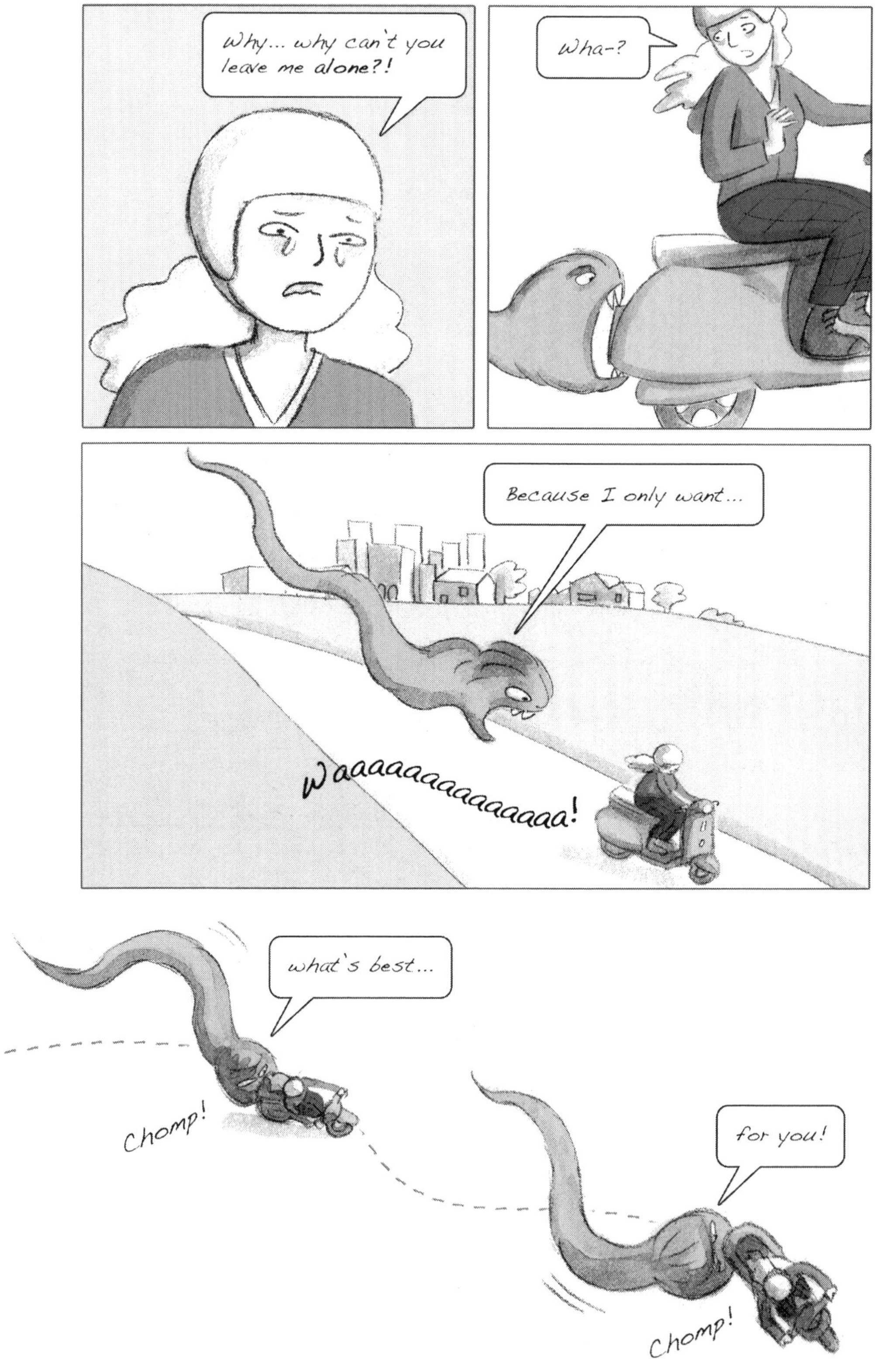
Why... why can't you leave me alone?!
Wha-?
Because I only want...
Waaaaaaaaaaaaaaa!
what's best...
Chomp!
for you!
Chomp!

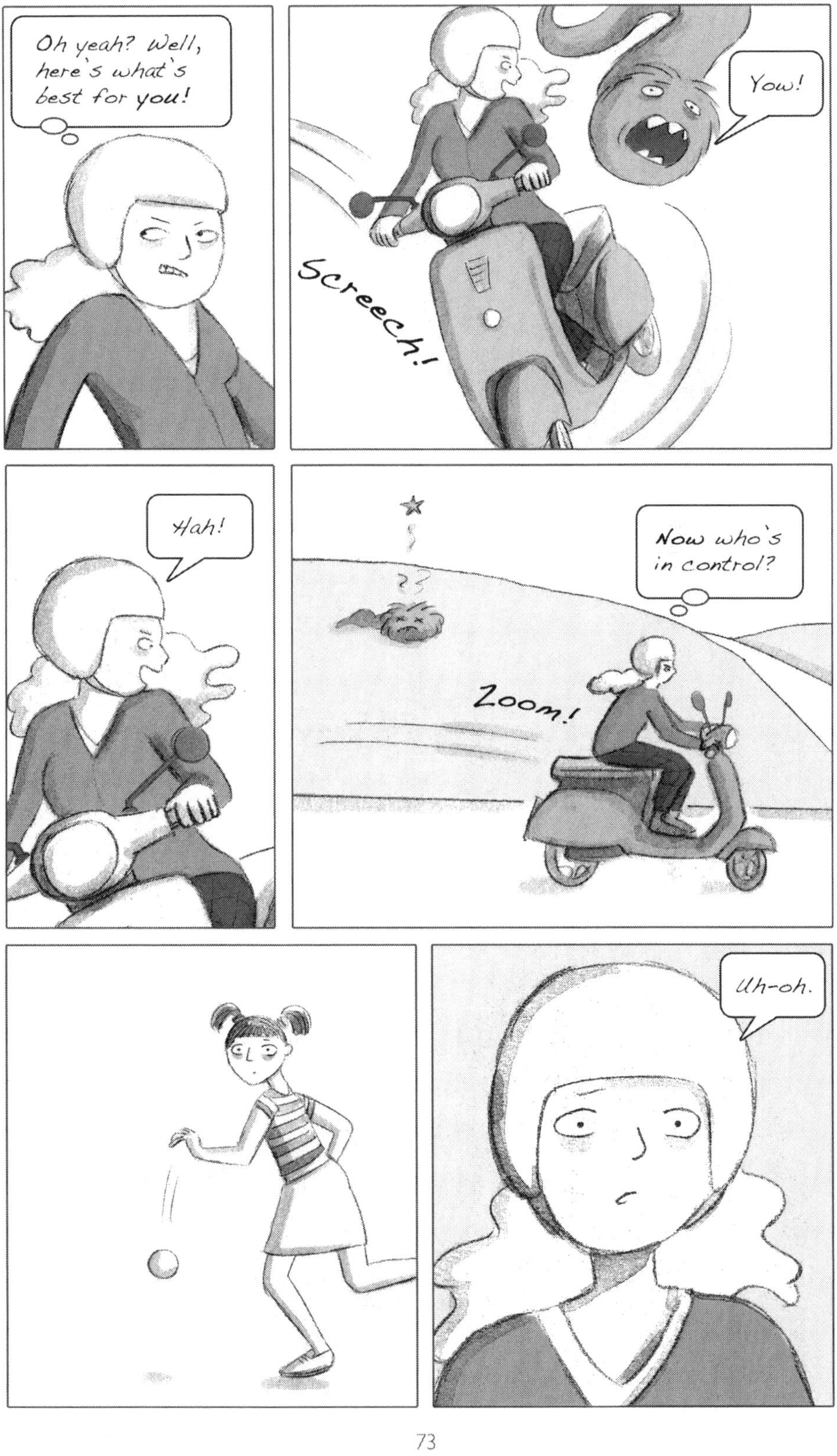
Oh yeah? Well, here's what's best for you!
Yow!
Screech!
Hah!
Now who's in control?
Zoom!
Uh-oh.

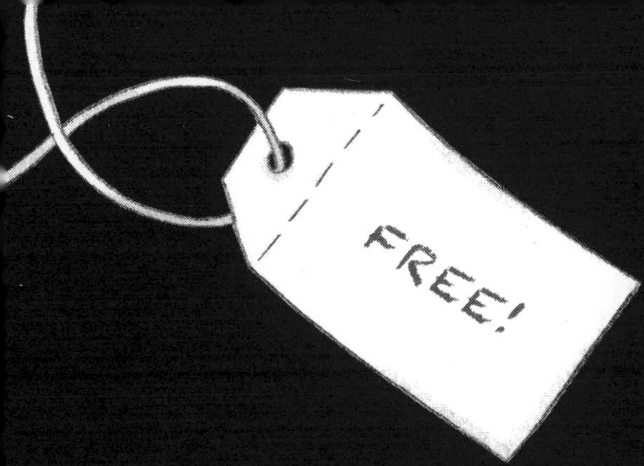
FREE!

In a true emergency, the mind stops; you become totally present... and something infinitely more powerful takes over.

ECKHART TOLLE

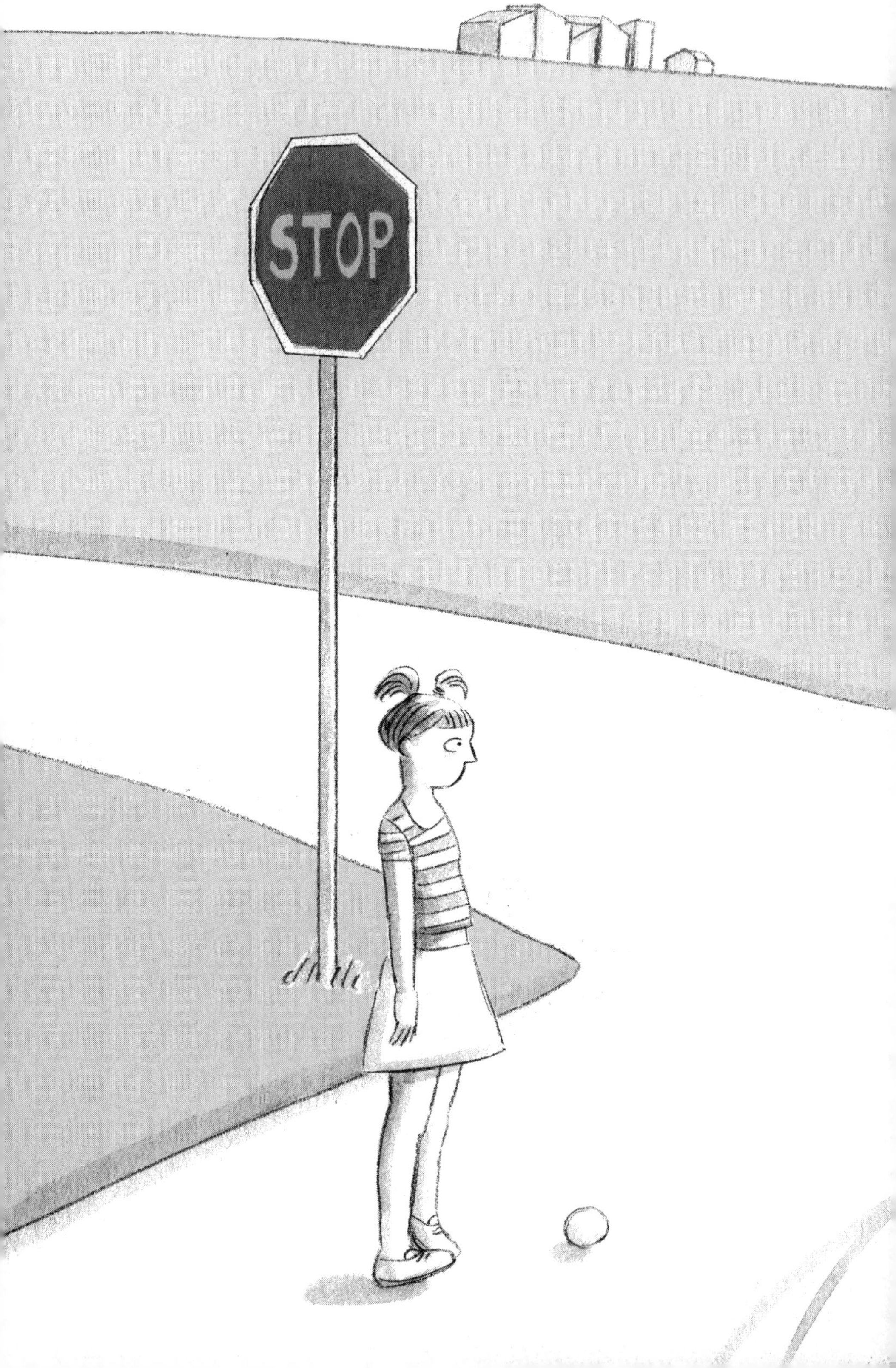
STOP

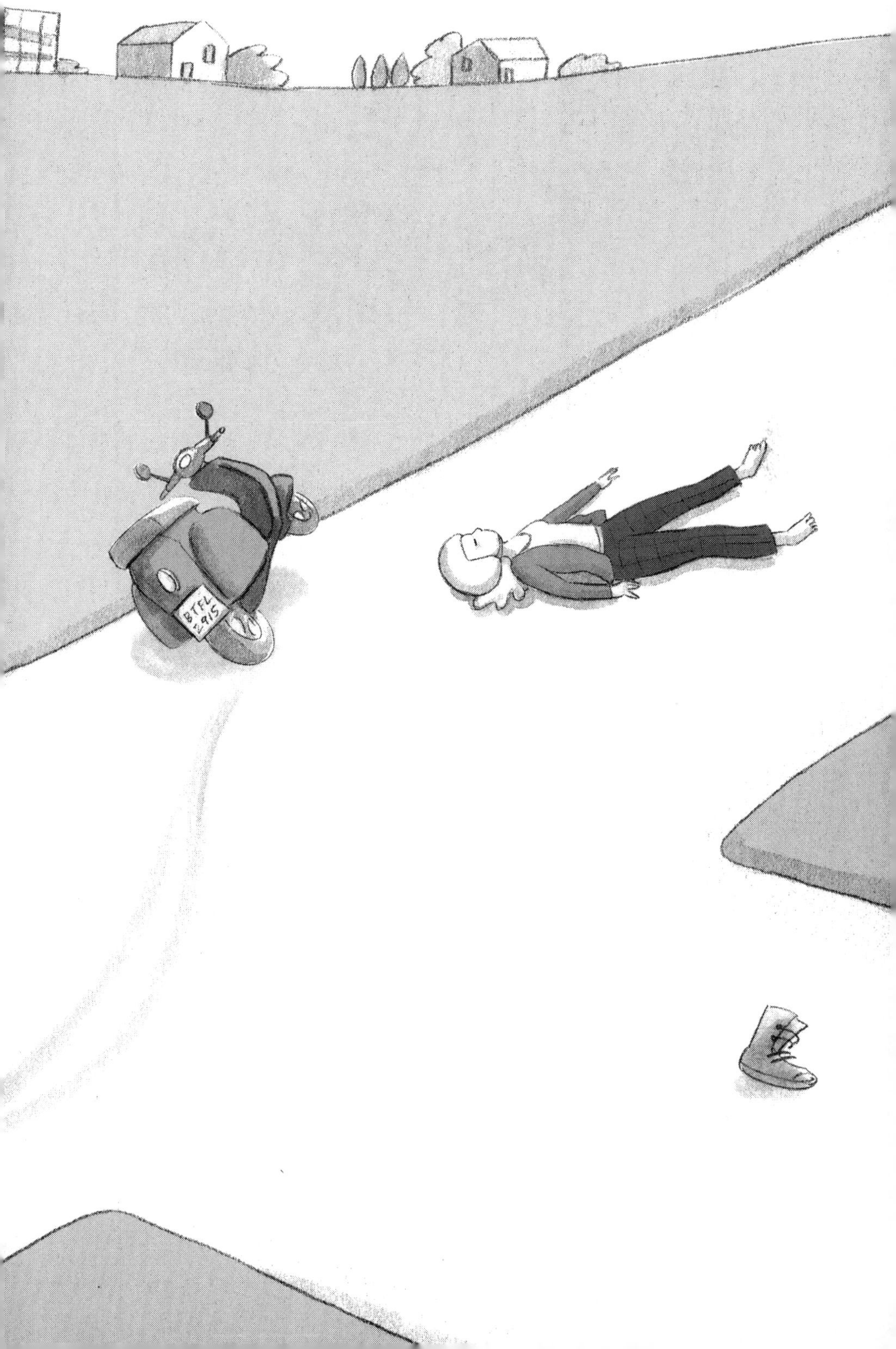
BTFL
915

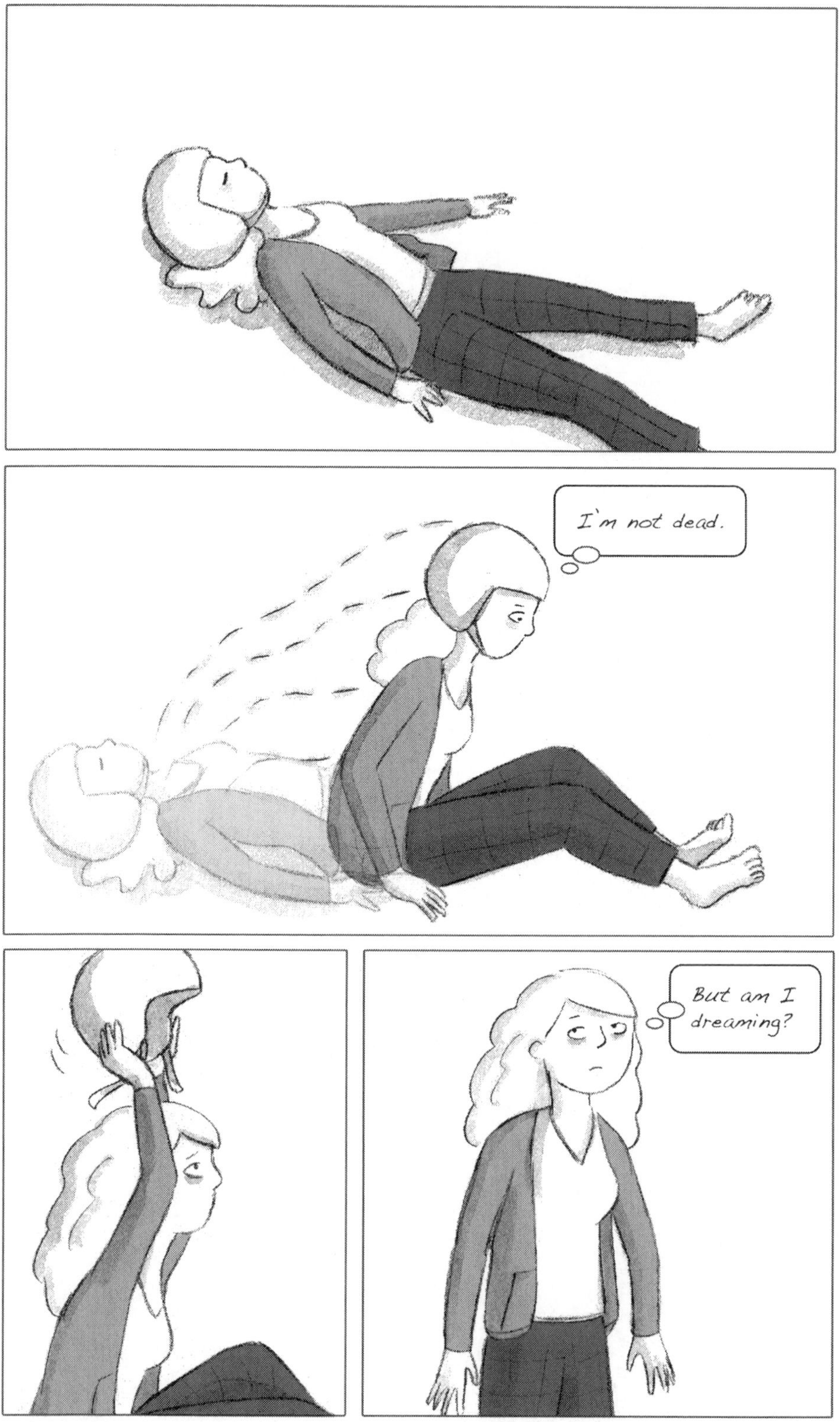
I'm not dead.
But am I dreaming?

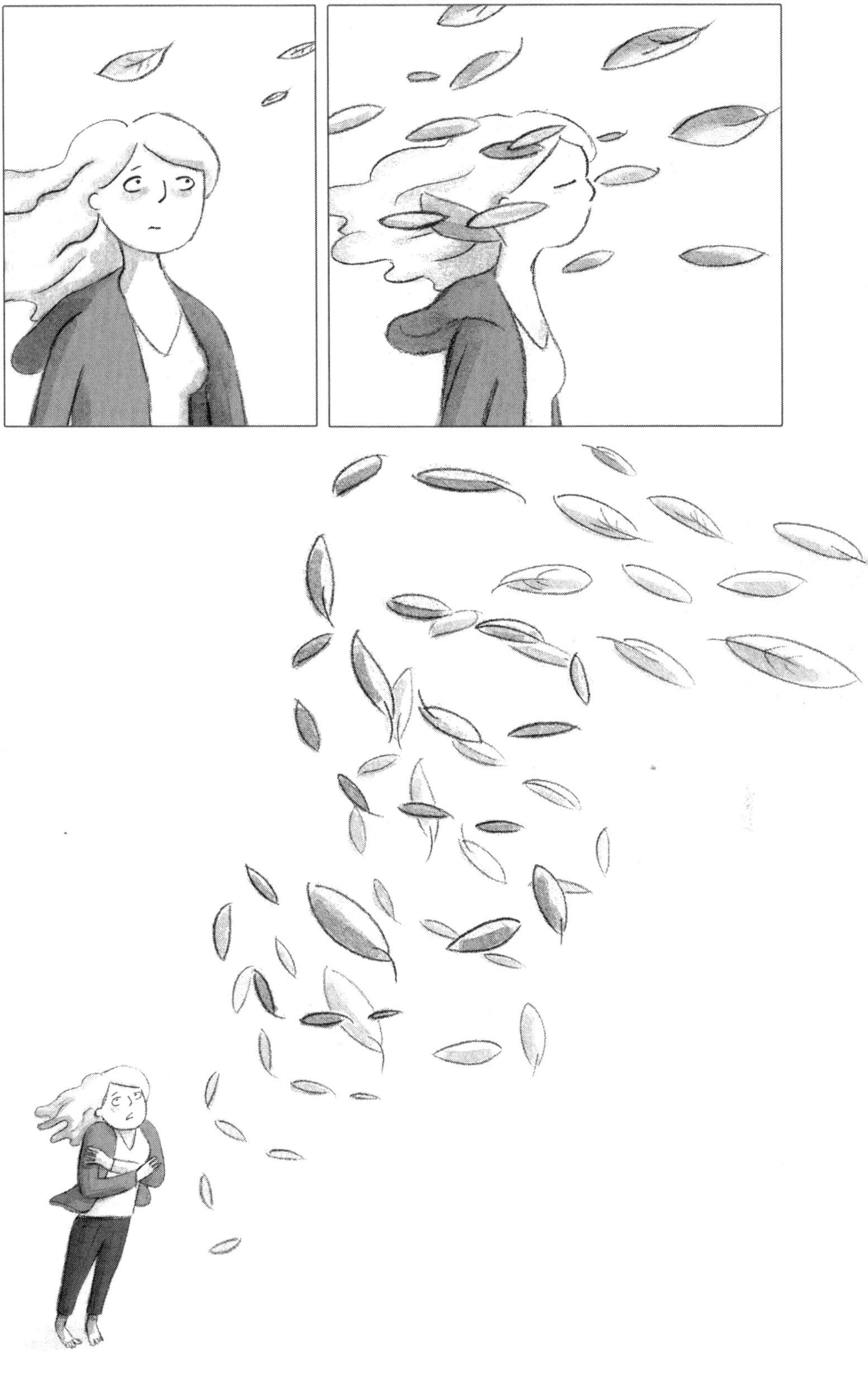

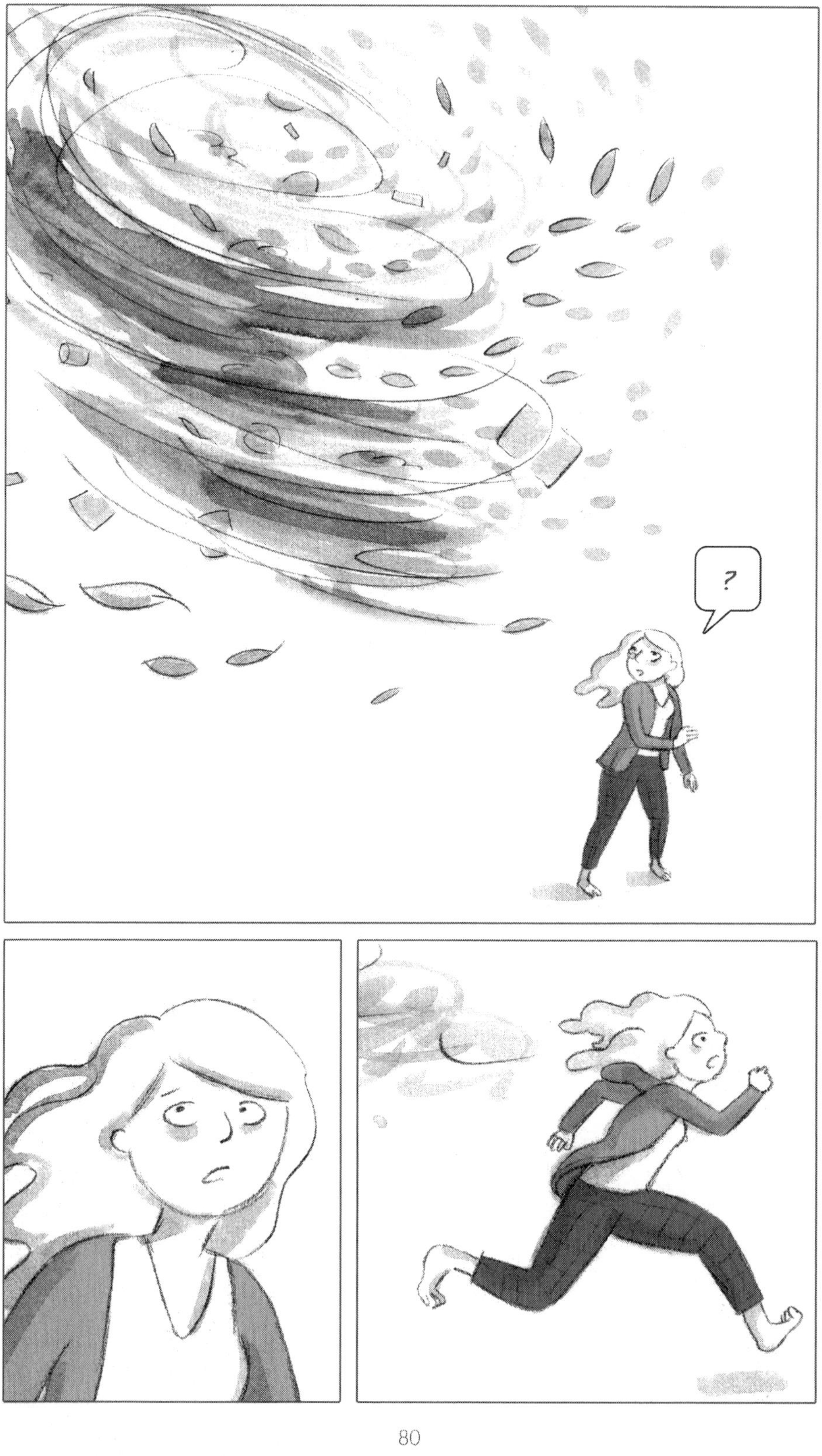
?

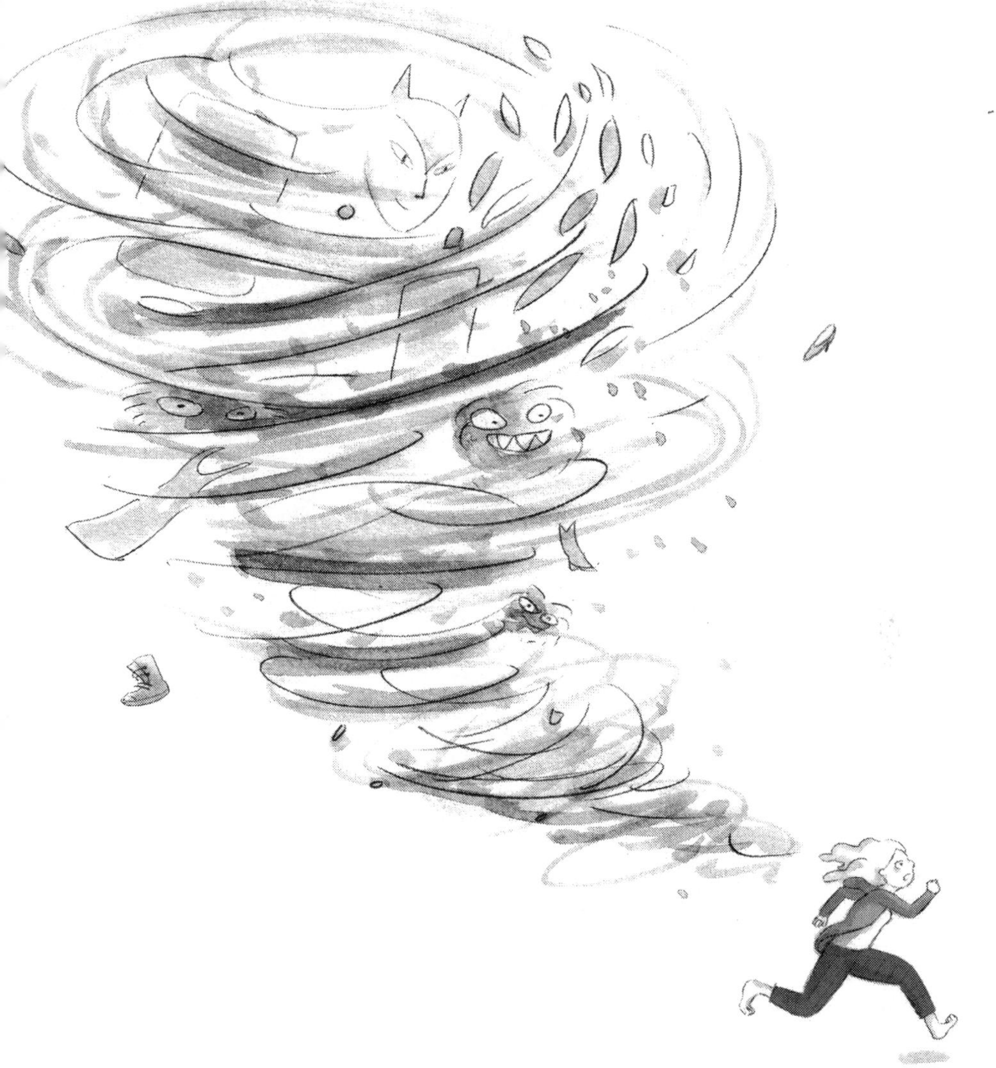

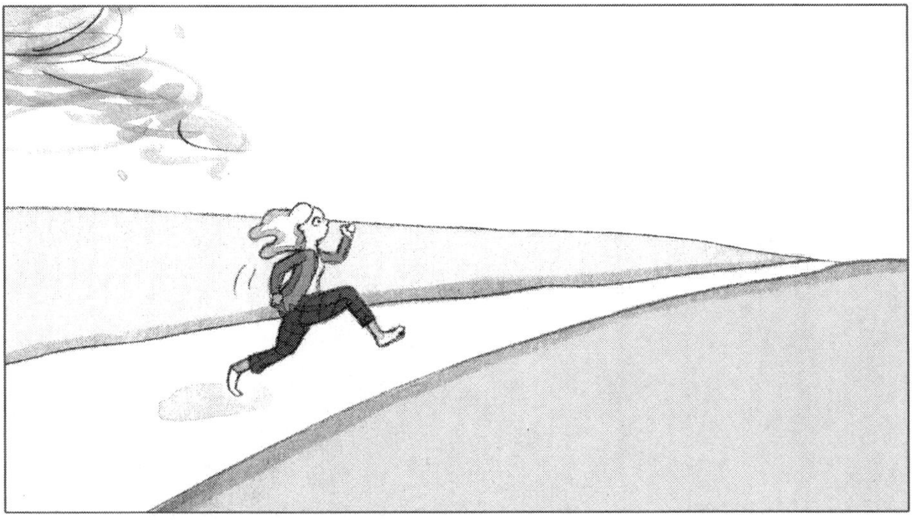

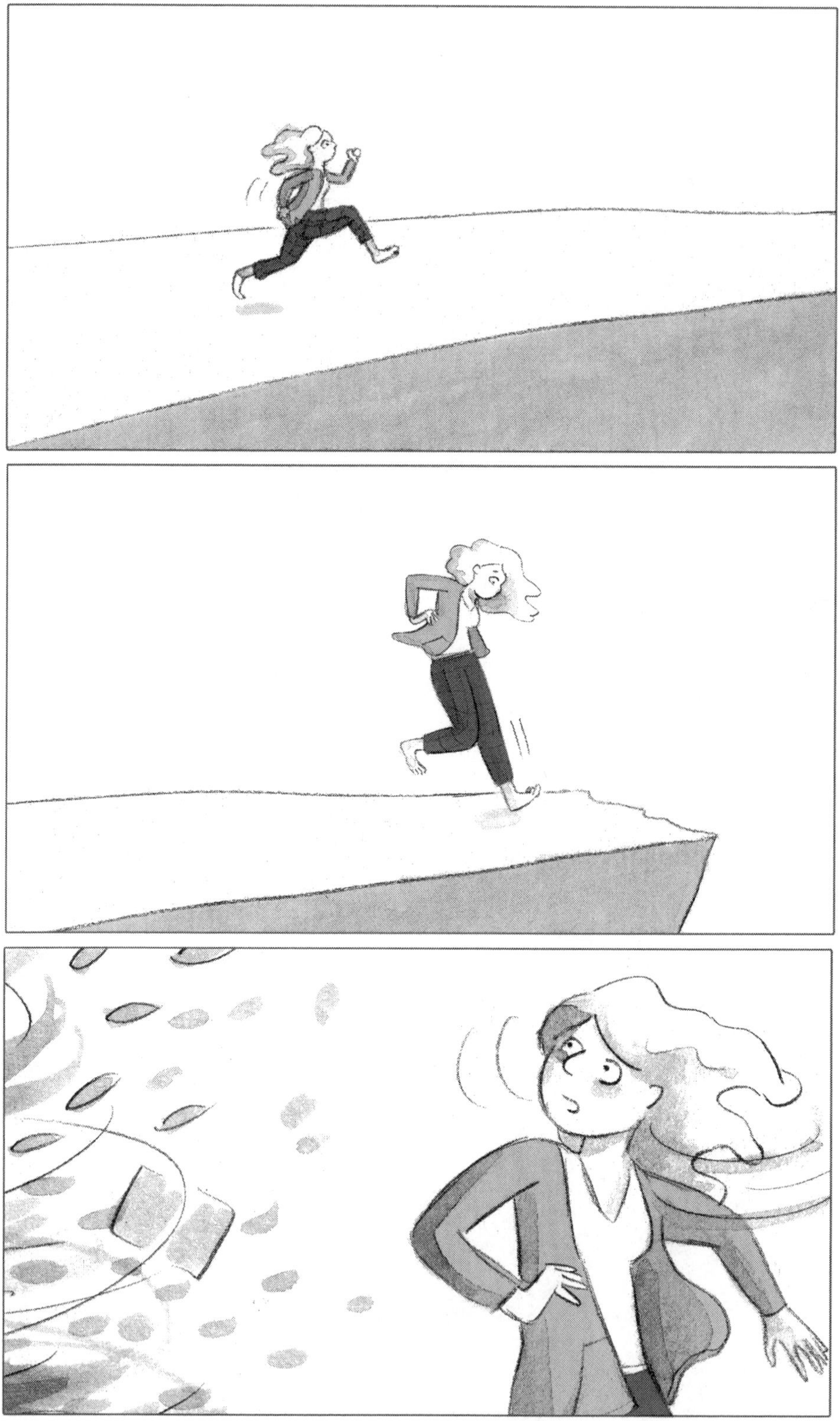

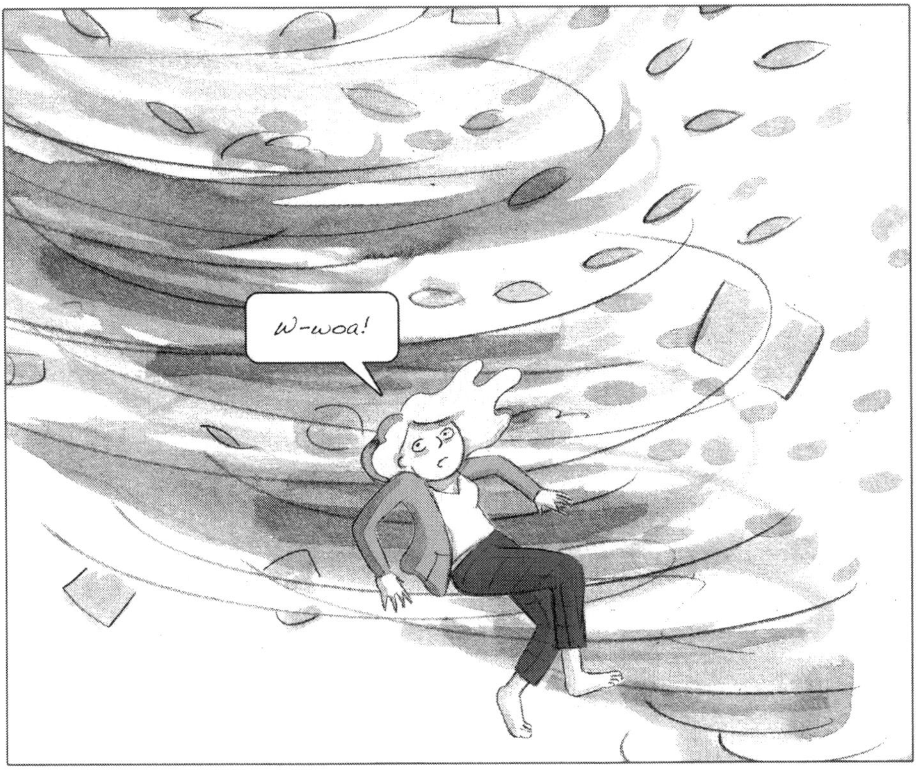
W-woa!

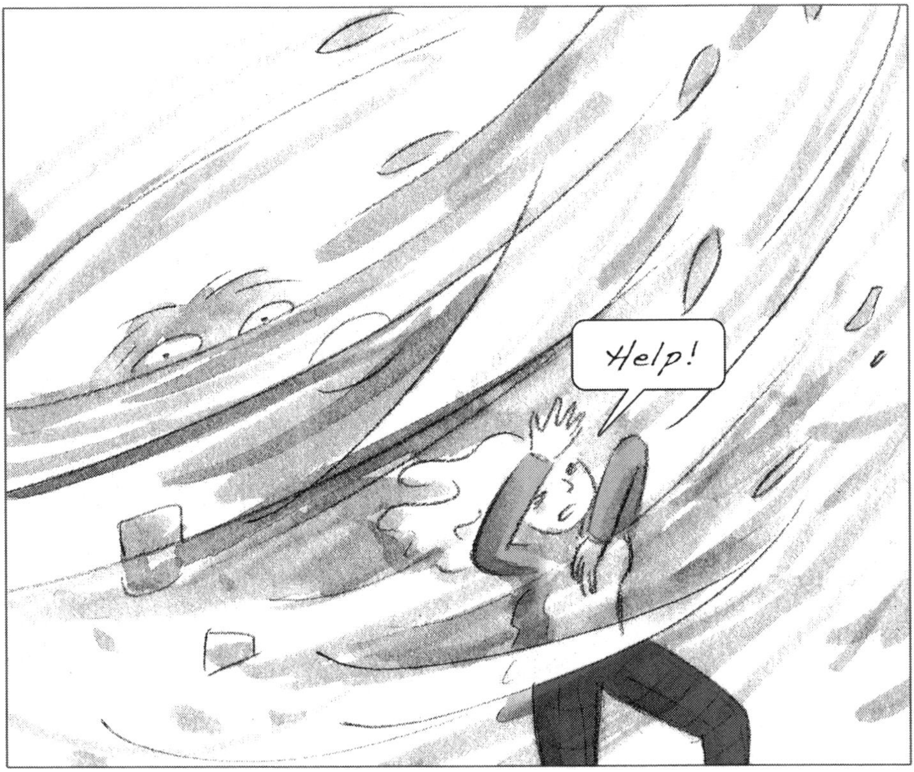
Help!

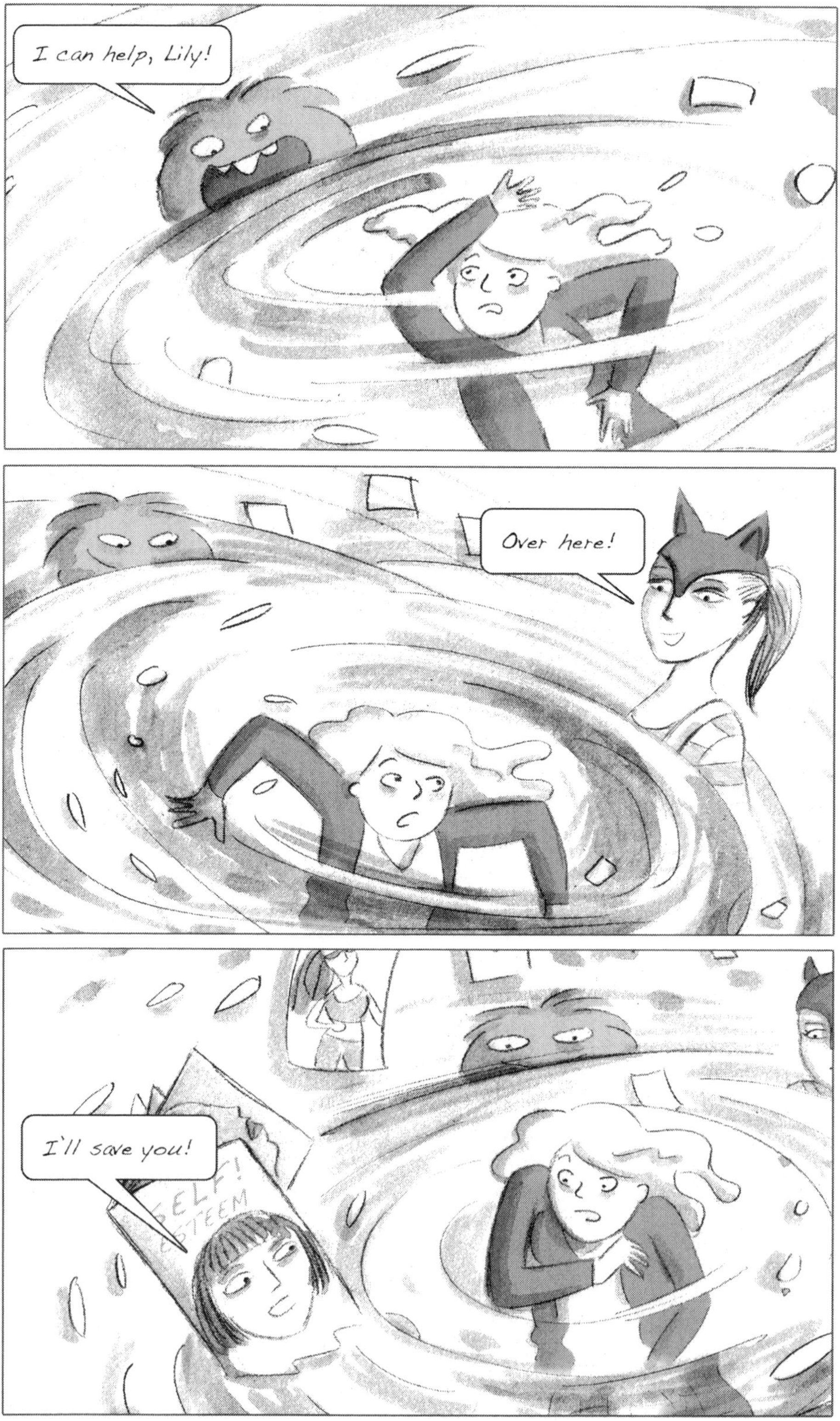
I can help, Lily!
Over here!
I'll save you!
SELF! ESTEEM

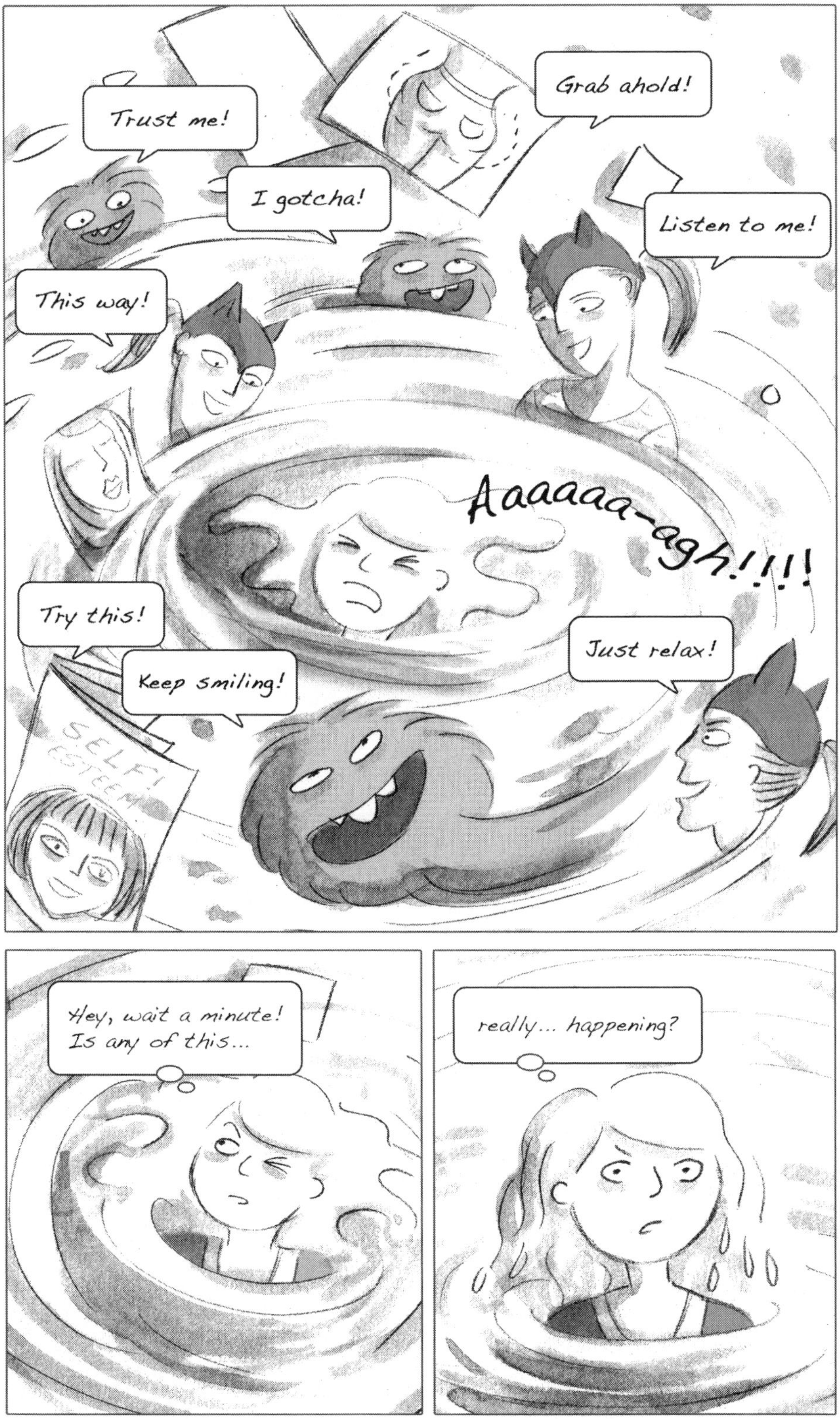
Trust me!
Grab ahold!
I gotcha!
Listen to me!
This way!
Aaaaaa-agh!!!!!
Try this!
Keep smiling!
Just relax!
SELF! ESTEEM
Hey, wait a minute!
Is any of this...
really... happening?

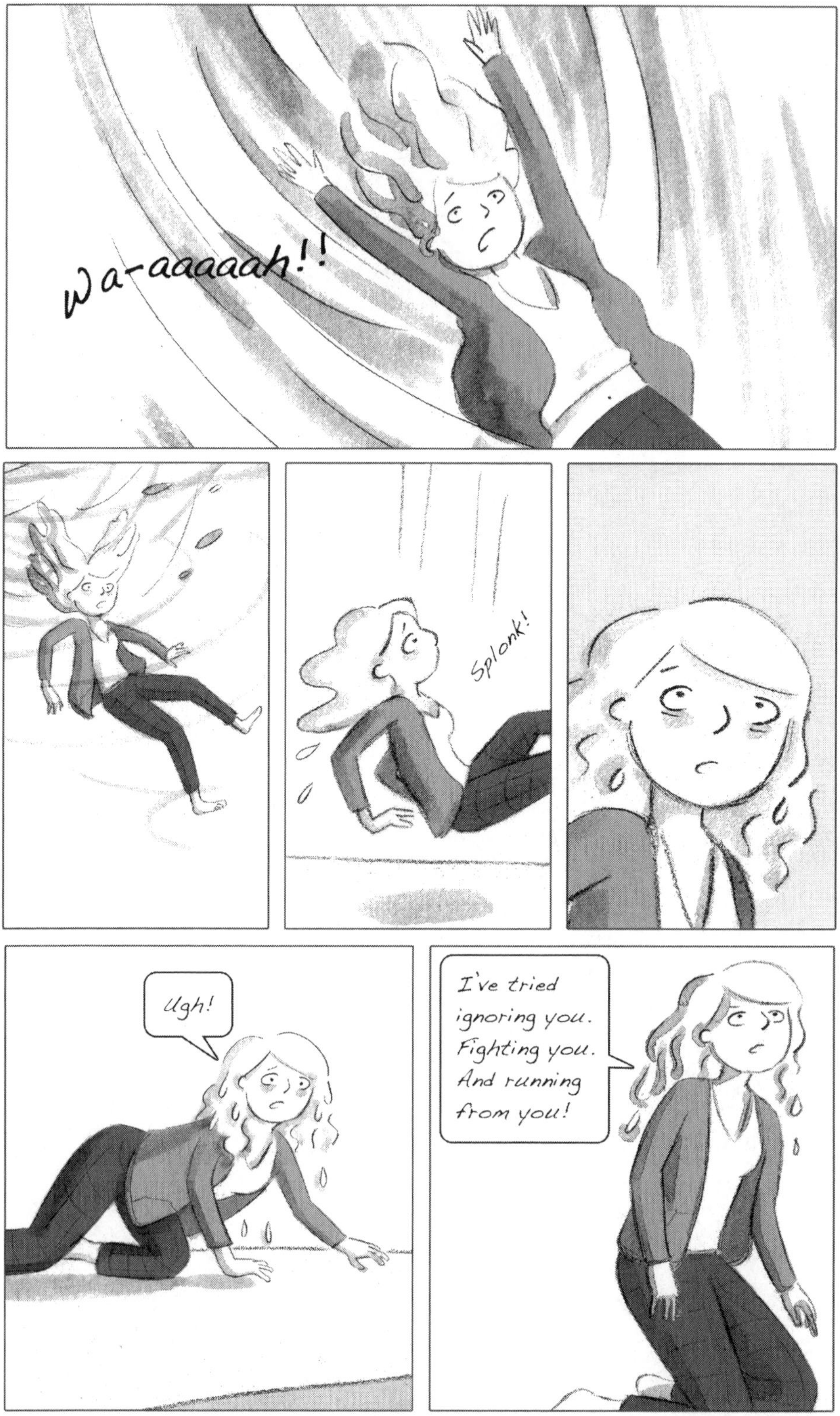
Wa-aaaaah!!
Splonk!
Ugh!
I've tried ignoring you. Fighting you. And running from you!

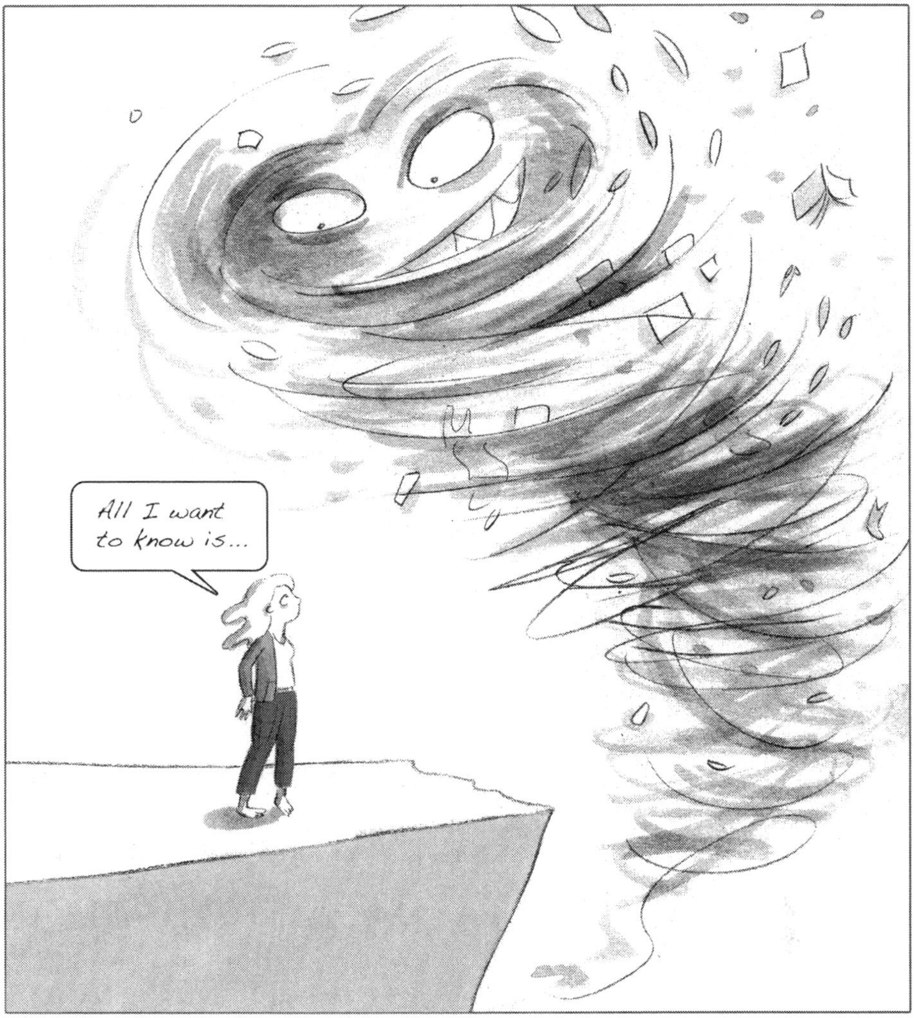
All I want to know is...

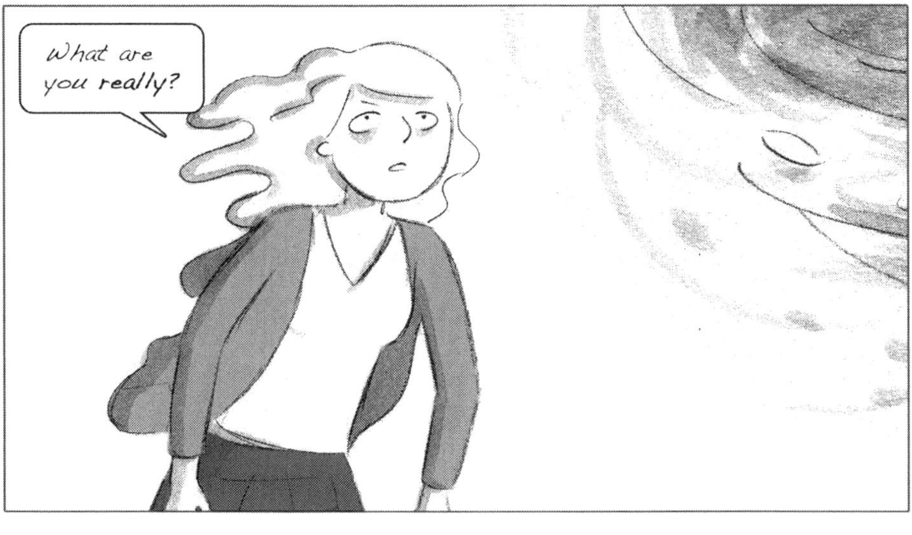
What are you really?

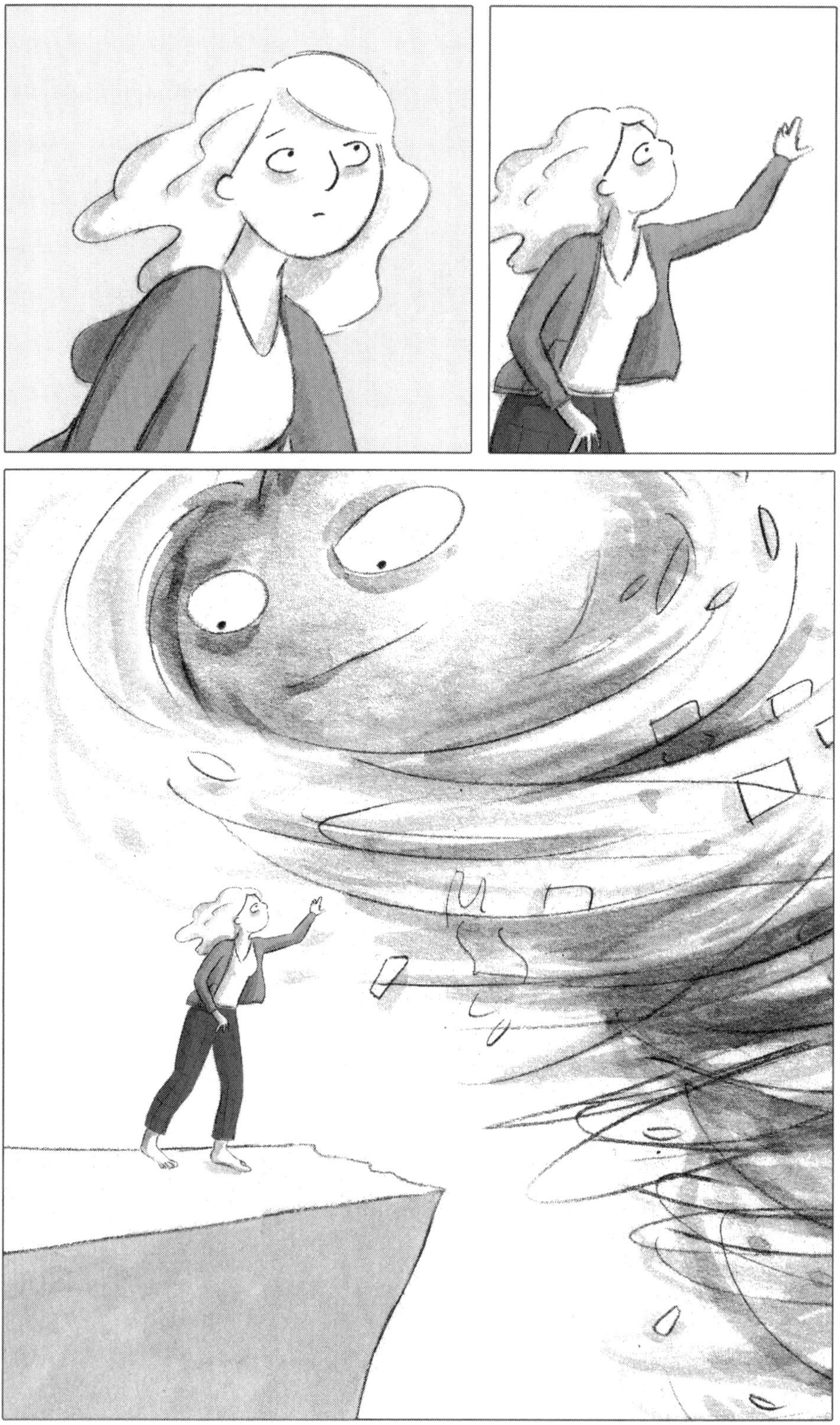

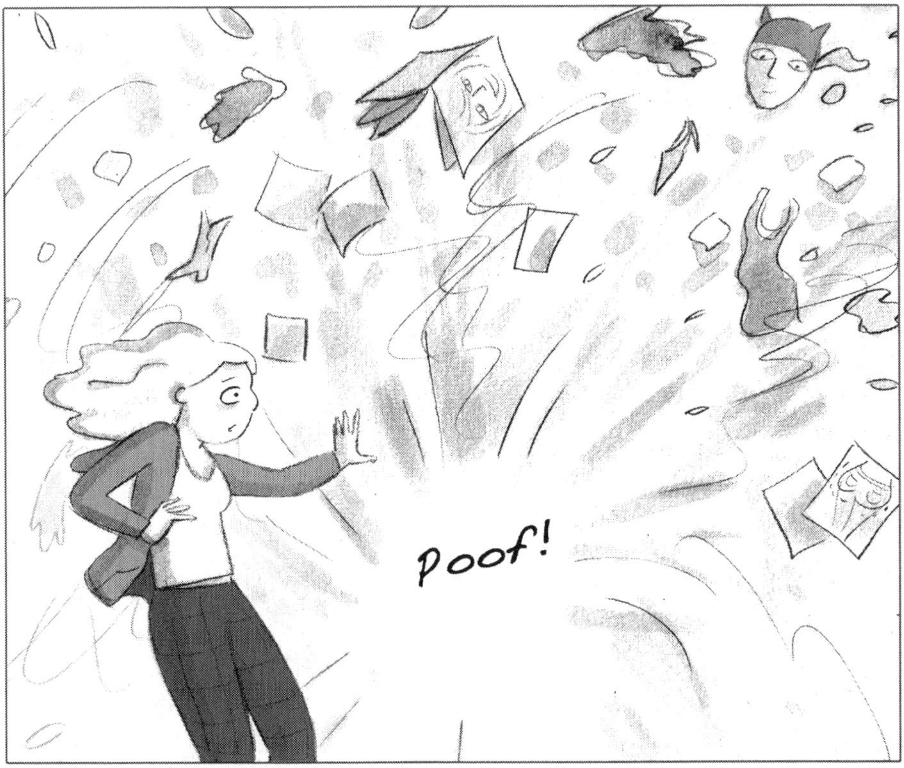
Poof!

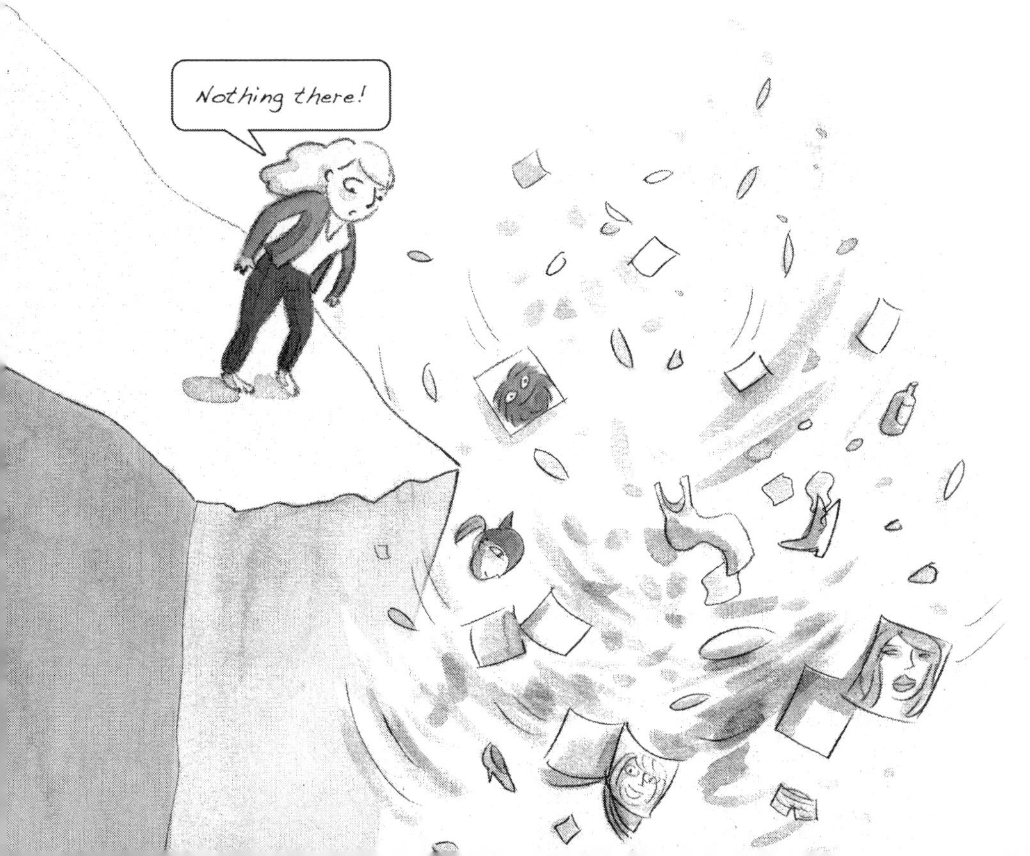
Nothing there!

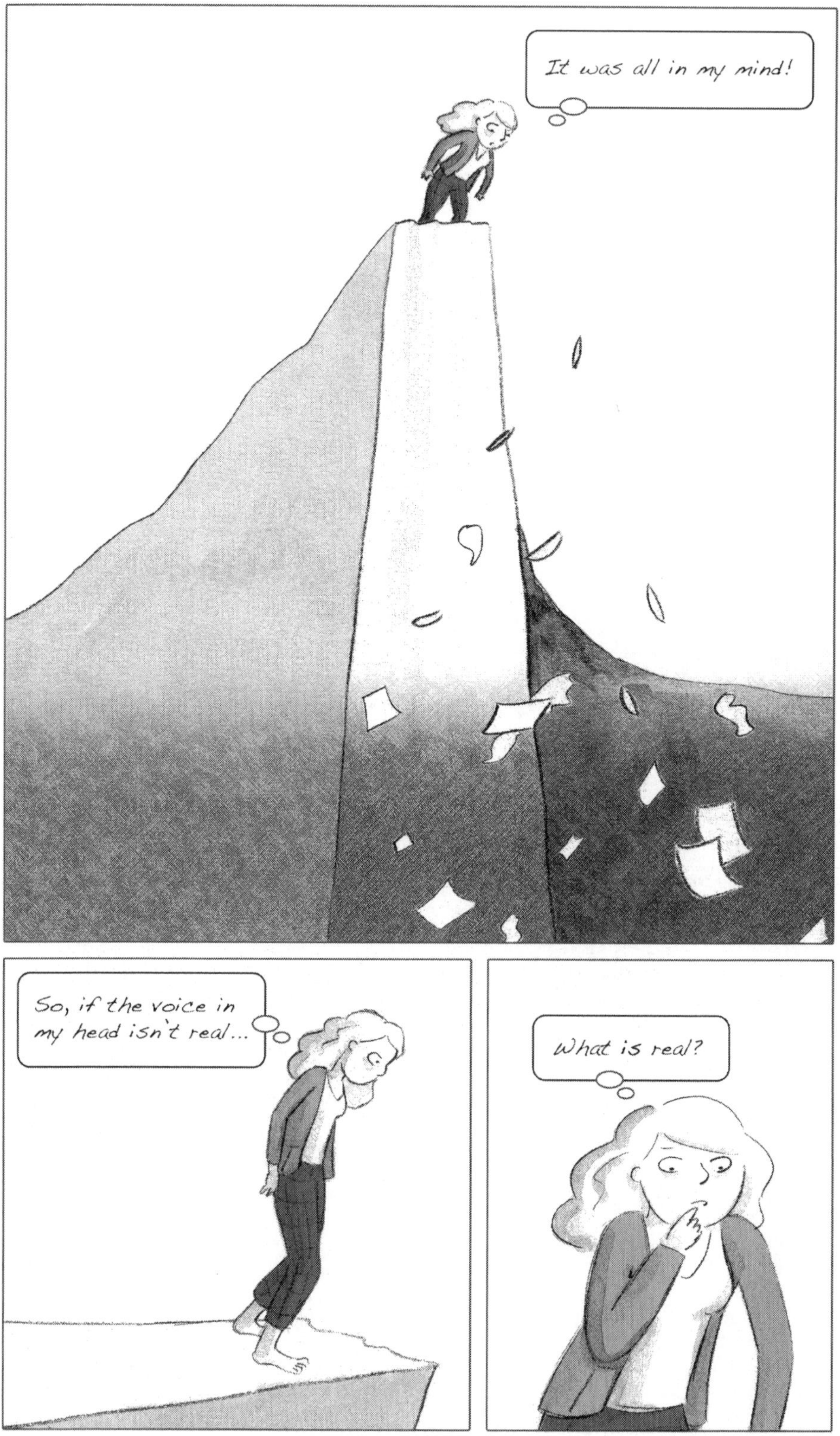
It was all in my mind!
So, if the voice in my head isn't real...
What is real?

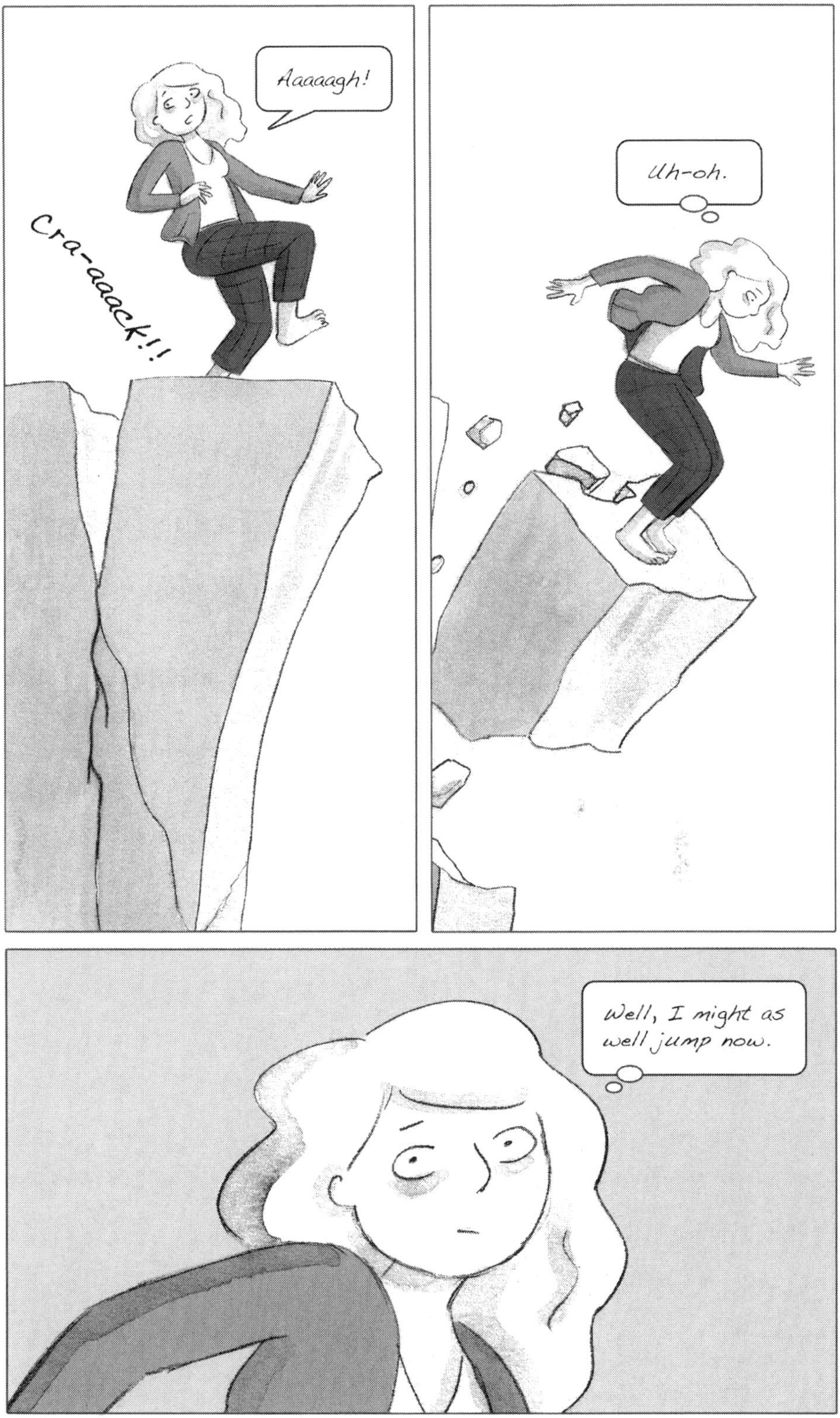
Aaaaagh!
Cra-aaack!!!
Uh-oh.
Well, I might as well jump now.

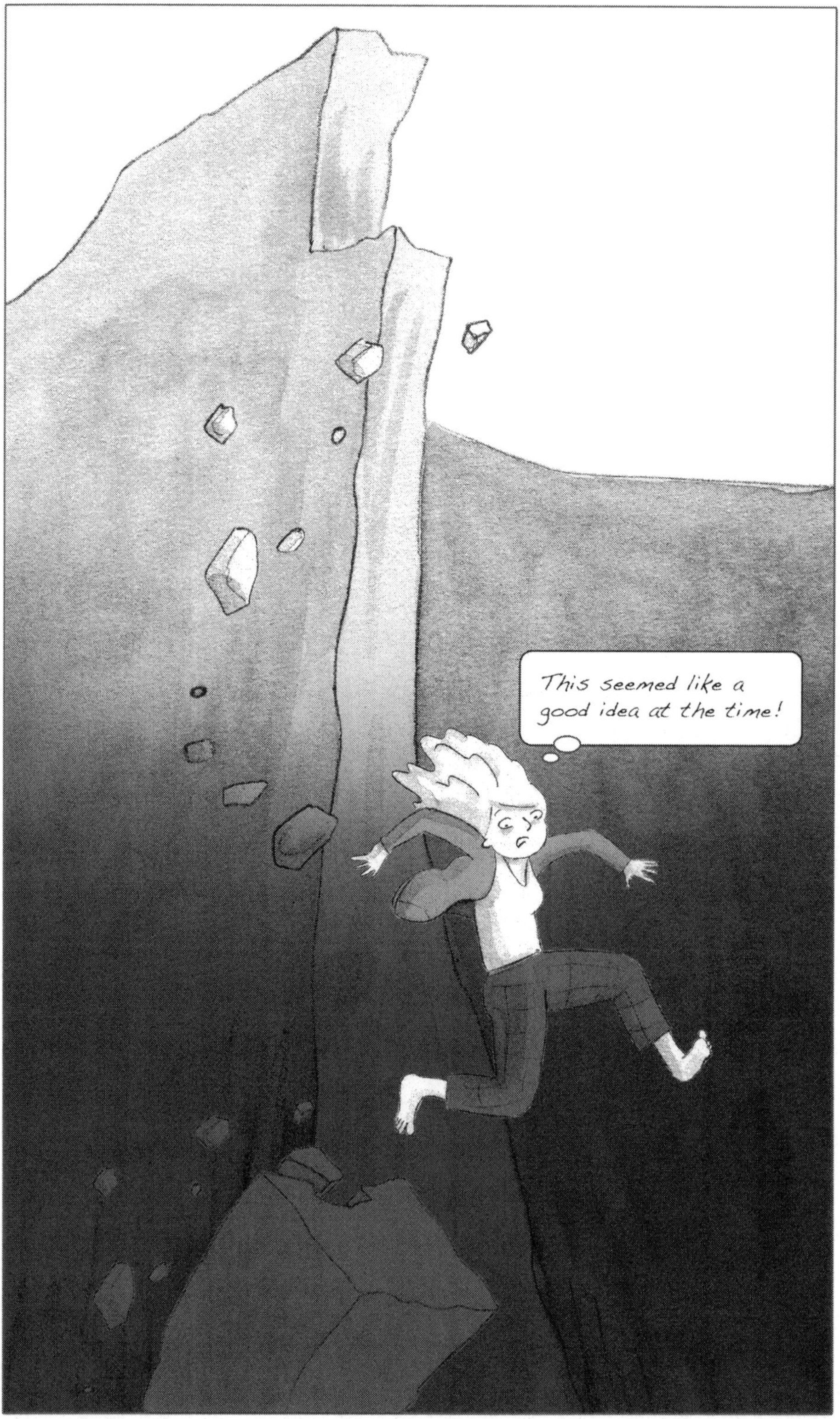
This seemed like a good idea at the time!

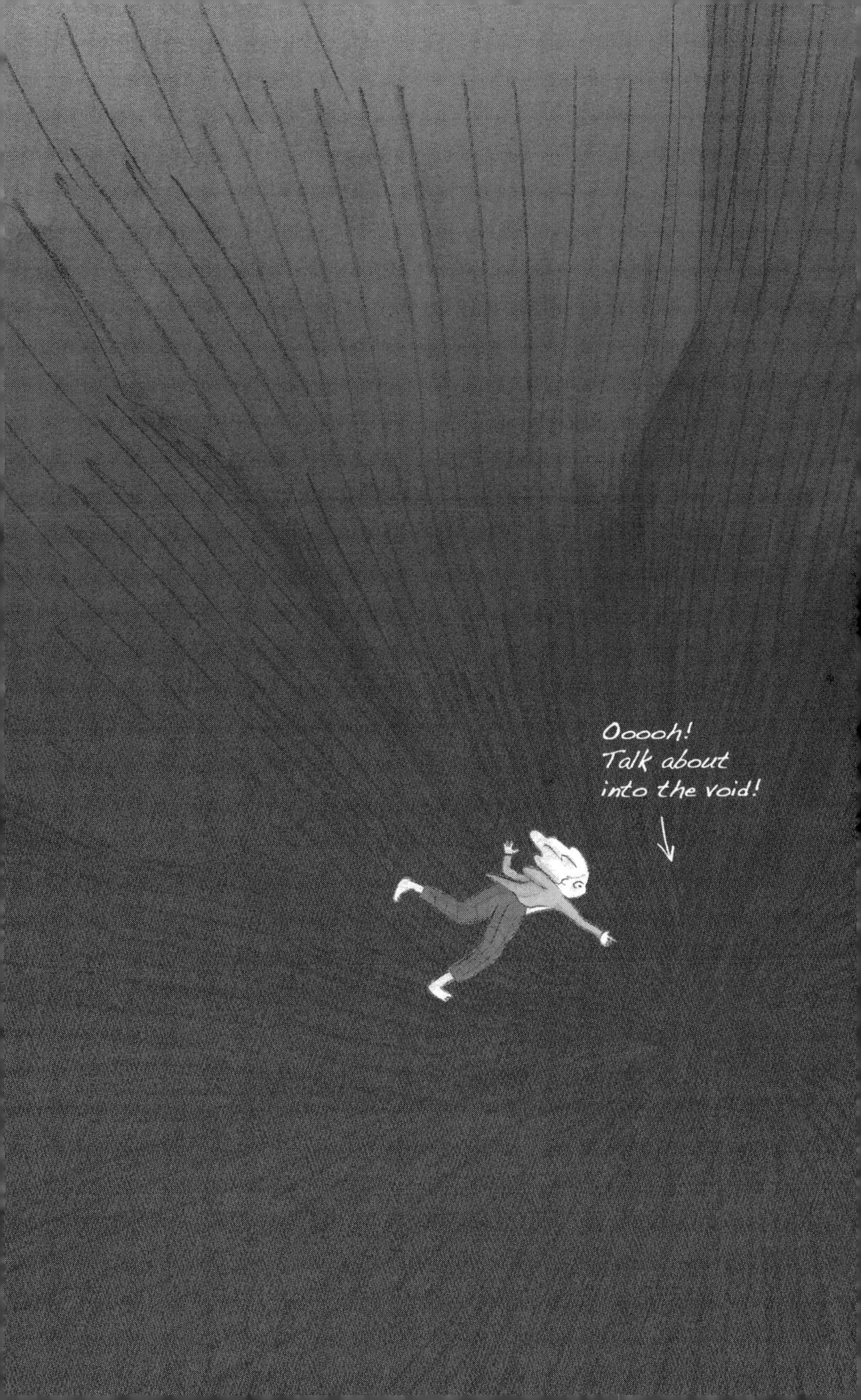
Ooooh!
Talk about
into the void!

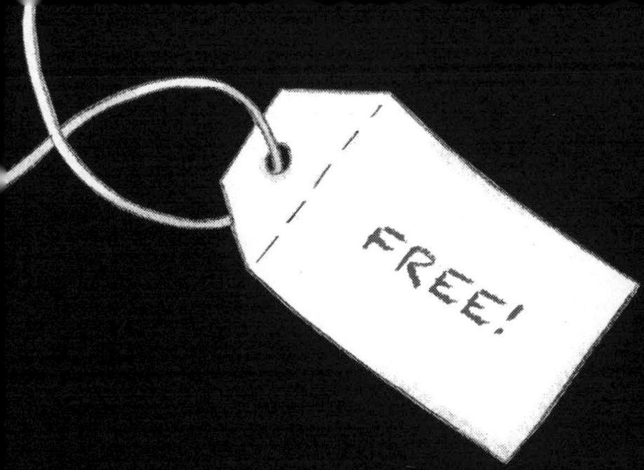
FREE!

The most intimate question
we can ask is this: who or
what am I?

ADYASHANTI

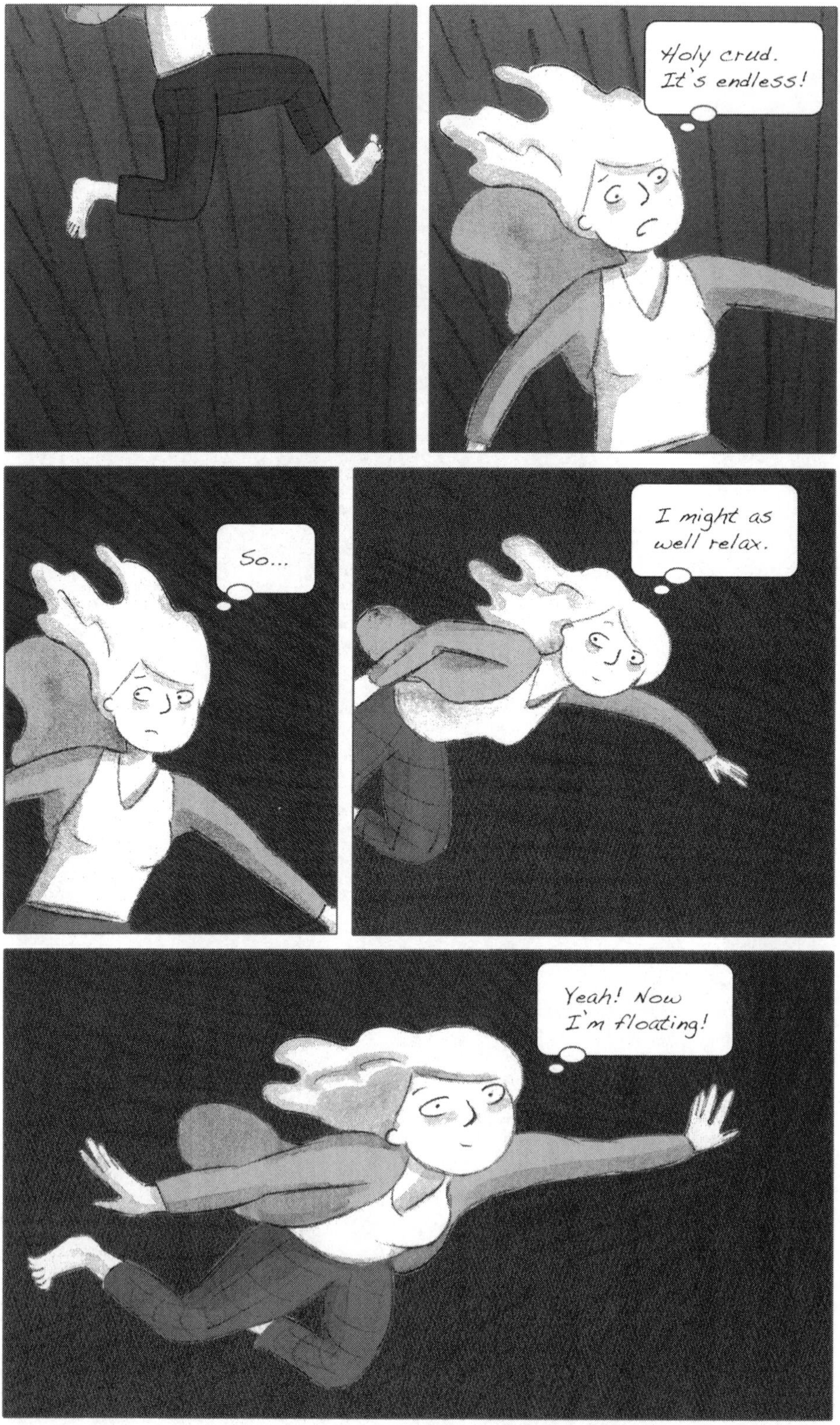
Holy crud. It's endless!
So...
I might as well relax.
Yeah! Now I'm floating!

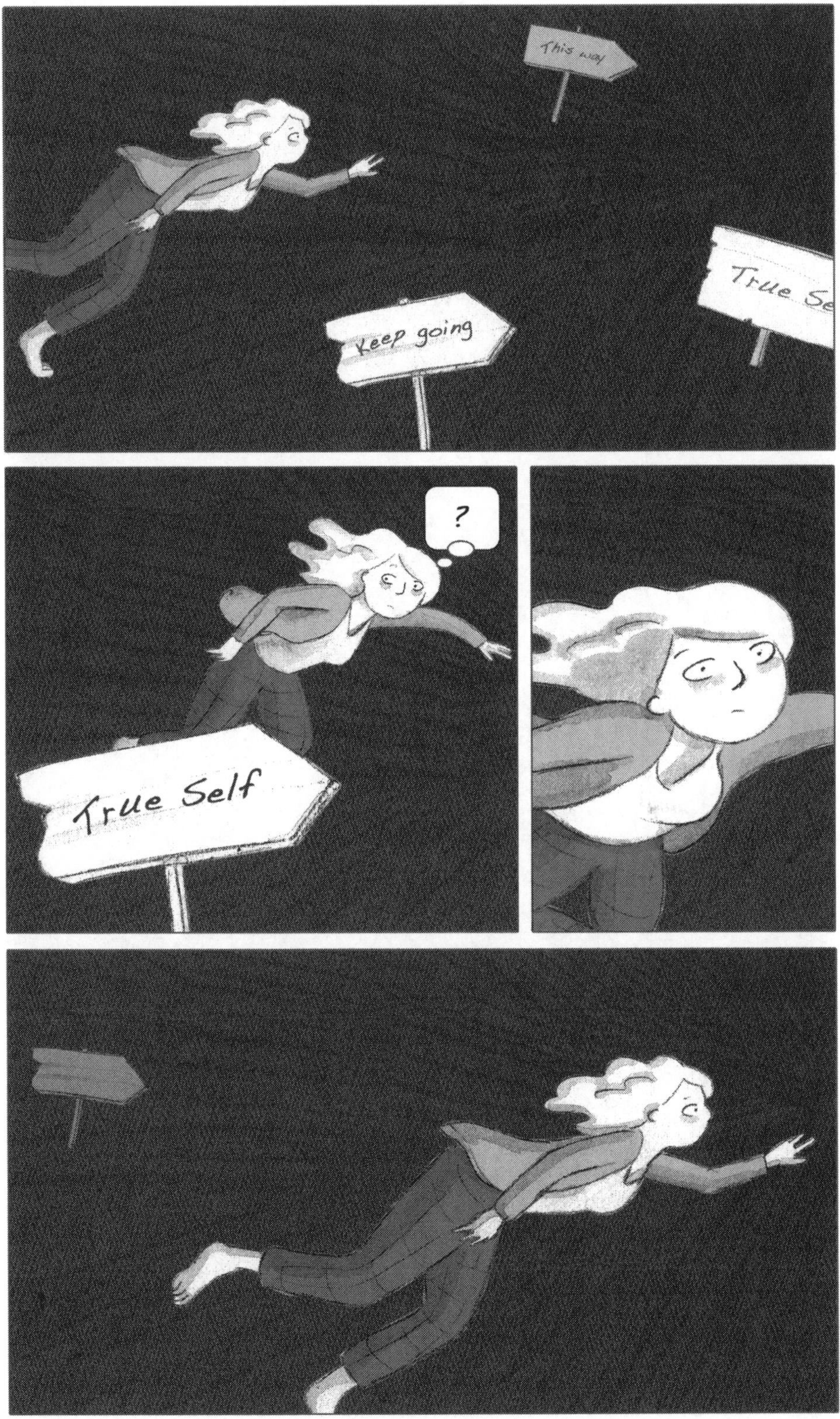
This way
Keep going
True Se
?
True Self

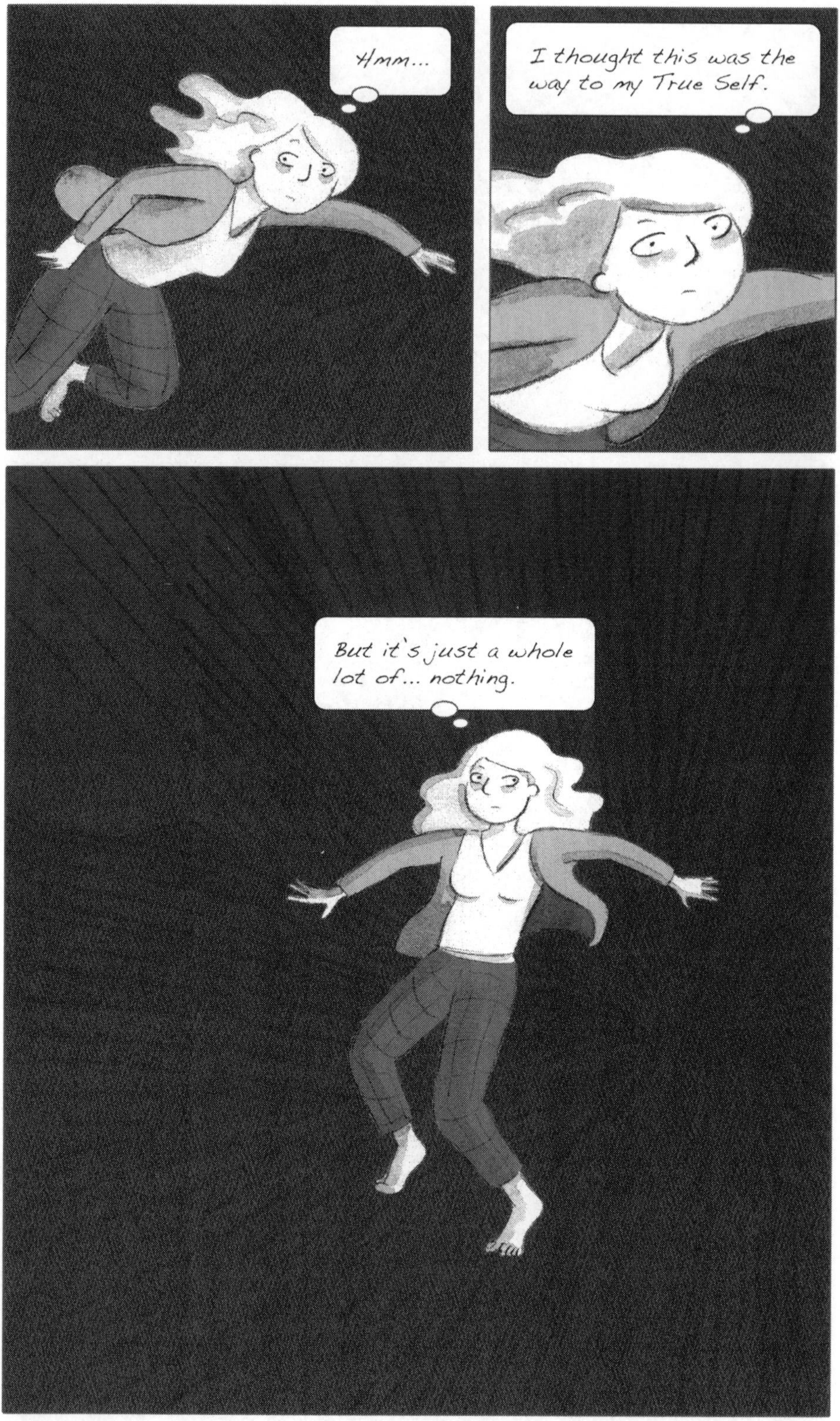
Hmm...
I thought this was the way to my True Self.
But it's just a whole lot of... nothing.

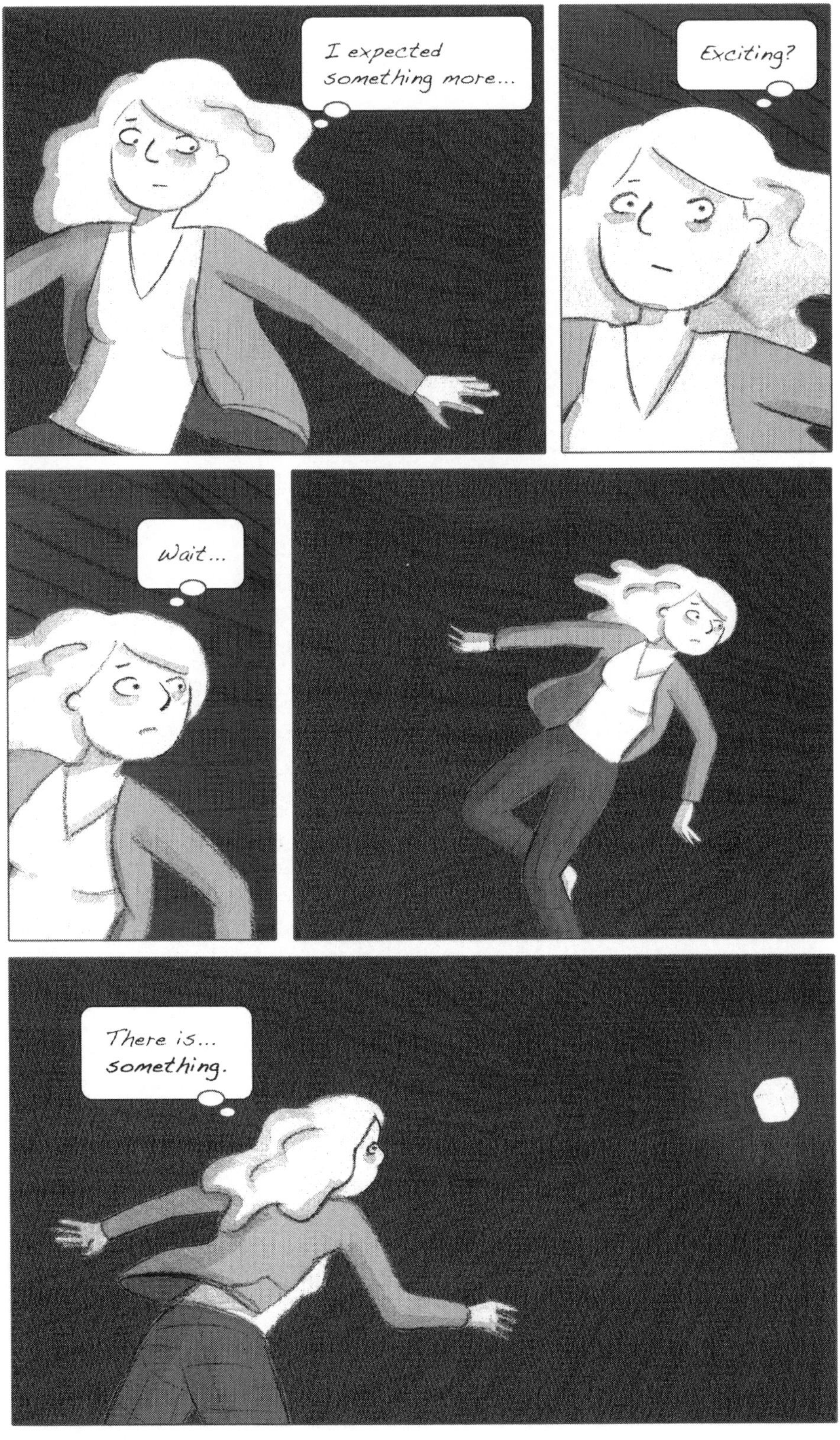
I expected something more...
Exciting?
Wait...
There is... something.

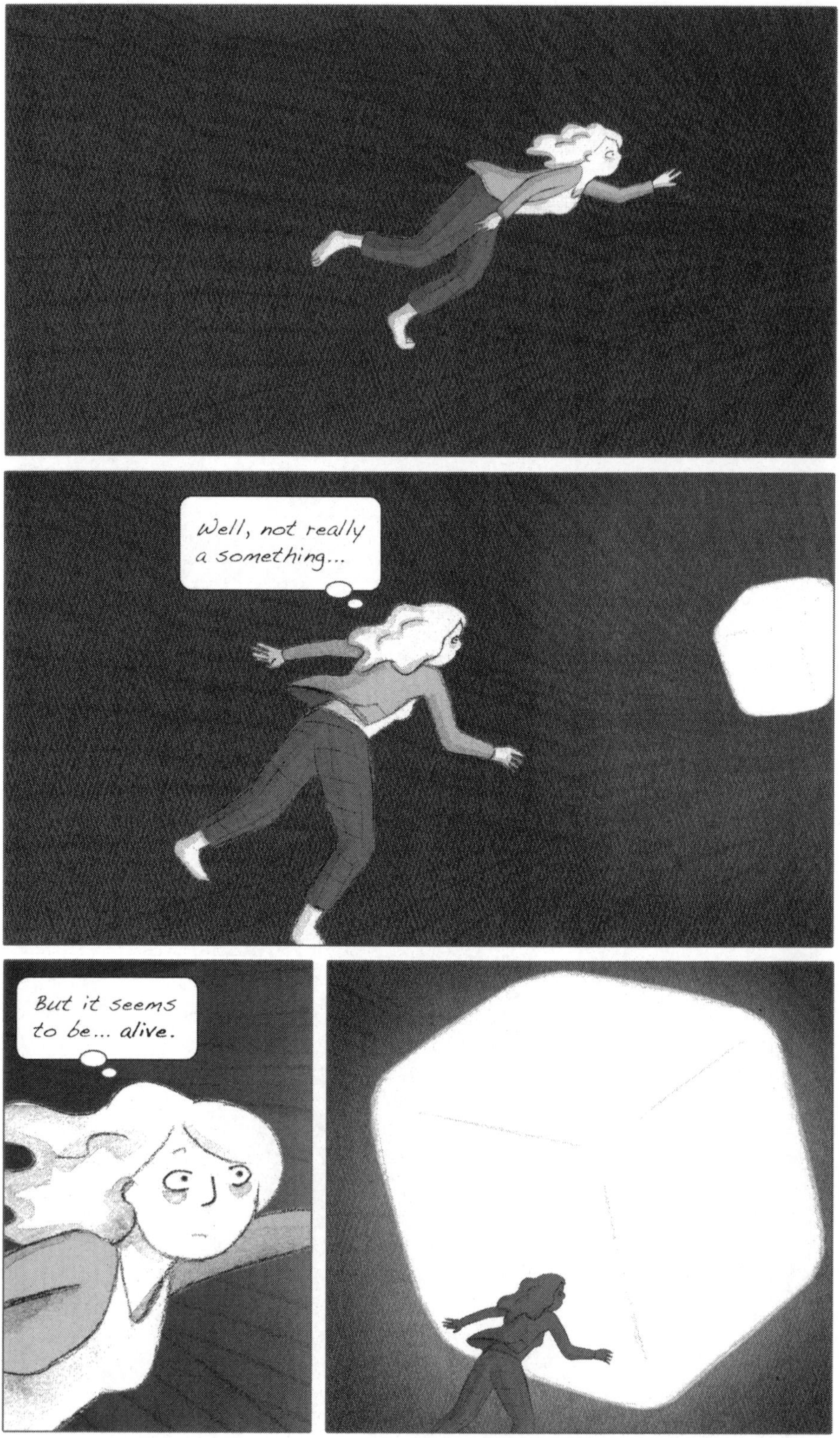
Well, not really a something...
But it seems to be... alive.

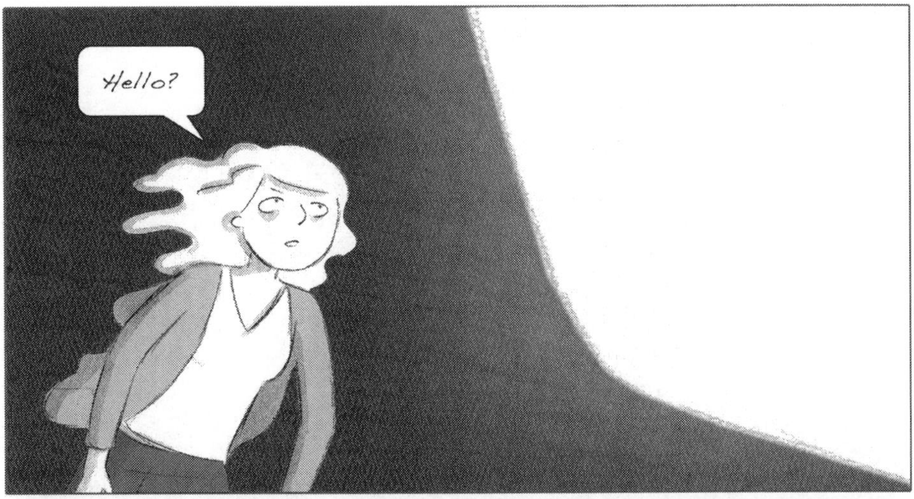
Hello?

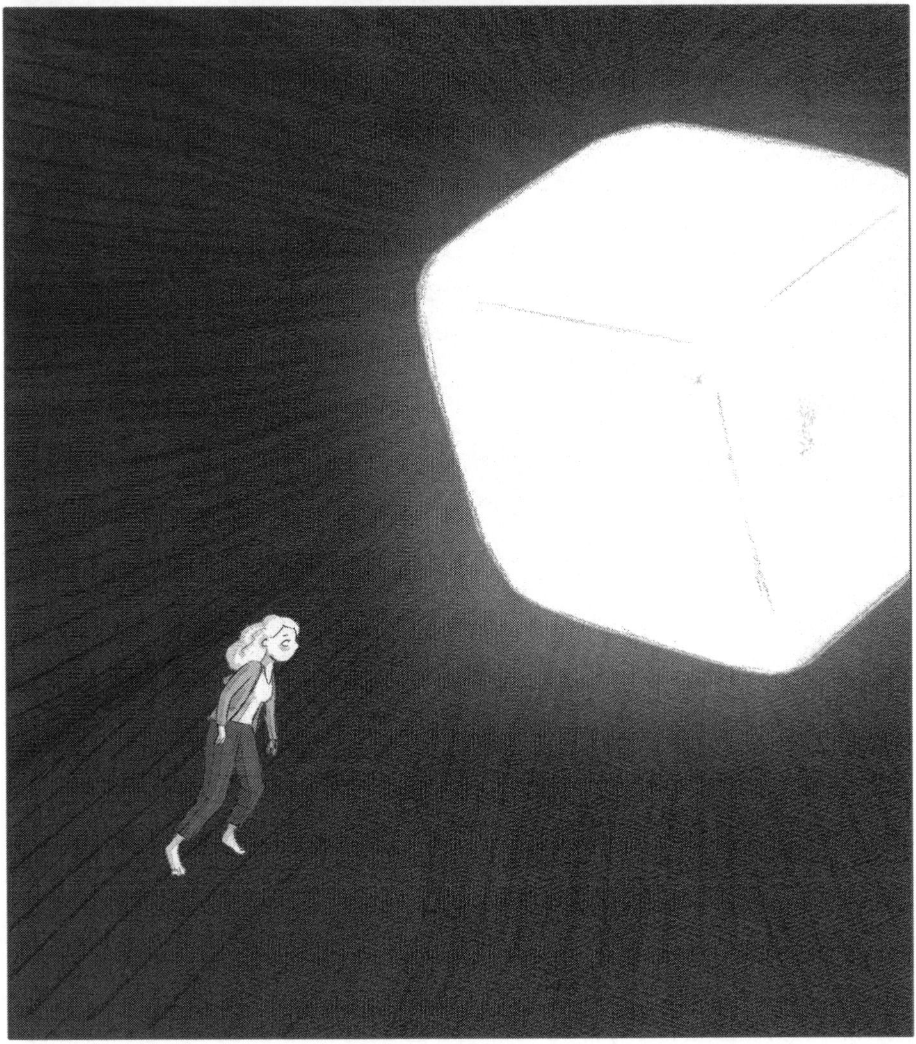

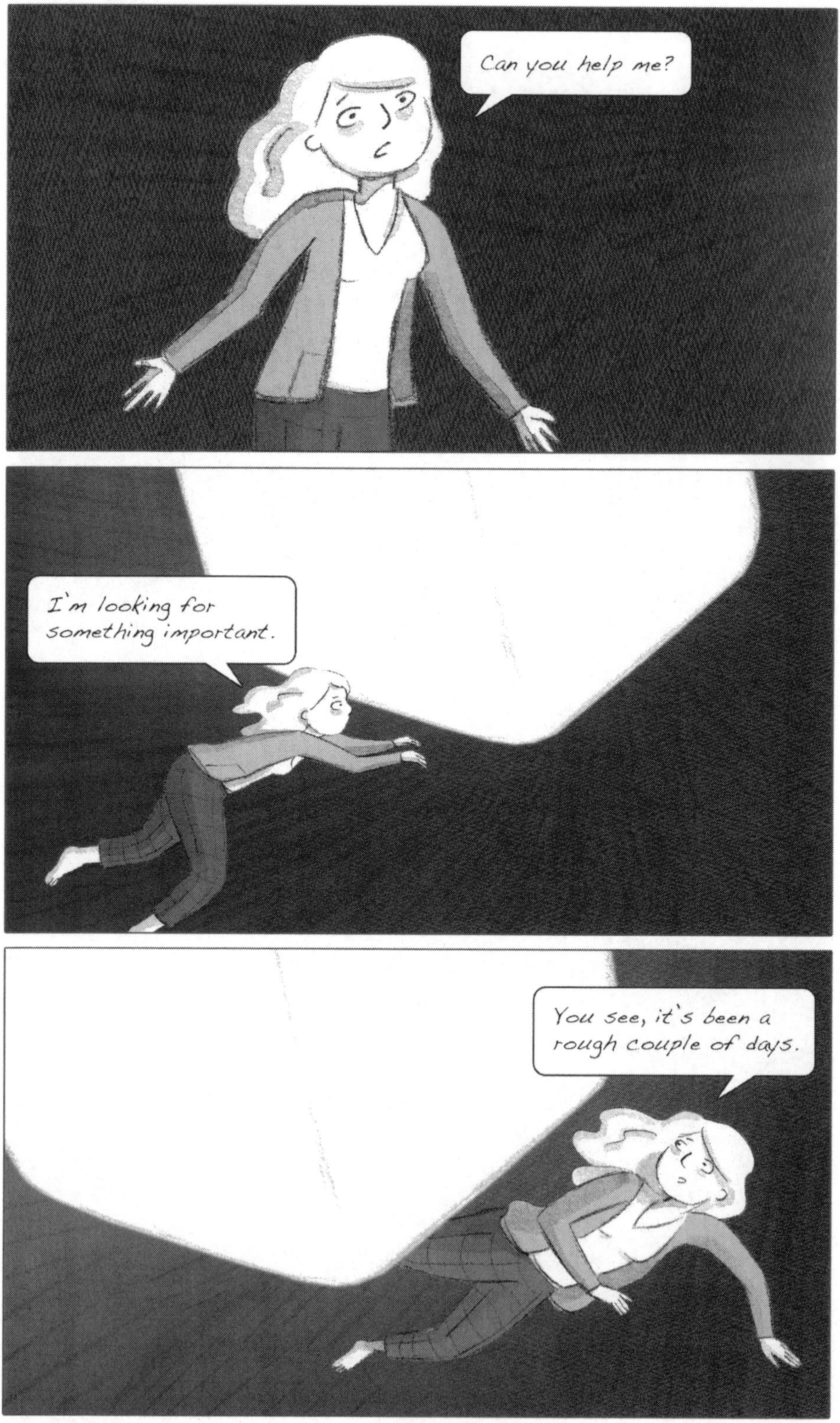
Can you help me?
I'm looking for something important.
You see, it's been a rough couple of days.

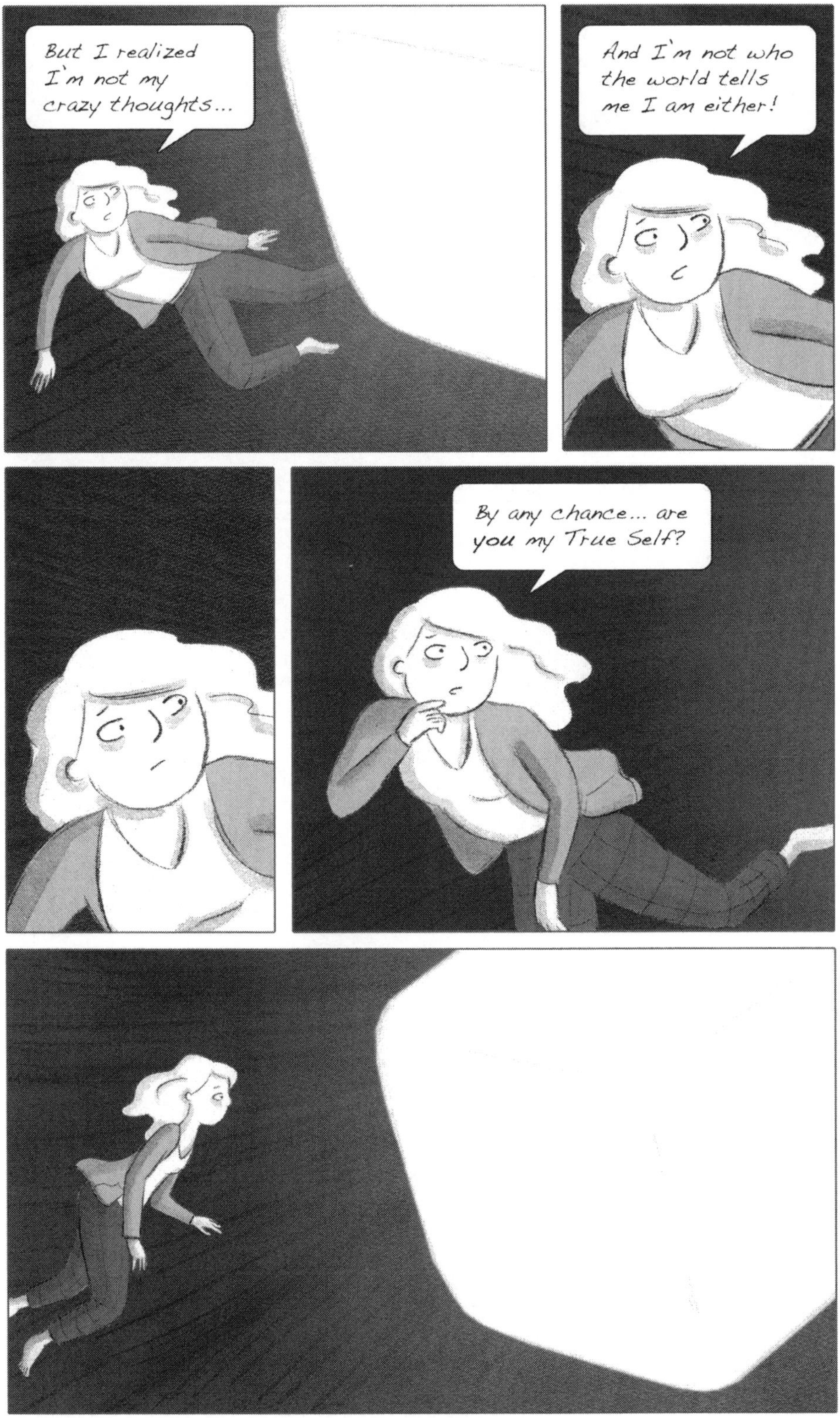
But I realized I'm not my crazy thoughts...
And I'm not who the world tells me I am either!
By any chance... are you my True Self?

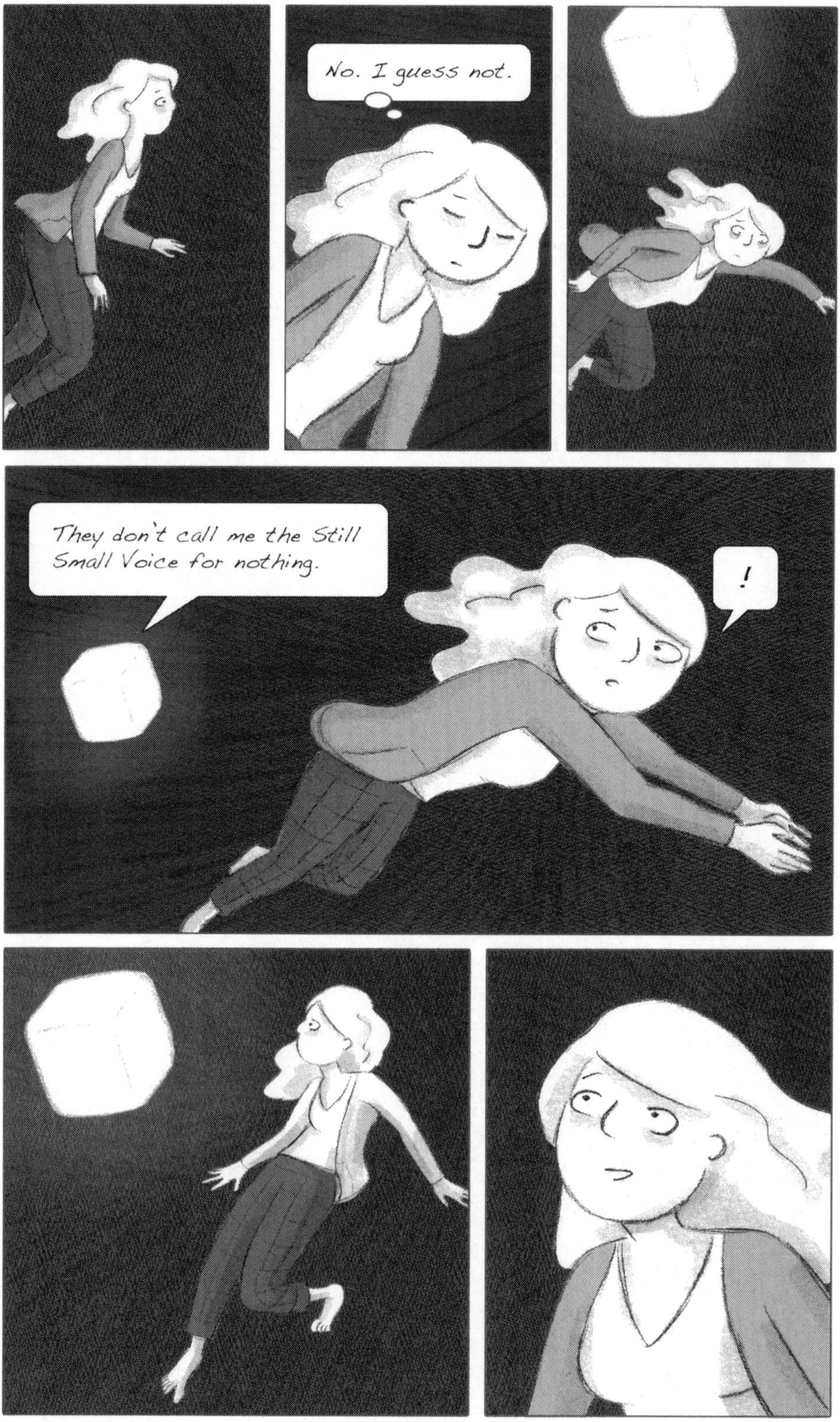
No. I guess not.
They don't call me the Still Small Voice for nothing.
!

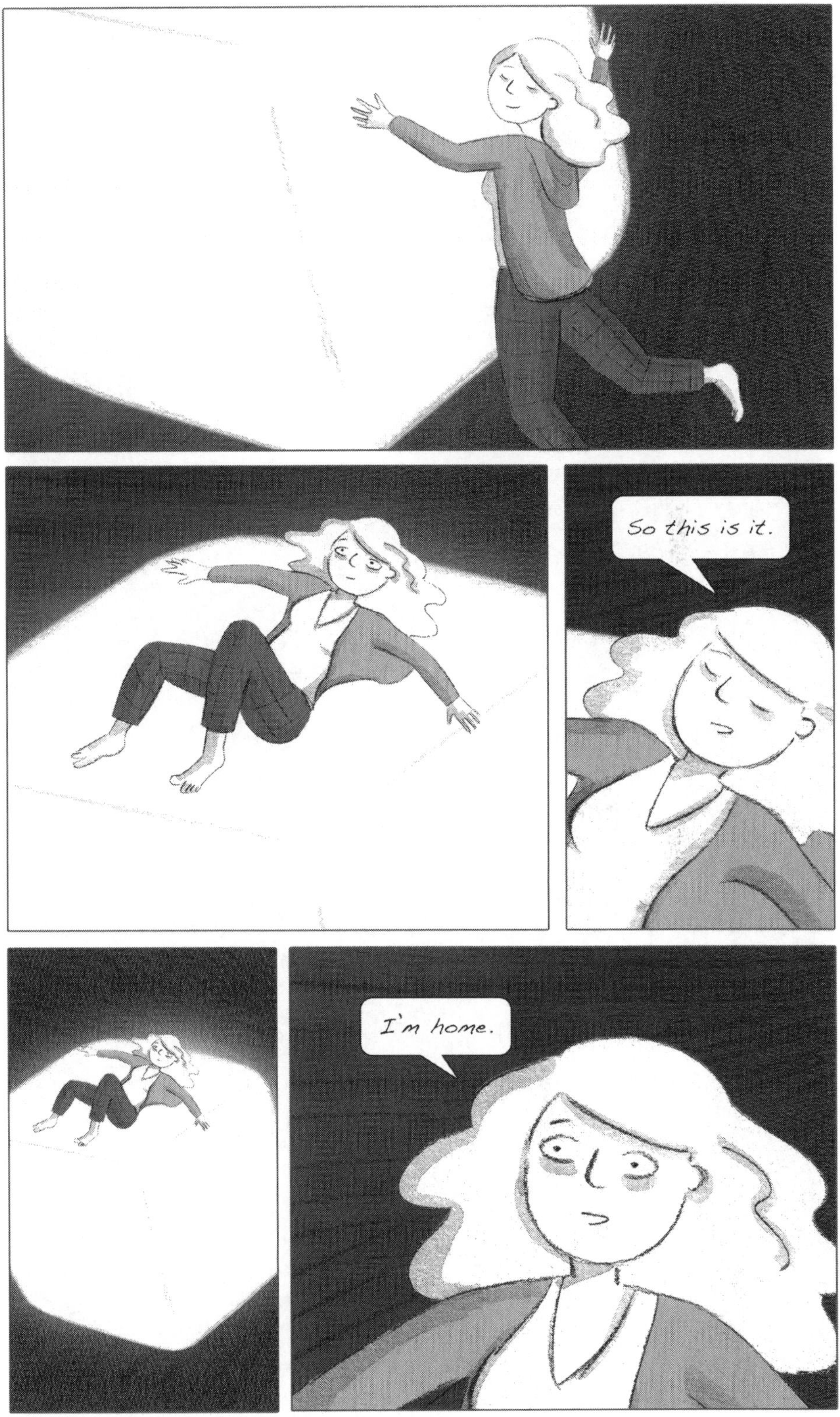
So this is it.
I'm home.

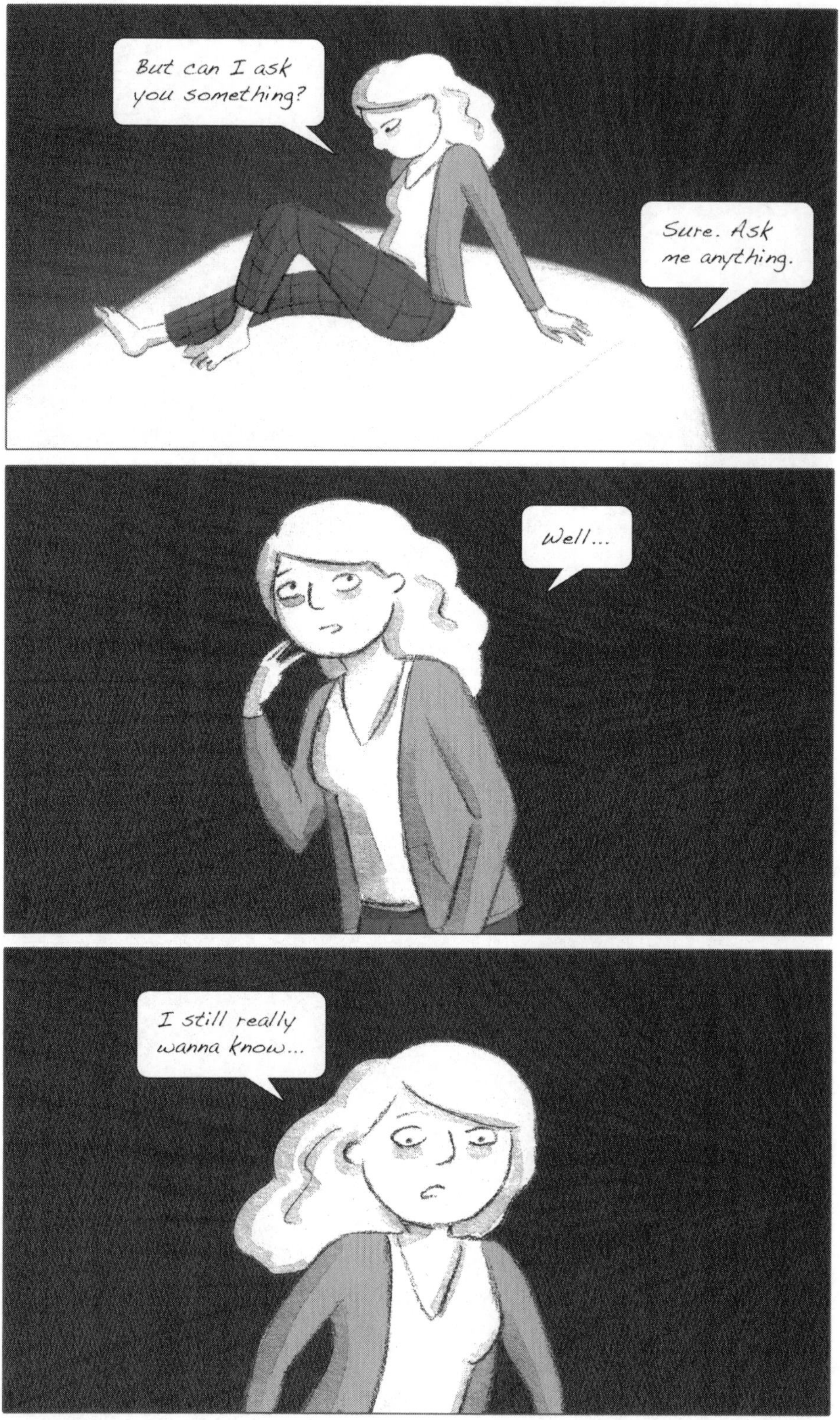
But can I ask you something?
Sure. Ask me anything.
Well...
I still really wanna know...

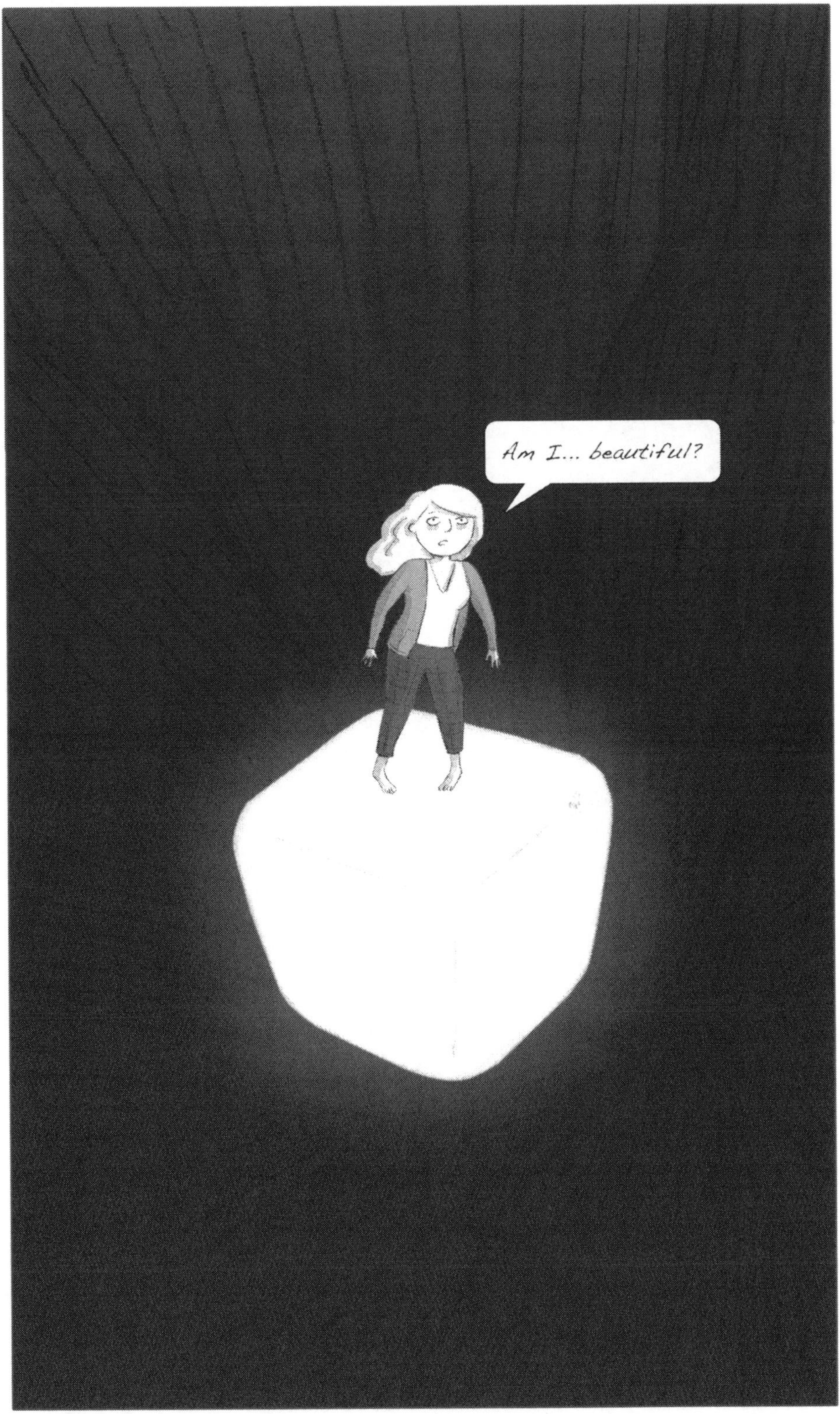
Am I... beautiful?

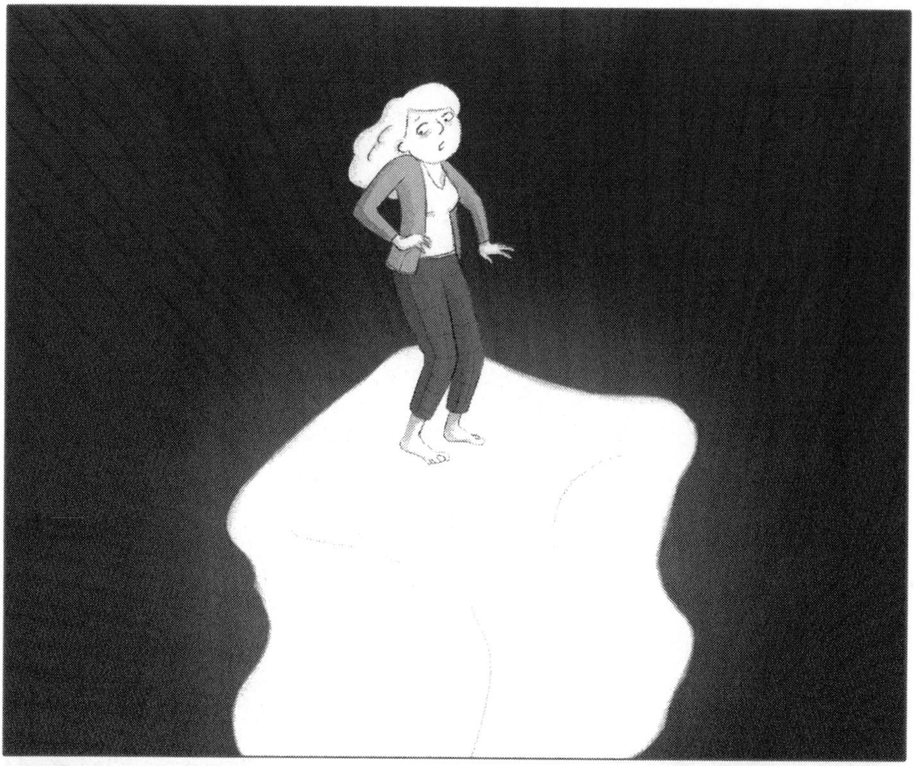

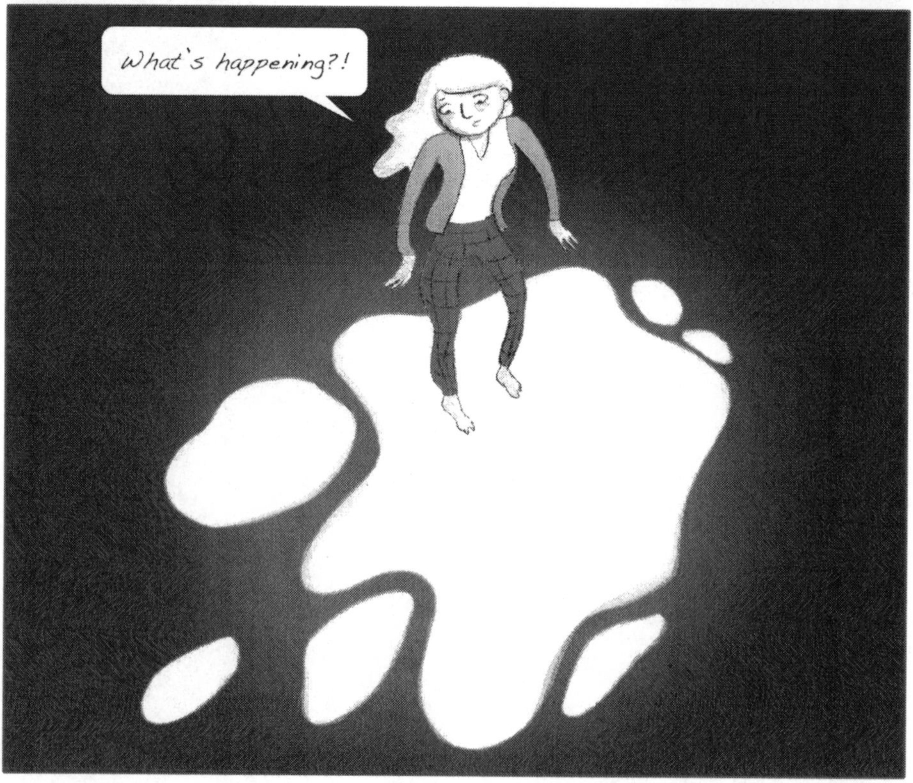
What's happening?!

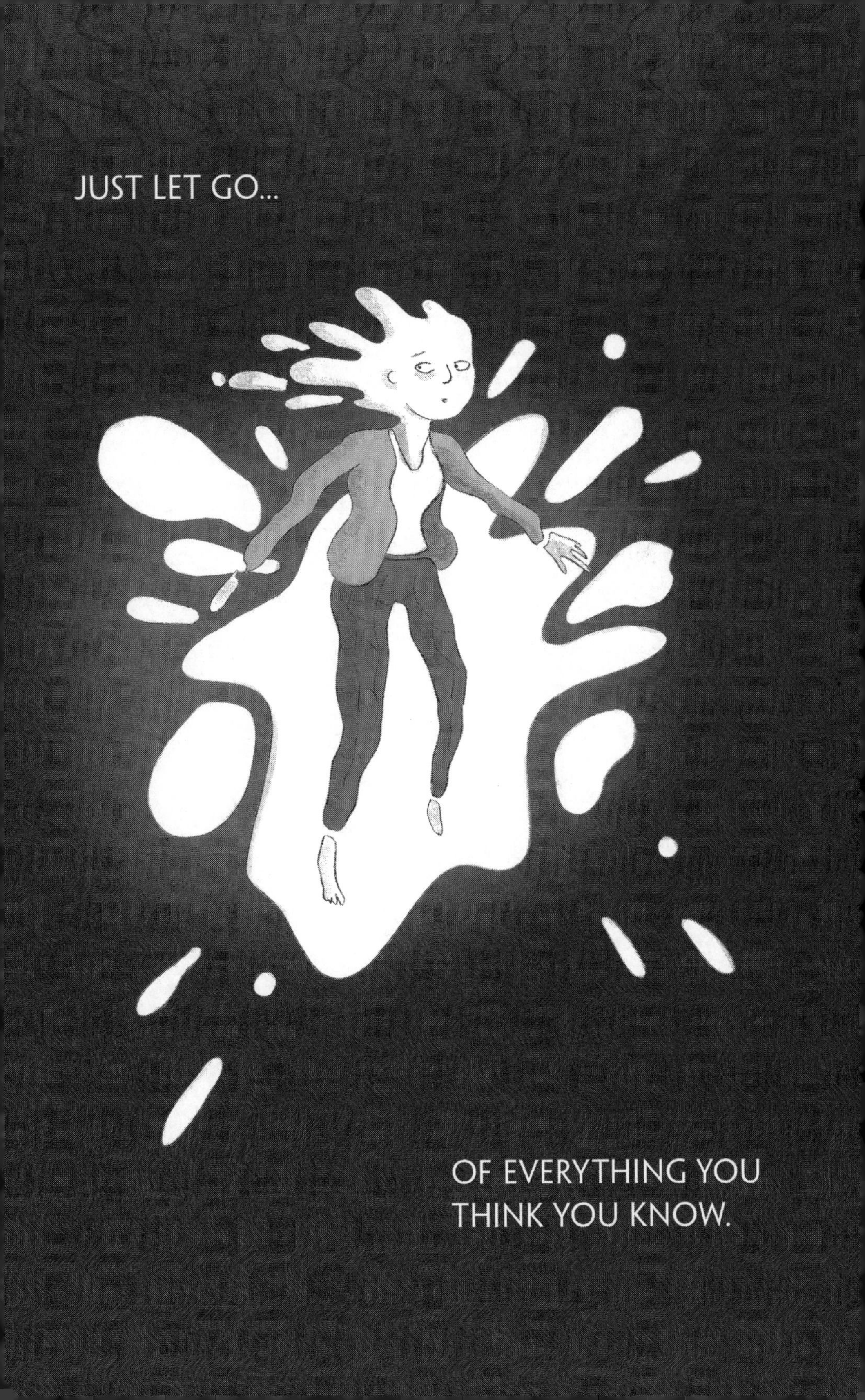
JUST LET GO...
OF EVERYTHING YOU THINK YOU KNOW.

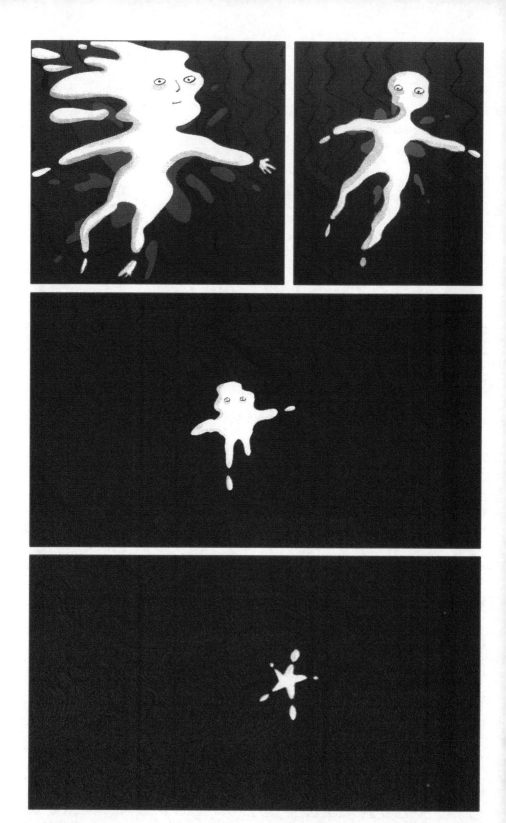

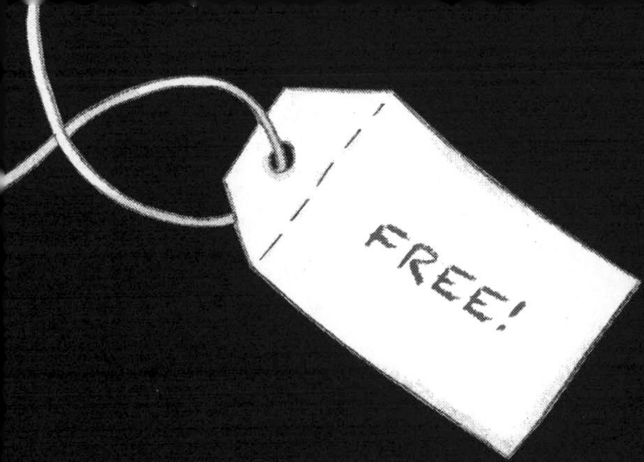
FREE!

I long, as does every human being, to be at home wherever I find myself.

MAYA ANGELOU

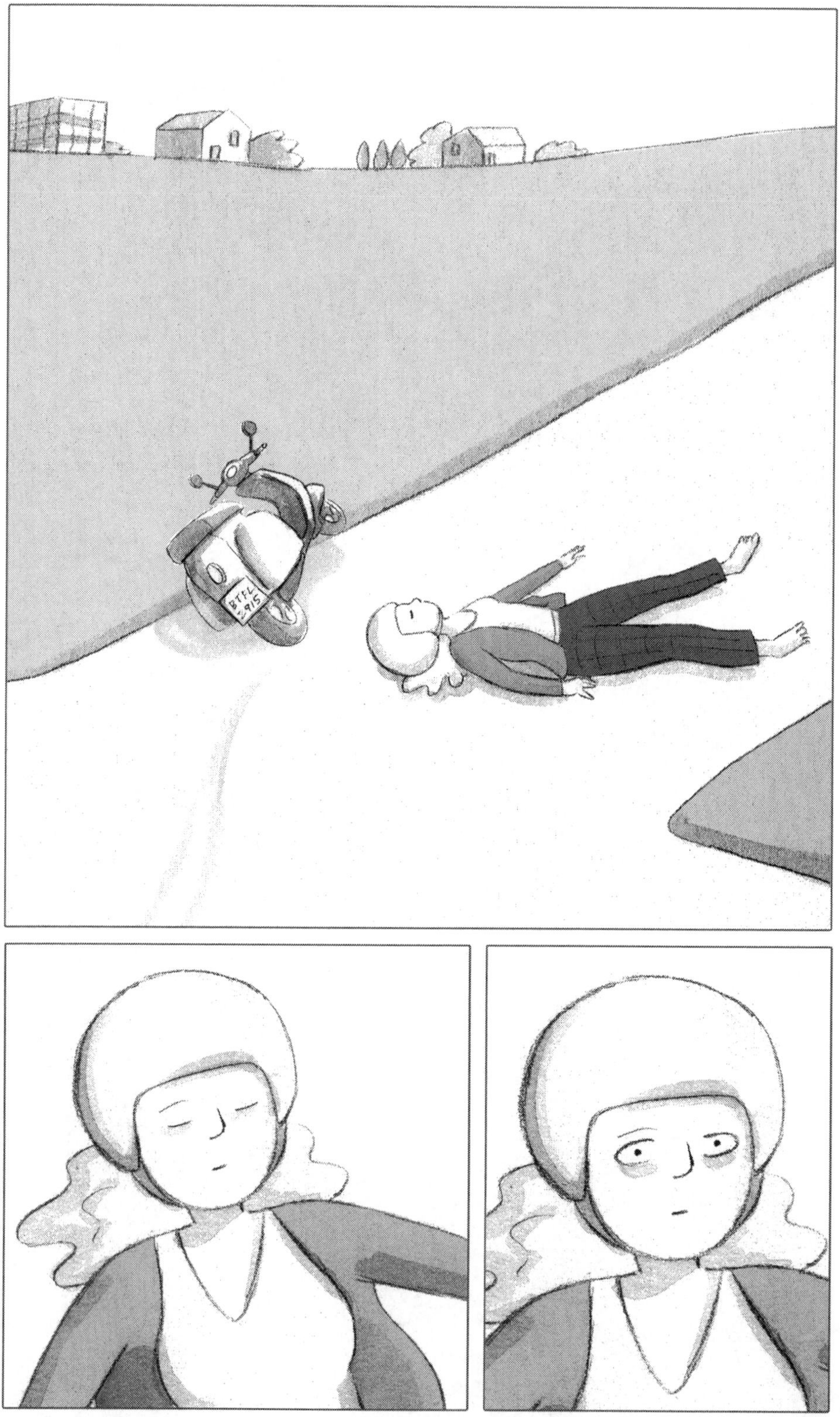

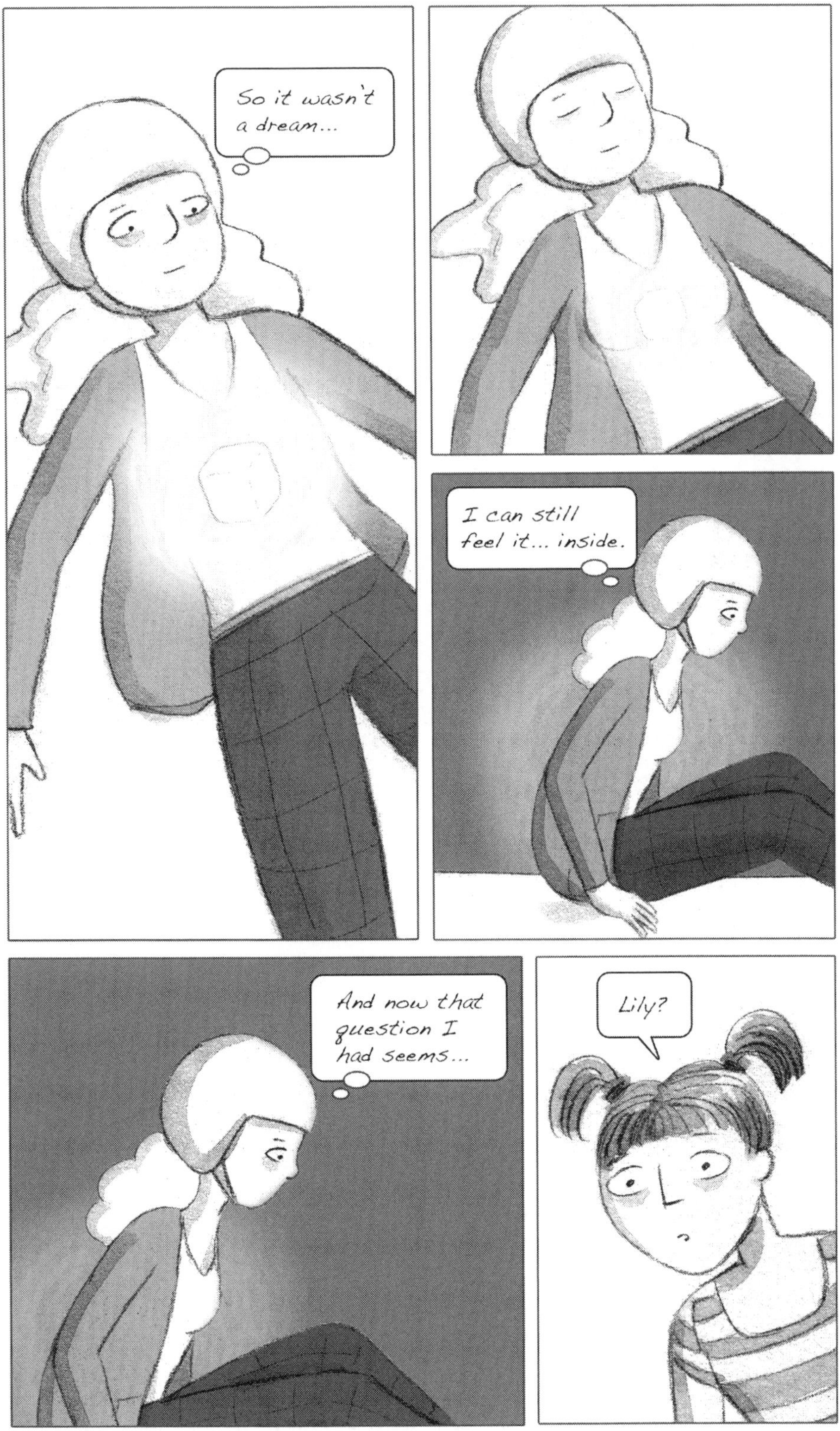
So it wasn't a dream...
I can still feel it... inside.
And now that question I had seems...
Lily?

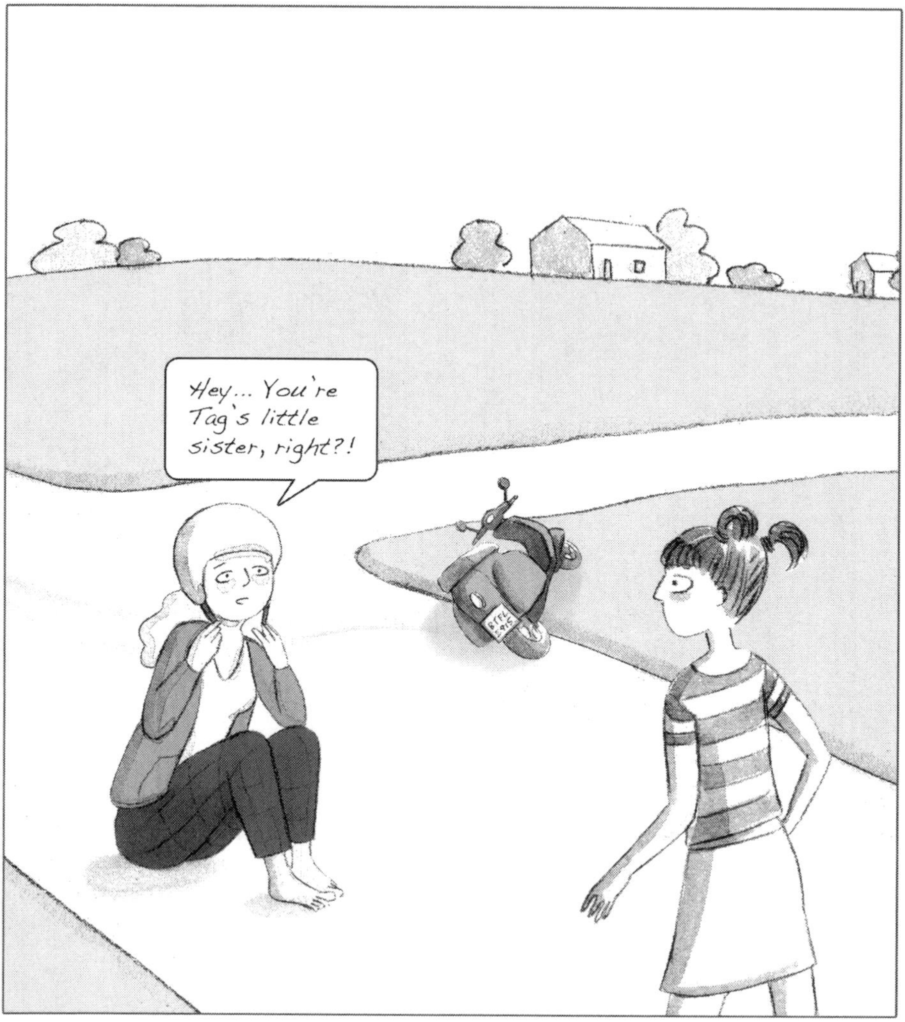
Hey... You're Tag's little sister, right?!

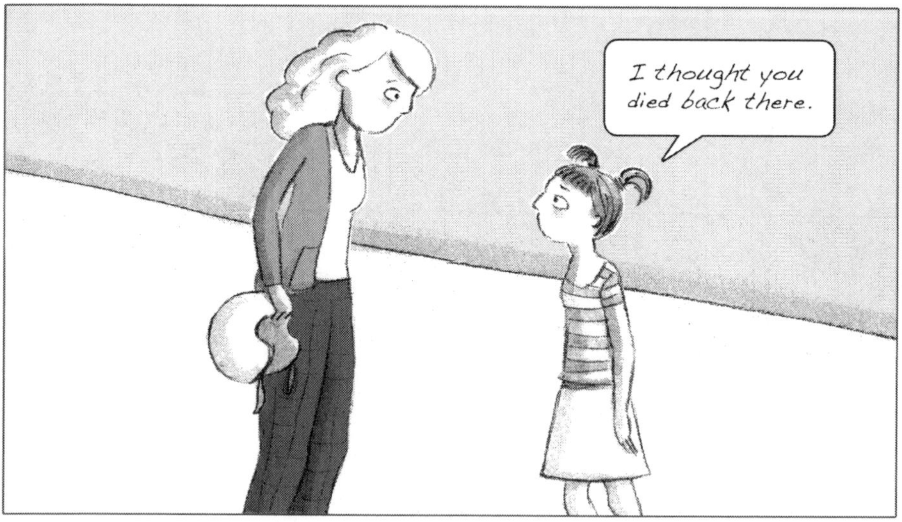
I thought you died back there.

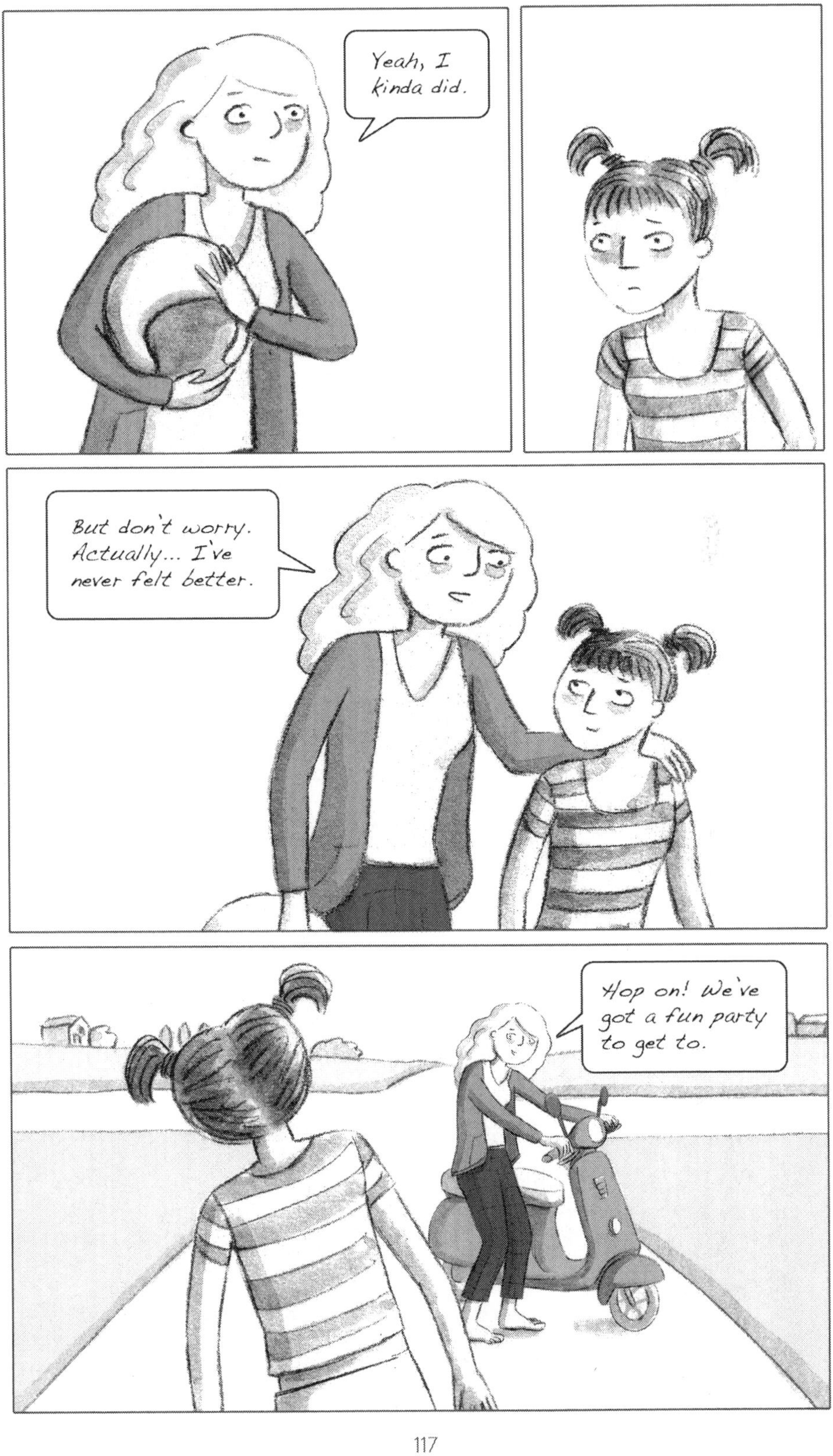
Yeah, I kinda did.
But don't worry. Actually... I've never felt better.
Hop on! We've got a fun party to get to.

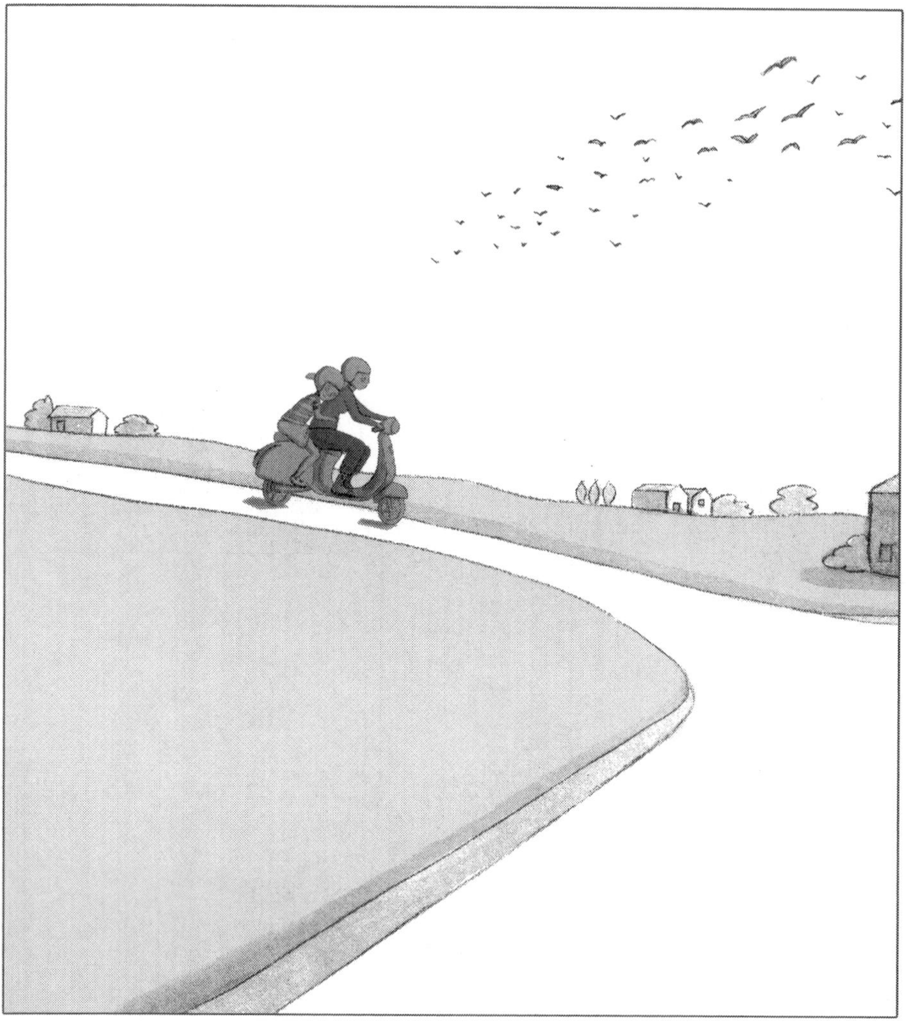

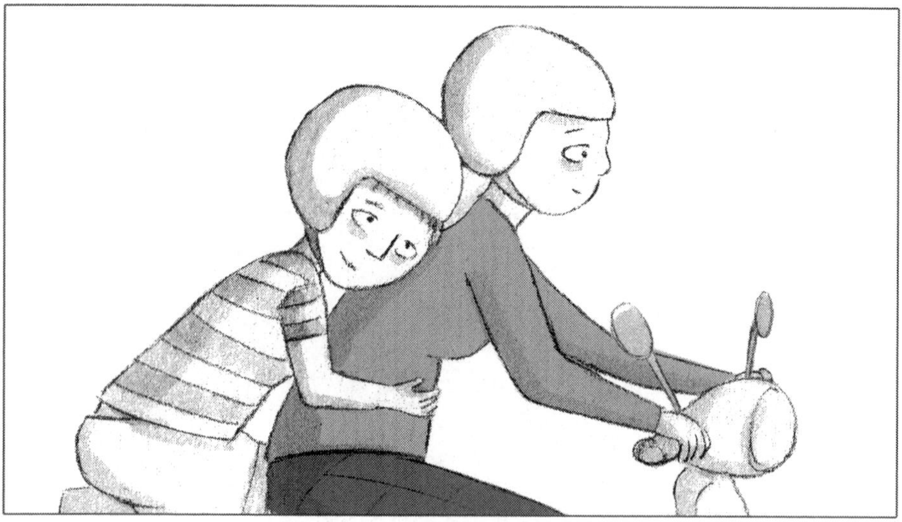

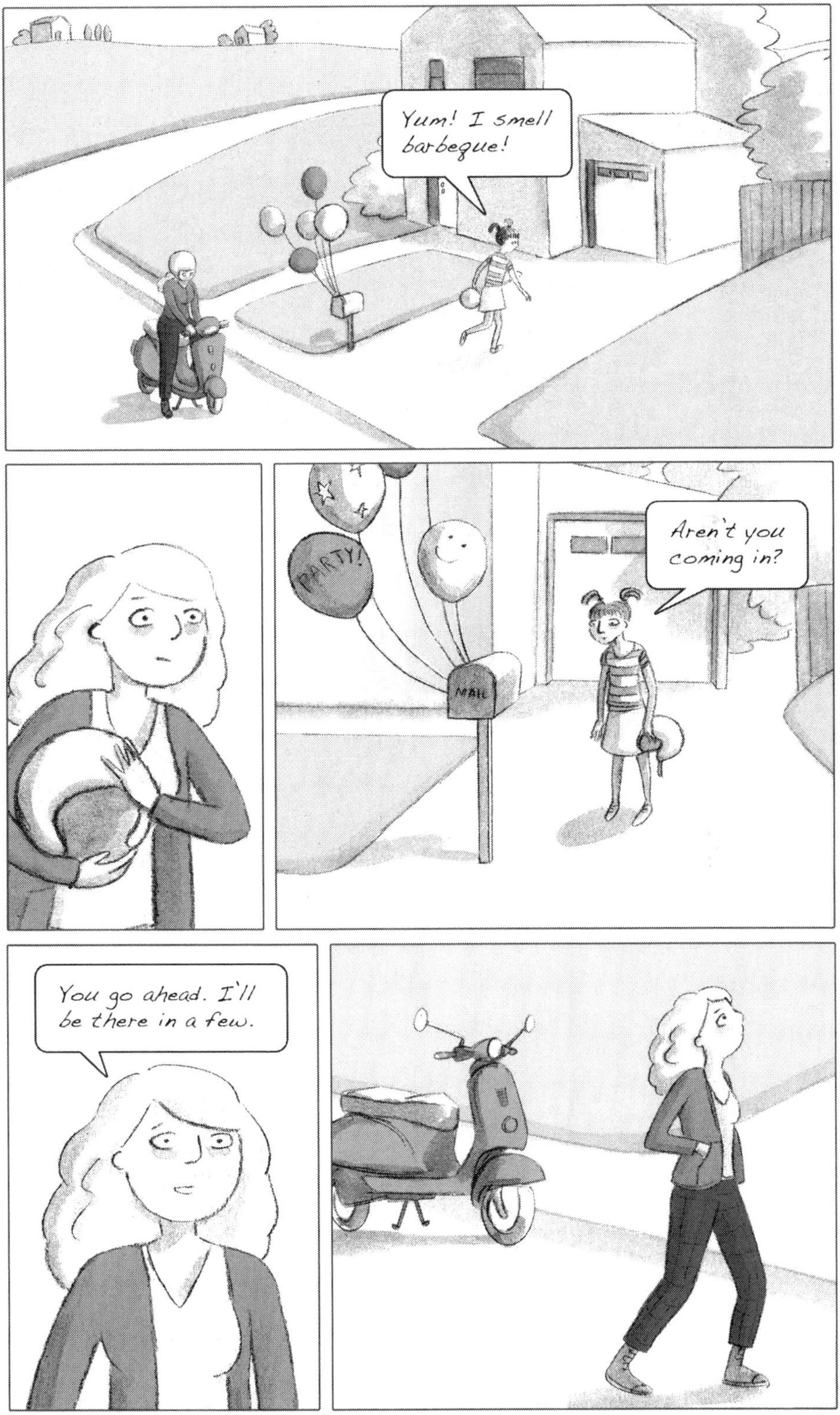
Yum! I smell barbeque!
PARTY!
MAIL
Aren't you coming in?
You go ahead. I'll be there in a few.

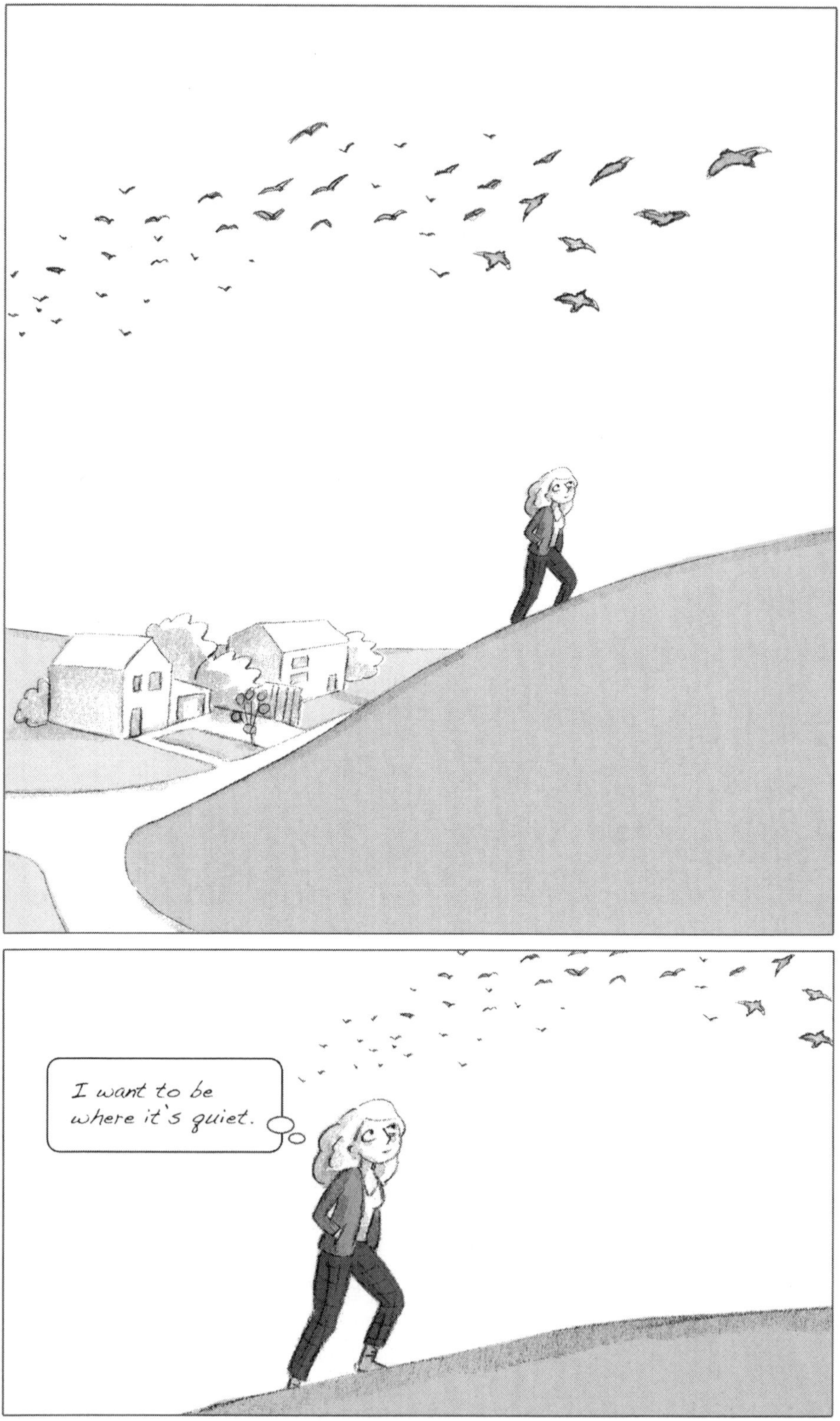
I want to be where it's quiet.

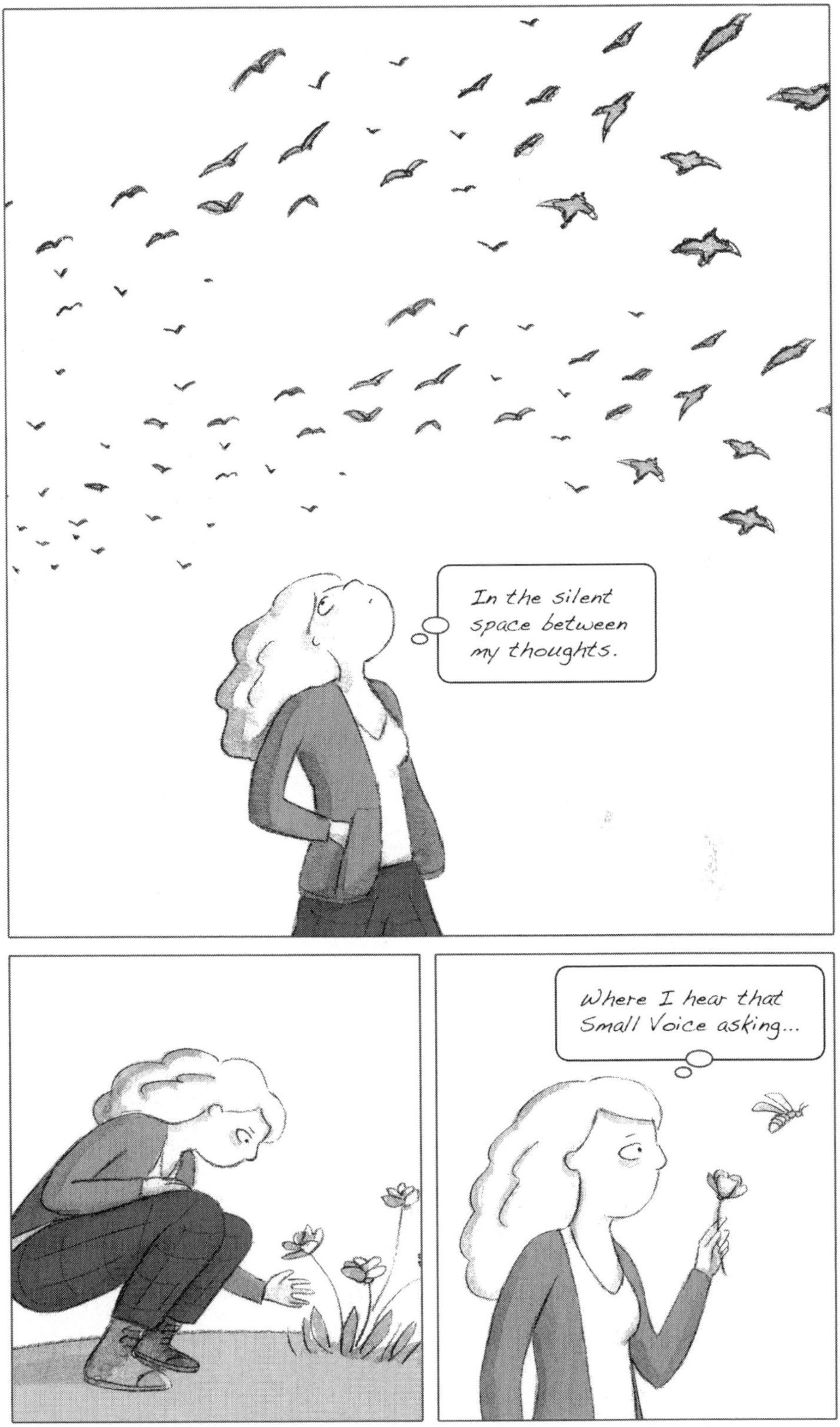
In the silent space between my thoughts.
Where I hear that Small Voice asking...

WHAT DOES BEAUTIFUL MEAN... TO ME?

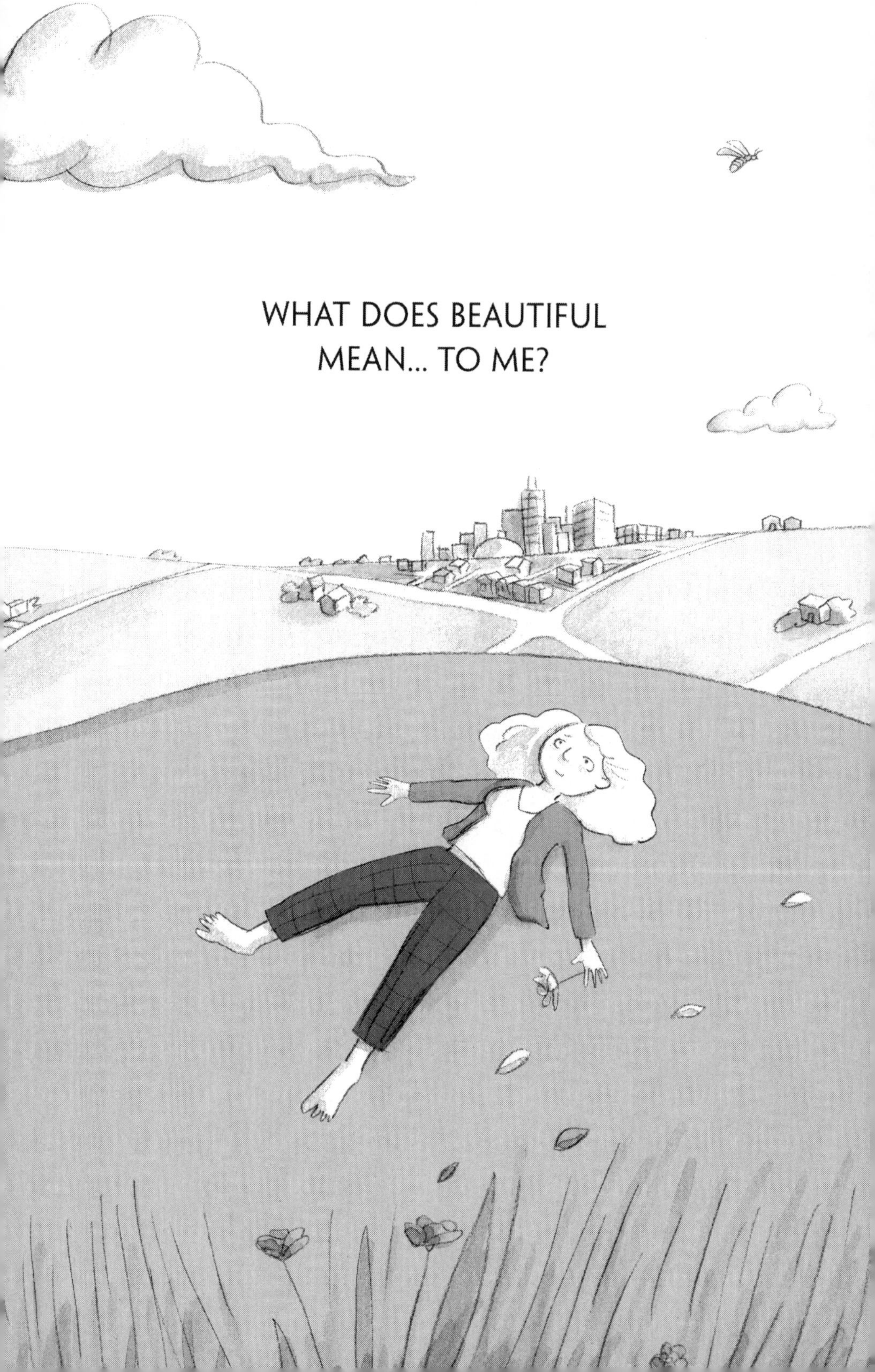

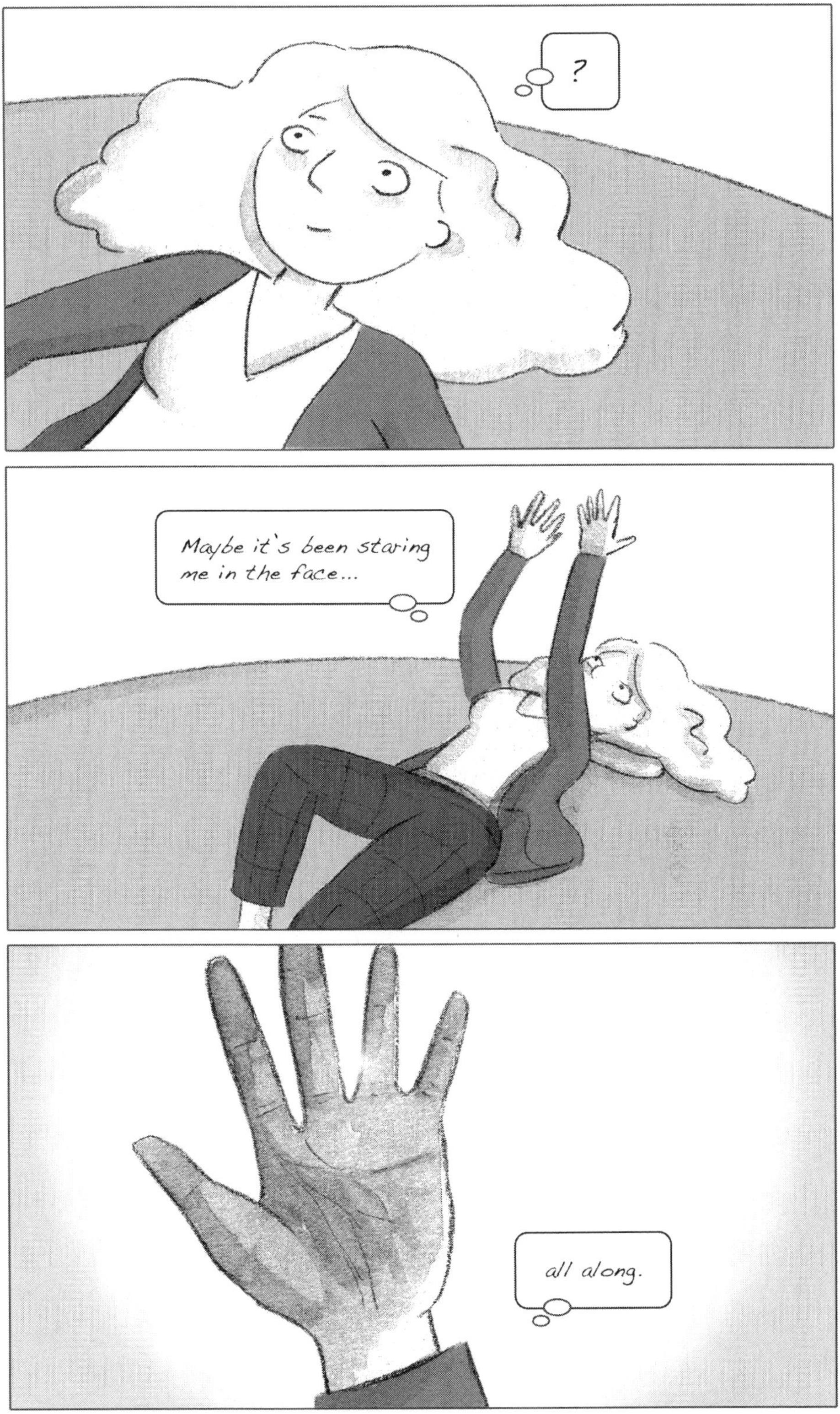
?
Maybe it's been staring me in the face...
all along.

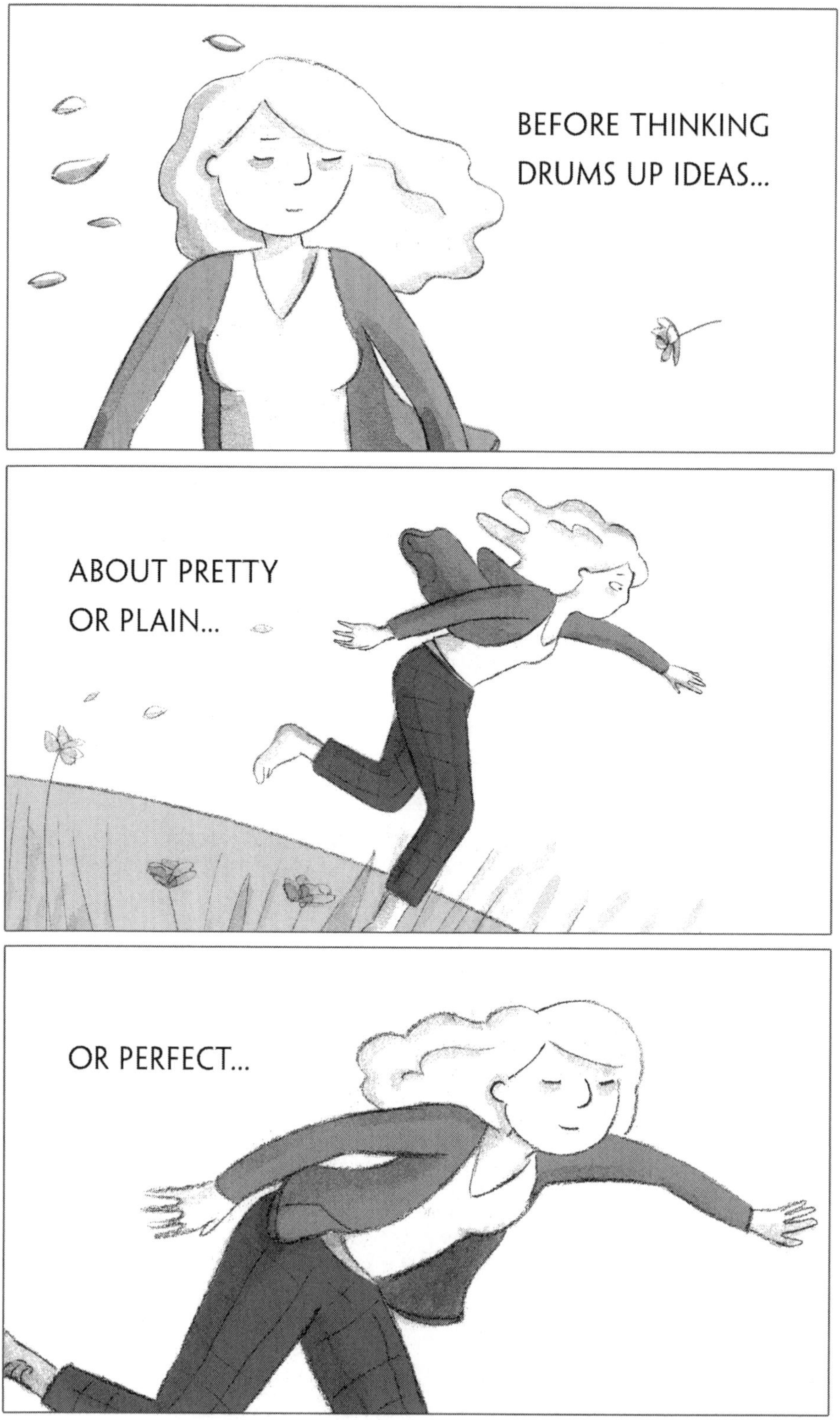
BEFORE THINKING DRUMS UP IDEAS...
ABOUT PRETTY OR PLAIN...
OR PERFECT...

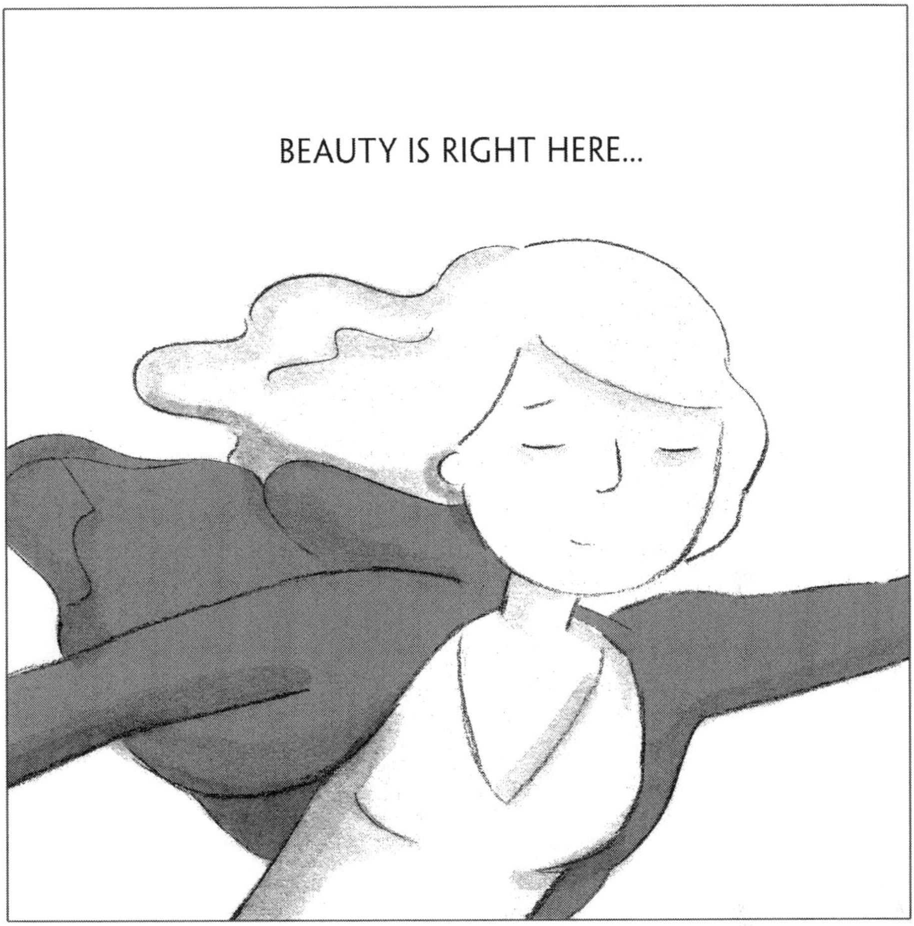
BEAUTY IS RIGHT HERE...

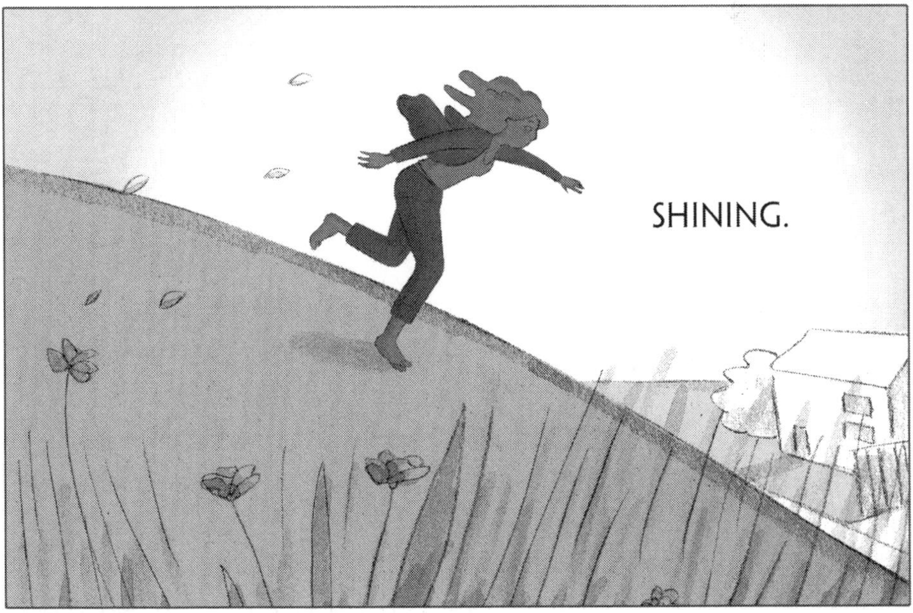
SHINING.

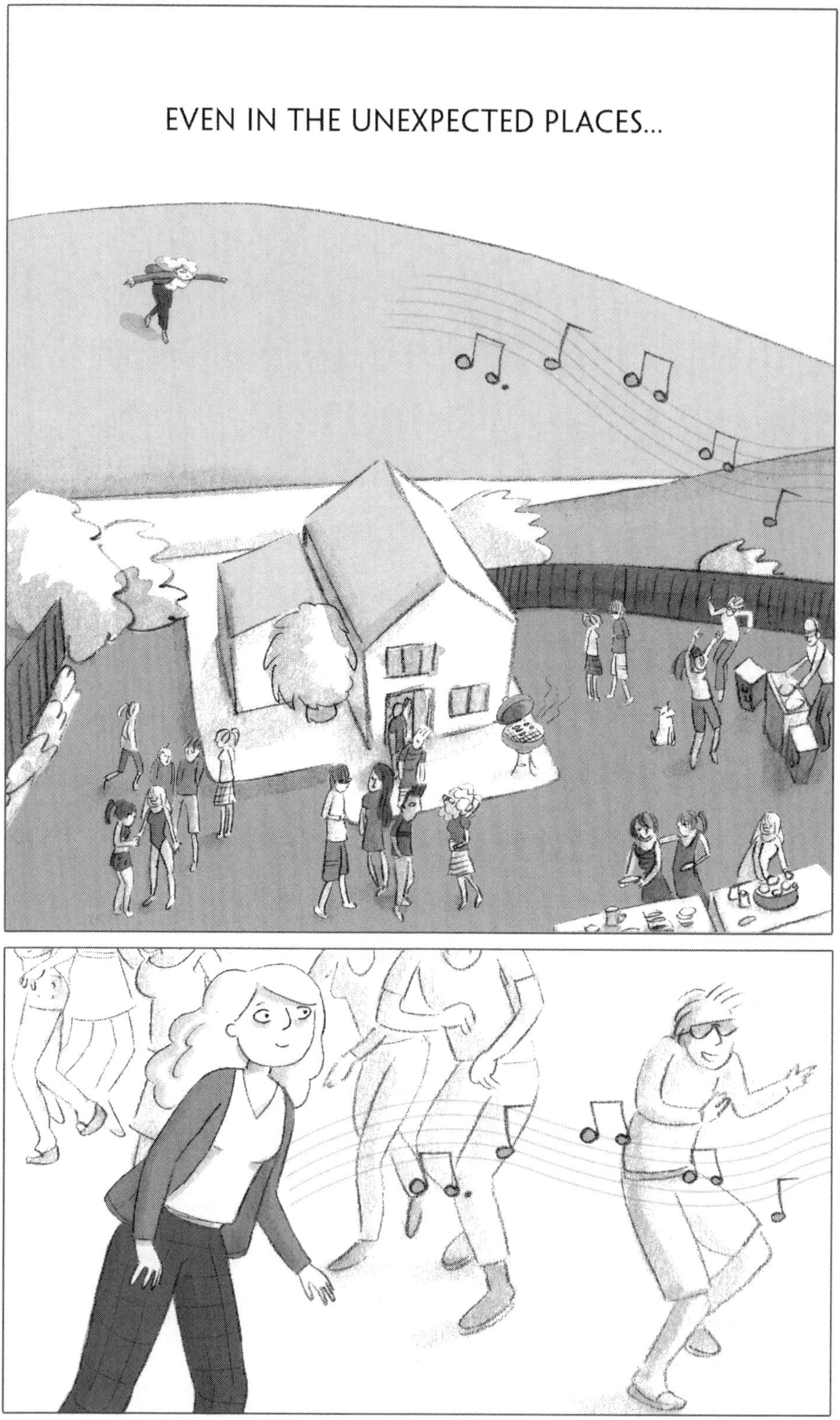
EVEN IN THE UNEXPECTED PLACES...

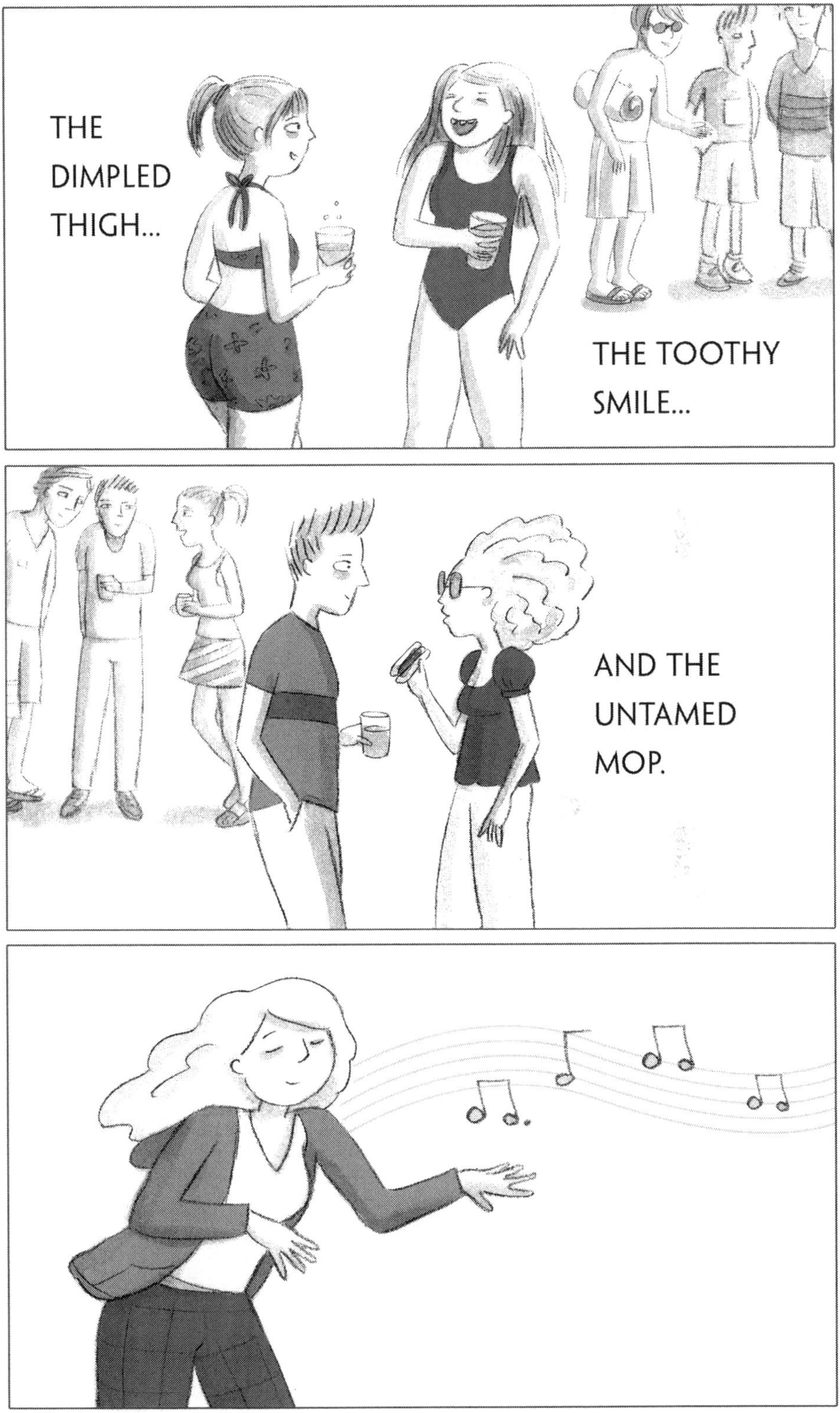
THE DIMPLED THIGH...
THE TOOTHY SMILE...
AND THE UNTAMED MOP.

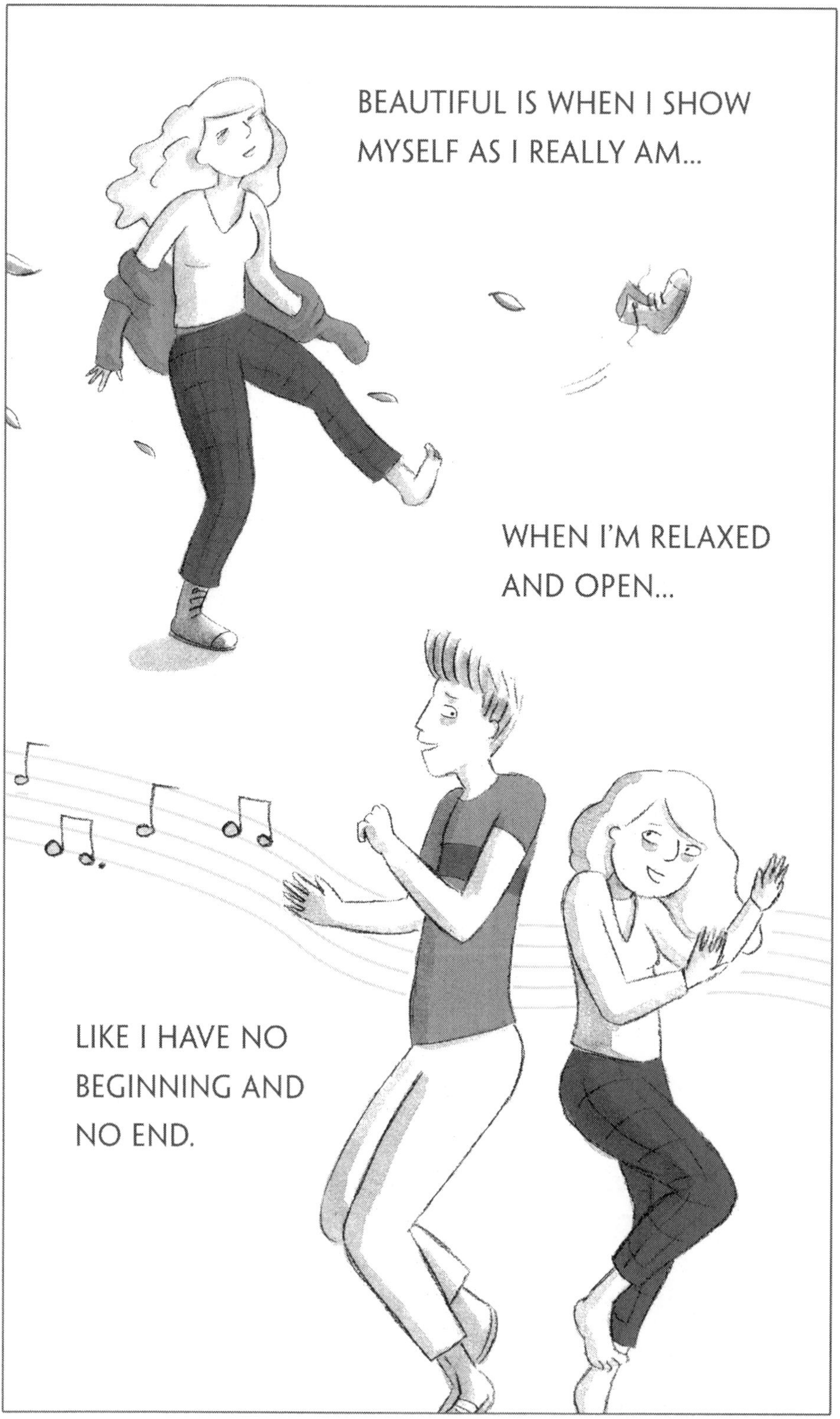
BEAUTIFUL IS WHEN I SHOW MYSELF AS I REALLY AM...
WHEN I'M RELAXED AND OPEN...
LIKE I HAVE NO BEGINNING AND NO END.

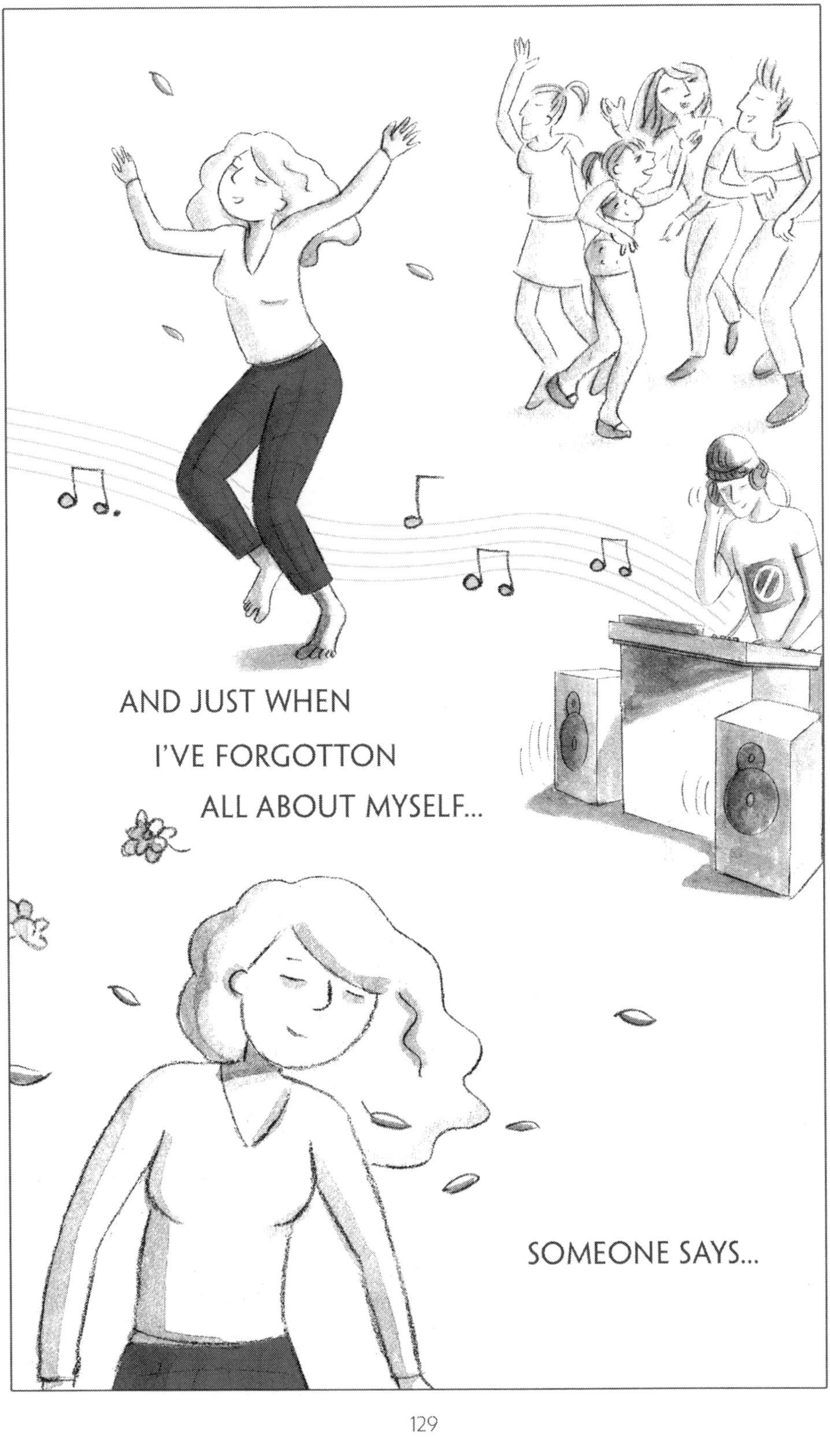
AND JUST WHEN
I'VE FORGOTTON
ALL ABOUT MYSELF...
SOMEONE SAYS...

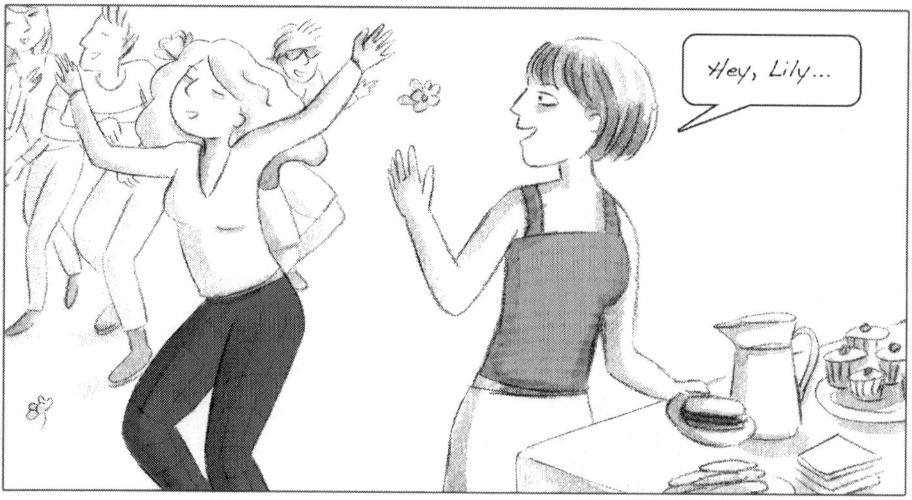
Hey, Lily...

YOU LOOK BEAUTIFUL!

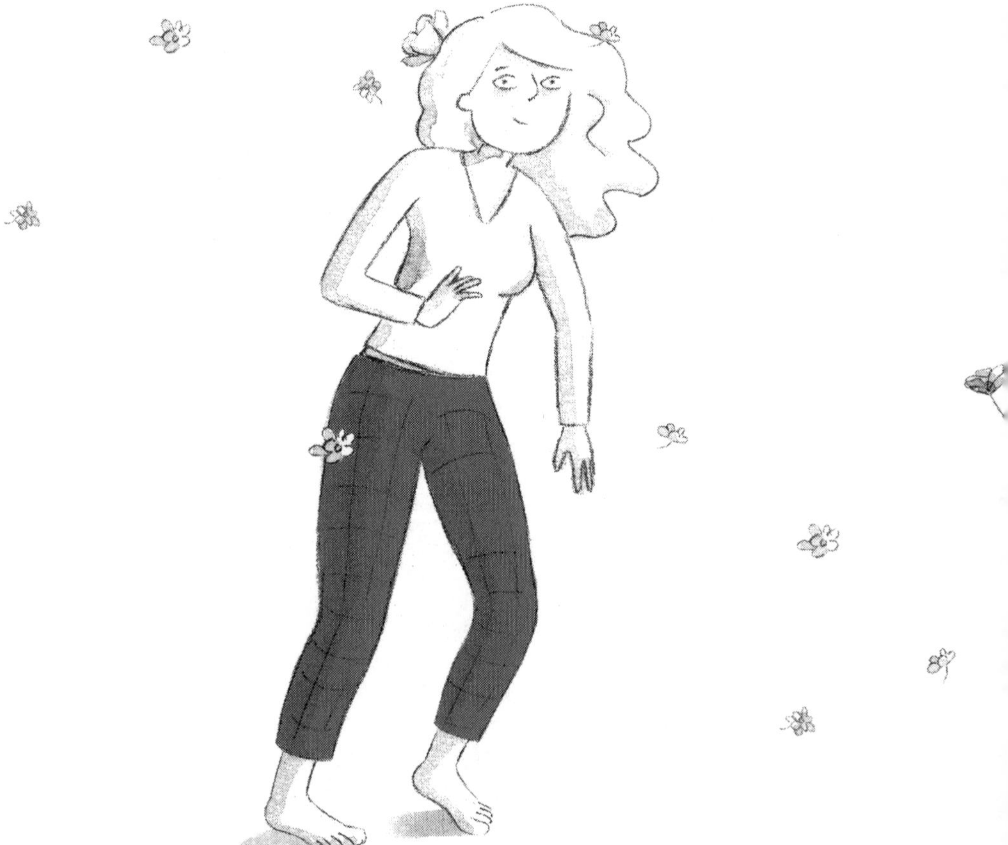

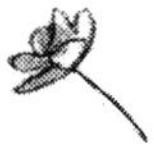

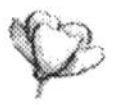

About the author

Marie D'Abreo is a writer, artist, and graphic designer. She grew up in Worthing, England, and later went on to get her Bachelor of Fine Arts at the Minneapolis College of Art and Design.

She now resides in San Francisco, California — a city that's expensive and chilly, but quite possibly too cool to leave.

Made in the USA
San Bernardino, CA
05 January 2018